Democracy and Poverty in Chile

Series in Political Economy and Economic Development in Latin America

Series Editor
Andrew Zimbalist
Smith College

†*Democracy and Poverty in Chile: The Limits to Electoral Politics,* James Petras and Fernando Ignacio Leiva, with Henry Veltmeyer

†*Inside the Volcano: The History and Political Economy of Central America,* Frederick Stirton Weaver

†*Sexual Politics in Cuba: Machismo, Homosexuality, and AIDS,* Marvin Leiner

"Everything Within the Revolution": Cuban Strategies for Social Development Since 1960, Thomas C. Dalton

Industrialization in Sandinista Nicaragua: Policy and Practice in a Mixed Economy, Geske Dijkstra

†*The Making of Social Movements in Latin America: Identity, Strategy, and Democracy,* edited by Arturo Escobar and Sonia E. Alvarez

Peasants in Distress: Poverty and Unemployment in the Dominican Republic, Rosemary Vargas-Lundius

The Latin American Development Debate: Neostructuralism, Neomonetarism, and Adjustment Processes, edited by Patricio Meller

Distorted Development: Mexico in the World Economy, David Barkin

State and Capital in Mexico: Development Policy Since 1940, James M. Cypher

The Peruvian Mining Industry: Growth, Stagnation, and Crisis, Elizabeth Dore

Cuban Political Economy: Controversies in Cubanology, edited by Andrew Zimbalist

†Available in hardcover and paperback

Democracy and Poverty in Chile

The Limits to Electoral Politics

James Petras and Fernando Ignacio Leiva

with Henry Veltmeyer

Westview Press
Boulder • San Francisco • Oxford

Series in Political Economy and Economic Development in Latin America

Copyright © 1994 by Westview Press, Inc.

Published in 1994 in the United States of America by Westview Press, Inc., 5500 Central Avenue, Boulder, Colorado 80301-2877, and in the United Kingdom by Westview Press, 36 Lonsdale Road, Summertown, Oxford OX2 7EW

Library of Congress Cataloging-in-Publication Data
Petras, James F., 1937–
   Democracy and poverty in Chile : the limits to electoral politics
/ James Petras and Fernando Ignacio Leiva, with Henry Veltmeyer.
      p.   cm. — (Series in political economy and economic
development in Latin America)
   ISBN 0-8133-8217-3 — ISBN 0-8133-8227-0 (pbk.)
   1. Chile—Economic conditions—1988–   . 2. Chile—Economic
conditions—1973–1988.   3. Chile—Economic policy.   4. Democracy—
Chile.   5. Chile—Politics and government—1988–   . 6. Chile—
Politics and government—1973–1988.   I. Leiva, Fernando Ignacio.
II. Veltmeyer, Henry.   III. Title.   IV. Series.
HC192.P48   1994
338.983—dc20   93-43013
                                                                                 CIP

Printed and bound in the United States of America

The paper used in this publication meets the requirements
of the American National Standard for Permanence of Paper
for Printed Library Materials Z39.48-1984.

10   9   8   7   6   5   4   3   2   1

Contents

Tables

Acronyms

ACI	Agencia de Cooperación Internacional
AFP	Administradoras de Fondos de Pensiones
AHC	Academia de Humanismo Cristiano
ASEXMA	Association of Exporters of Manufactures
BID	Banco Interamericano de Desarrollo
CASEN	Caracterización Socio-Económica Nacional
CED	Centro de Estudios del Desarrollo
CEP	Centro de Estudios Públicos
CEPAL	Comisión Económica para América Latina
CIEPLAN	Corporación de Investigaciones Económicas para América Latina
CLACSO	Consejo Latinoamericano de Ciencias Sociales
CLAEH	Centro Latinoamericano de Economía Humana
CNC	Comisión Nacional de Campesina
CNI	Central Nacional de Informaciones
CODELCO	Corporación del Cobre
CODEPU	Comite Nacional de Defensa de los Derechos del Pueblo
Concertación	Concertación de Partidos por la Democracia
CPC	Confederación de la Producción y el Comercio
CPI	Consumer Price Index
CUT	Central Unitaria de Trabajadores
DINA	Dirección de Inteligencia Nacional
DNS	Doctrine of National Security
ECLAC	United Nations Economic Commission for Latin America and the Caribbean
ENADE	Annual National Assembly of Private Enterprise
ERP	Economic Recovery Program
FDI	foreign direct investment
FLACSO	Facultad Latinoamericana de Ciencias Sociales
FOSIS	Fondo de Solidaridad e Inversión Social
GDP	gross domestic product
GEA	Grupo de Estudios Agro-Regionales
GIA	Grupo de Investigaciones Agrarias

GISTRADE	Grupo de Investigación Sobre los Trabajadores Desplazados
GNP	gross national product
ICAL	Instituto de Ciencias Alejandro Lipschutz
IChEH	Instituto Chileno de Estudios Humanistas
IDB	Inter-American Development Bank
IFC	International Finance Corporation
ILET	Instituto Latinoamericano de Estudios Transnacionales
IMF	International Monetary Fund
INDAP	Institute for the Development of Agriculture
INE	Instituto Nacional de Estadística
INJ	Instituto Nacional de la Juventud
ISI	import-substitution industrialization
LASA	Latin American Studies Association
M1A	private money
MAPU	Movimiento de Acción Popular Unitario
MAS	Movimiento por la Autonomía Sindical
MDP	Movimiento Democrático Popular
MIDA	Movimiento de Izquierda Democrático Allendista
MIDEPLAN	Ministry of Planning and Cooperation
MIR	Movimiento de Izquierda Revolucionaria
NATO	North Atlantic Treaty Organization
NED	National Endowment for Democracy
NGO	nongovernmental organization
ODEPA	Bureau of Agricultural Policy and Analysis
PEM	Programa de Empleo Mínimo
PET	Programa de Economía del Trabajo
PIRET	Promoción e Intercambio de Recursos Educacionales y Tecnológicos
POJH	Programa Ocupacional para Jefes de Hogar
PPD	Party for Democracy
PREALC	Programa Regional de Empleo para América Latina y el Caribe
PRIES-CONO SUR	Programa Regional de Investigaciones Económicas y Sociales del Cono Sur
SAP	structural adjustment programs
SENAEM	Servicio Nacional de Empleo
SERNAM	Servicio Nacional de la Mujer
SOCHEP	Sociedad Chilena de Economía Política
SOFOFA	Society to Promote Manufacturing
SUR	SUR Profesionales

UDI	Unión Demócrata Independiente
UF	Unidad de Fomento
UNDP	United Nations Development Program
UNESCO	United Nations Educational, Scientific, and Cultural Organization
UNIFEM	United Nations Development Fund for Women
UNRISD	United Nations Research Institute for Social Development
USSR	Union of Soviet Socialist Republics, or Soviet Union

1

Introduction

Pain and Prosperity in Chilean Development

Chile has once again captured the hearts and minds of the U.S. establishment: From Wall Street to Washington, in the *New York Times,* and in the mainstream academic journals, Chile's economic model is being hailed as a successful case of free market economics with democracy. In the 1960s, facing a strong Socialist challenge, the same crowd described the Christian Democratic reformers as Chile's "last best hope." In the 1990s, after a decade of negative growth rates, cholera epidemics, and social regression throughout most of Latin America, the U.S. establishment is desperate to find a success story. And it has struck on the "Chilean miracle." The official story is that Chile has achieved, as one *New York Times* journalist has described it, "prosperity through pain." Although most Chileans—including the 45 percent below the poverty line—might disagree and rephrase it as "pain through prosperity," the success story has so often been repeated and unquestionably accepted that it is time for a critical reassessment—for an evaluation that takes into account the trajectory of the whole period (1973–1992), examining not only the booms but also the busts; that looks at the continuities of authoritarian institutions (the army, the police) as well as at the spaces of free expression; that looks at the social impact of macrosocial policies and not only at the external balance sheets.

The purpose of this book is to provide an in-depth analysis of the economic and political restructuring experienced by Chilean society since the 1970s. Many studies of Chile's recent history are one-sided. Unilateral explanations for complex events abound: It is not uncommon to read that neoliberal economic policies succeeded in giving Chilean society the dynamism and prosperity it lacked; or that the "triumph of democracy" was the expression of the capacity for dialogue, compromise, and negotiation by Chile's reemergent political class. Though rich in self-serving rhetoric, these interpretations provide scant analytical bite. To address these many limitations, we have chosen an approach that emphasizes the intricate interaction of ideological and political, as well as structural and strategic, factors that shaped the changes experienced by Chilean society between

1973 and 1992. We have opted for examination, not papering over, of the profound contradictions that constitute Chilean society and that give life to the oppositional movements that are emerging in the 1990s. We believe that a comprehensive understanding of Chile's recent history requires a critical reassessment of the relationship between the export-oriented economic model and electoral politics. Seeking to understand the relationship between democracy and poverty today in Chile has been the driving motivation behind this book. In the process we have challenged many of the facile interpretations of the Augusto Pinochet dictatorship, the transition, and the current Patricio Aylwin government.

Irony and Paradox in Chilean Politics

Throughout the past decades, Chilean politics and economic development have frequently attracted attention far beyond national borders. In contrast to its neighbors, Chile had, prior to 1973, the longest tradition of electoral regimes of any country in all of Latin America. Yet it was the last country to make the transition from a military to an electoral regime. Historically, Chile was noted for its civic culture, yet its class structure was among the most rigidly defined and most staunchly defended on the continent.

The ironies and paradoxes continue in more recent years. From the late 1960s to 1973, Chile's electoral system became a vehicle for major changes: in land tenure, including extensive land redistribution; in large-scale social organization of the urban poor and landless peasants; and in successful experiments in worker-managed industrial enterprises. Electoral politics seemed to provide opportunities for long-term, large-scale changes in the social system as well. But with the coup of 1973, Chile marked the beginning of the bloodiest and most repressive military regime in its history—a regime that would become one of the most authoritarian systems in the hemisphere.

The contrast between democratic change from below and elite authoritarian policies from above defines the two souls of Chilean politics—a political distinction that does not rigidly separate civilians from the military. The striking aspect of Chile's rightist turn in 1973 was the degree of support the coup and the subsequent bloody repression secured from Chile's respected propertied and professional classes and from sectors of the Christian Democratic leadership. Large majorities in the upper- and upper-middle-class suburbs (the *barrio alto*) supported the coup and continued to support Pinochet right up to his eventual defeat in the plebiscite at the end of the 1980s.

The return to a civilian electoral regime in Chile has been deeply marked by the authoritarian regime that preceded it: Most of the basic institutions established by the dictatorship remain, acting as formidable barriers to any resurgence of transformative social movements. The long-term effects of the authoritarian period are found not only in the state institutions but also in the social structure, social relations, and economic institutions established during the reign of terror: Chile's agricultural sector today, with its wealthy agro-export elite and atomized seasonal farm workers, resembles the economy and social structure of Central America. The economic policies favoring large-scale foreign investment in the extractive industries resemble late nineteenth century Latin American practices in Mexico and Bolivia. Equally significant, living through dictatorship has had the effect of *domesticating* the parties, the political class, and the intellectuals who were at the forefront of transformative politics in the 1960s and 1970s. Repressive policies have become part of the political consciousness and condition the behavior of the former center-left parties: Critics of Pinochet—both Socialist and Christian Democratic—have embraced the elitist socioeconomic strategies of their former adversaries. They have absolved the military and the torturers of the human rights crimes they committed (the politics of "reconciliation") and are working closely with the intelligence agencies to create new institutions of political surveillance, recruiting former antidictatorial militants to inform on their still-active comrades.

The paradox is clear: Chile, the most advanced social democracy of the early 1970s, has become one of the most conservative electoral regimes on the continent in the early 1990s.

Assessing the "Chilean Miracle"

We begin exploring the "Chilean miracle" with a chapter on the Chilean transition. Stressing the need to differentiate between "state" and "regime" in order to grasp the contradictory nature of Chile's passage from military to civilian rule, Chapter 2 provides the analytical framework for the rest of the book. In Chapter 3, on the Pinochet regime, Henry Veltmeyer examines Chile's other transition: from democratic socialism to a free market military dictatorship. He focuses on the conflict between free market opportunities for domestic and foreign investors and the social needs of the majority of the working population; he examines as well the boom and bust character of the model and the lopsided emphasis on prime material exports at the expense of the domestic market and industry. Veltmeyer's contribution stresses the role played by state terror and repression in the different stages of restructuring Chilean capitalism after the 1973 military coup.

In Chapter 4, we analyze the spectacular ideological shift among Christian Democratic and Socialist economists and intellectuals—a shift from

national industrial welfare strategies to free market export approaches—
that transpired in the 1980s while Pinochet was still in power. One of the
greatest achievements of the Pinochet dictatorship was precisely its capacity to redefine the parameters of theoretical endeavor and political discourse engaged in by Chile's intellectuals and political class. We examine
the itinerary that produced a new conception of both economics and politics; we show how the willingness of key civilian politicians and intellectuals to endorse the existing socioeconomic configuration of power and
the export-oriented model of capital accumulation constituted one of the
key prerequisites for the military's agreement to hand over the government to a civilian political class.

In Chapter 5, we highlight the impact of the electoral transition on social classes and movements, on political institutions, and on the mechanisms of political representation. The essentially conservative nature of
the transition—characterized by the continuity of state institutions and
economic elites—is seen as a trade-off for the opening of the political system. We discuss several decisive issues crucial to understanding the Chilean transition. The first is the conflict created by an emerging technocracy
that has accumulated decisionmaking powers at the expense of the social
movements that brought the Aylwin regime to power. The second issue
concerns the conflict between the Aylwin regime's export strategy, based
on temporary low-paid labor, and the demands of farm workers for a return to social legislation abolished by the dictatorship. The third conflict is
between the regime's policy of de facto impunity granted to the military
for its massive violation of human rights and the demand for the democratic principle of equality before the law.

Chapter 6 focuses on the Aylwin government's economic strategy of
"growth with equity." Although macroeconomic variables have achieved
equilibrium and show evidence of "economic success," this has been at
the cost of continuing large-scale poverty. Massive inflows of capital in
short-term notes, nonrenewable resources, and foreign takeovers of critical growth sectors point to the medium-term constraints of the development model. Our assessment of the Aylwin regime's economic performance during its first two years reveals a distinct continuance of the
neoliberal-inspired open economy development strategy. Behind the
much-touted discourse on "capitalism with a human face" lies the abys-
mal failure to generate a diversified, equitable, and productive economy.

Chapter 7 offers an in-depth examination of the relationship between
electoral politics and social movements. On the basis of extensive interviews and meetings that we held with union and community leaders in
1990 and 1991, we analyze the expectations, disenchantment, and reactivation of mobilization movements by urban shantytown dwellers, temporary farm workers in the agro-export sector, and copper mine workers.

These mobilizations are placed in the more general framework of the growth, replacement, crisis, and reactivation of mass mobilization movements in Chile over the last decade. Here the two souls of Chilean politics are clearly delineated: On the one hand, we find a political class interested in an elite democracy that gives it permanent control over popular and social movements; on the other hand, we see working class and popular movements that, with varying degrees of autonomy and effectiveness, keep alive the historical possibility of democratic social transformation from below, as well as the extension of participatory democracy. The chapter concludes with an analysis of the tensions between the political class embedded in the regime and social movements growing out of the unresolved contradictions in civil society.

The limits of Aylwin's "growth with equity" development strategy are explored in Chapter 8. Here we focus on the following unresolved economic conflicts: (1) export competitiveness, versus improved real wages, (2) macroeconomic balances, versus instability induced by the inflow of speculative short-term capital encouraged by Chile's open-economy strategy, (3) allocation of public resources to cover lingering financial costs from the state's bail-out of private banks, versus increased funding for social programs, and (4) entrenchment in low-wage, resource-intensive exports, versus moving on to a higher value-added second phase of the export model. We then outline the components of an alternative economic and political model that would be more effective in attacking poverty and promoting democracy.

Chile's Two Transitions

Over the past two decades, Chilean society has undergone tremendous social, economic, and political changes. Chile experienced two transitions: The first moved the nation from a democratic socialist economy into neoliberal terror; and the second transformed it from a dictatorial military regime to an elected-civilian regime. The two transitions establish a benchmark that allows us to examine how these deeply structural changes have affected the quality of political and social life in Chile, beginning with the terrorist and free market policies of Pinochet and ending with the contemporary technocratic electoral regime of Aylwin. In the concluding chapter, we analyze the ways in which the political opening has allowed the educated middle class, with its political leverage, to prosper, while leaving behind the majority of Chileans—a process that can be described as political renovation of the political class and disarticulated representation of the lower classes. This situation creates a tremendous challenge for the social and political forces interested in bringing about a full and comprehensive democratization of Chilean society.

Although Chile's dominant political culture today speaks to elitist neoliberal policies, Chile's social movements have once again taken to the streets in an effort to recover the legal rights, dignity, and material living standard lost during the dictatorship. If official Chilean politics has largely been a series of compromises between a domesticated Left and entrenched privileged classes, where democracy is subordinated to property, then unofficial Chilean politics, the politics of the social movements, has been a search by a cumulative set of democratic grass-roots organizations hoping to create a political system in which property privileges are subordinated to democracy, in the broadest social, economic, and cultural sense.

2

The Chilean Transition

State, Regime, and Democratization

Our analysis of the Chilean transition focuses both on elaborating an analytical framework to examine the different stages of this change and on clarifying basic conceptual issues regarding the use and abuse of the notions of "regime" and "state" in analyzing the transitional process. We consider this clarification crucial for a comprehensive understanding of the transition: it is imperative to slice through the dense rhetoric about the "return to democracy" in order to analytically reveal the concrete relations of power among social classes and political forces in this process.

In the first section of this chapter we will discuss conceptual distinctions among the key components of the political system—state, regime, and government—and in the second part we will address elements of continuity and change in the different stages of the processes of transition. We will apply this framework to an analysis of the transition from the military to the electoral regime in Latin America with special emphasis on the Chilean case.

Though it has become fashionable to write about the state, most of this writing is based on a great deal of confusion about essential concepts. The "state" refers to the *permanent* institutions of government and the concomitant ensemble of class relations that have been embedded in these same institutions. Such permanent institutions include those that exercise a monopoly over the means of coercion (army, police, judiciary), as well as those that control the economic levers of the accumulation process.

The "government" refers to those political officials that occupy the executive and legislative branches of government and are subject to renewal or replacement. There are various types of government classified along several dimensions. For example, there are civilian or military regimes; and elected or self-appointed regimes. These different kinds of regimes pursue a variety of socioeconomic strategies, ranging from welfare capitalist to neoliberal types.

In analyzing the process of political change, it is important to recognize the different levels at which political transformations take place in order

7

both to determine the scope and direction of policy and to be able to adequately characterize the process. For example, in the second half of the 1980s in Latin America in general, and in Chile in particular, there have been a number of political changes that have been dubbed "democratization" processes that have produced "democratic states." In terms of our conceptual distinctions, however, these political changes have not in the least changed the nature of the state but rather have led to changes at the level of government or regime. The military, police, and judicial officials in the overwhelming majority of cases have remained in place, with the same controls over "security," with the same values and ideologies, and without having been brought to justice for their terrorist behavior. Moreover, the same class linkages that defined the state before the political changes occurred continue under the new regimes. The continuities of the basic state structures define the essential components of the political system: the boundaries and instrumentalities of social action. The new political regimes exercise their prerogatives, as well as their executive and legislative initiatives, within the framework established by the preexisting configuration of power. This means that any characterization of the political configuration and the process of political change must include both the continuities of the state and the changes at the regime level. Moreover, since the state exists prior to and is more basic than the regime in the functioning of the social system, it is the nature of the state to be the "noun," and of the regime to be the "adjective," in characterizing the political configuration. Thus in the case of Chile, for example, the continuities in the state apparatus—organizationally and ideologically intact, carried over from the period of terrorism—provide the key to defining the political system, whereas the change from an appointed military to the elected Aylwin regime provides the modification. Hence the Chilean political system could be referred to as an elected-civilian regime embedded in an authoritarian state.

The accommodation between an elected-civilian regime and an authoritarian elitist state is based on converging socioeconomic agendas—and not, as simplistic analysts would argue, on circumstances "forced" upon reluctant reform-minded civilians. In the case of Chile and other Southern Cone countries, incumbent civilian regimes have elaborated development strategies that are essentially directed toward integrating the export-oriented growth programs of their predecessors, to achieve more "rational management" of the domestic economy and more effective mobilization of outside economic resources. Since a civilian regime's economic models are built on supply-side incentives, using the premise of creating a favorable climate for external funding, this sort of regime engages in the same restrictive domestic income policies as its predecessors did. Upon taking office the civilians are very aware that their popular "political capital" is based on their displacement of the terrorist military regime and will, sooner or later, begin to dissipate. In anticipation of popular protest and in defense of their economic strategy, elected-civilian regimes choose to retain their ties to the existing state apparatus. The socioeconomic continuities serve to bridge the political differences between the military and civilian, particularly as the military element retains preponderant influence in the state, whereas the civilian sector is relegated to managing the regime.

Changes of regime are not always congruent and compatible with the preexisting state: Elected regimes may attempt to restructure both the state apparatus and the linkages between classes and that apparatus to bring them all in line with their socioeconomic agenda. When the agenda of a new regime diverges substantially from the basic orientation of the state upon which it rests, a period of "instability" begins, and "conflict" ensues between the different "branches" of the government—but invariably it is the state apparatus that wins and either overthrows or forces a modification in the behavior of the regime. For example, the conflict between the state and the regime in Chile during the Allende regime was resolved by the state (the military), which overthrew the democratically elected regime and proceeded to form a new authoritarian regime in the image of the structure of the repressive apparatus. Likewise, in Cuba, in the period following the Batista regime, the revolutionary army became the base for the new state, whereas the liberals formed the regime. In the ensuing conflict between the state and regime over social policy, it was the state, linked to the working class and peasantry, that prevailed. The composition, orientation, and class relations of the state shape the long-term, large-scale policies of a political system. That is why Washington is willing to accept changes in regime (be they from military to civilian) in order to preserve the continuity of the state; conversely, and for the same reason, Washington is adamant in opposing political changes that dismantle the existing state, particularly when the new state is organized to sustain a regime with a nationalist and Socialist platform. Washington is willing to sacrifice the Ferdinand Marcos, François Duvalier, and Augusto Pinochet dictatorships and accept civilian regimes—as long as such new regimes can preserve the state apparatus.

Discussions of political regimes, whether electoral-civilian or military, need to refer to the state-class relations upon which they depend. Regimes cannot defend themselves or promote the accumulation process when they act contrary to state interests. This is understood by incoming civilian politicians as they proceed to fashion development agendas and political relations adapted to these institutional realities. In many cases the need to "adapt" is very minimal since the civilians share a common perspective with the state elites. However, this agreement over policy between the regime and state is obscured by the ideologues of civilian regimes (such as Guillermo O'Donnell, Manuel A. Garretón, and others), who promote the ideology of "democracy without adjectives"—who attempt to narrow the discussion of the political system to regime changes and the accompanying electoral procedures without examining the larger historical-structural configuration within which those changes take place. A major problem in this discourse is the marked tendency to dichotomize the political process by categorizing according to an authoritarian-democratic dimension. This form of analysis is flawed at several levels. First, authoritarians are active negotiators and facilitators of the transition. Second, authoritarians continue to exercise power and control over the instruments of violence. Third, there are issue areas (punishment of military human rights violators, debt obligations, agrarian reform) that are off-limits to civilian regimes. Fourth, in some cases, human rights violations continue under civilian regimes, and in some cases they increase massively (Peru under Fernando Belaunde, Alan García, and Alberto Fujimori; and El Salvador under Napoleón Duarte and Alfredo Cristiani are two clear examples). In other cases political terror has become more selective: in Brazil under José Sarney and Fernando Collor, killings of peasant advocates of agrarian reform continued; hundreds of political murders took place during Marco Cerezo's regime in Guatemala. In Chile, although police repression has lessened, torture of political arrestees is frequently reported and the essential rights of farm workers are still systematically denied. The continuation of repressive institutions, policies, and practices expresses the interpenetration of elected-civilian regimes and authoritarian institutions.

The facile equating of elected-civilian regimes with "democracy" or with "democratization"—and with concomitant respect for elementary rights (security of one's physical state)—runs counter to numerous examples in recent Latin American history. The civilian Joaquín Balaguer regime in the Dominican Republic—elected in the aftermath of the 1965 U.S. invasion—oversaw the emergence of paramilitary death squads responsible for several hundred political murders. The Julio César Méndez Montenegro regime in Guatemala, elected in 1966, presided over one of the bloodiest chapters in that country's gory history. If we add the Belaunde regime in Peru, with its more than eight thousand civilian deaths, and the Duarte regime, with over sixty thousand civilian deaths, we get some notion of the gap between electoral processes and the most elementary ingredient of citizenship—the right to life. In some cases, in fact, one could argue that certain "authoritarian" military regimes provided more of the essential conditions for citizen participation than the elected regimes that succeeded them. This is clearly the case if we compare the Juan Velasco Alvarado military regime in Peru with the Belaunde elected-civilian regime. Under Velasco a vast number of neighborhood, trade union, peasant, and professional associations emerged, and, despite efforts at co-optation, have managed to establish broad areas of popular social participation and even control over decisions affecting their lives, without any of the terrorism so common under an elected-civilian regime. Under Belaunde, trade unions were undermined, shantytowns were assaulted, and hundreds, if not thousands, of peasant activists were assassinated. Likewise, under Colonel Francisco Caamaño's leadership in the Dominican Republic during the ill-fated popular uprising in Santo Domingo in 1965, there was far more freedom and citizen involvement than was to emerge during the subsequent "civilian" regime.

The presence or absence of civilians, or of military, or even of elections, is less important in shaping the democratization process than is the relationship of the state to the class structure and the underlying relationship of power between classes within the state. Both present experience and history demonstrate that elected-civilian regimes linked to class, as well as states promoting repressive socioeconomic policies, frequently rule within an authoritarian framework. Conversely, on rare occasions we find military regimes linked to popular classes—a combination that opens up the opportunity for extending and deepening citizen participation and extending popular control over important areas of social life.

The regime changes that have taken place in Latin America in general, and in Chile in particular, are almost totally divorced from any profound changes in the rest of society. The elitist restructuring and reorganization of society and the economy that was completed by military regimes have become both the point of departure for these new civilian regimes and the elaboration of their socioeconomic policies. In fact, these civilian regimes have assumed the burden of securing financial assistance, which was unavailable to the military regimes, to finance the "modernization" of the elitist development model. Moreover, faced with the broad societal delegitimation of the military, civilian regimes have assumed the task of absolving the military of all responsibility for massive criminal offenses through quasi- or open amnesties. What some analysts describe as the "democratization process" has a dual character: reconsolidating authoritarian state power—in both the military institution and the accumulation model—while conceding political space for individual expression and limited social mobilization. The contradictory nature of this conjunctural process creates the basis for deepening the alienation of those majoritarian social movements that conceived of democratization as a process in which regime change would be accompanied by profound change in the state apparatus and the accumulation model. In current theorizing about democracy, centrist intellectuals opposed to the military regimes remove class conflict from politics and obfuscate the role of political structures that function as apparatuses of corporate capitalist domination; thus they fashion an ideology to legitimate the new amalgam of authoritarian state and civilian liberal regimes.

This reversion to the vacuous rhetoric of Anglo-American liberal ideology is a far cry from the efforts of progressive Latin American intellectuals from the late 1940s through the 1970s, who worked from a perspective that defined both the nature and process of the class struggle and the insertion of that struggle into the process of state formation and class transformation. A rich theoretical, empirical, and historical literature was accumulated in Latin America that systematically criticized conventional North American conceptions of "state" as government; of government as an "Open Sesame" device for competing interest groups; of civil and military bureaucracies as "neutral actors" merely pursuing their professional "institutional interests." The rise of mass social movements in the 1960s and the success of the Cuban Revolution spelled the demise not only of liberal ideology in the social sciences but also of neoclassical economic dogma.

The counterresponse to the ascendancy of class analyses was the emergence of two alternative frameworks. The notions of "bureaucratic-authoritarianism" and "corporatism" subsumed class relations and class differences into supraclass political categories that cut across basic class cleavages. During the early 1970s, because of the intellectual pressure emanating from the influential class analysis paradigm, these precursors of contemporary neoliberalism combined Weberian categories of bureaucratic authority with competing and conflicting Marxian classes. Early on, these intellectual currents devised categories that underplayed the centrality of class struggle and modified the class nature of state power through the mystification of the state as an autonomous bureaucratic actor. This intellectual current reified the state, emptying it of any class content. This was accomplished through the use of geographic metaphors—instead of sociological analysis—in which notions of "political space" took the place of concrete relations between classes and state and introduced ideas about the arbitrary separation of the electoral process from real power vested in the armed forces. Cutting off "political analysis" from its long-standing and deeply entrenched power matrix, these theorists focused on the epiphenomena of narrow electoral interests, personalities, and partisan party concerns—the stuff of North American political science, vintage 1950 (passed off as the most up-to-date post-Marxist intellectual innovation).

Neoliberalism's revival in the 1980s and 1990s is an attempt to regain intellectual hegemony and occurs as a consequence of the military defeat and extermination of the revolutionary Left during the 1970s. The military defeat and the terror imposed by the military succeeded in defining new boundaries for political discourse.

Neoliberal concepts of politics emerge in a transitional period in the aftermath of the military terror and at the beginning of the revival of mass social movements. The new civilian regimes promote the idea of "democracy without adjectives" by capitalizing on the temporary impotence of the bourgeois-military, which can no longer directly rule unchallenged, at the time that the mass movements cannot yet effectively project their own political program. Although the ideology of civilian regimes may speak to a "classless democracy," the political practice of these regimes involves imposing class-selective austerity programs to pay foreign bankers, promoting multinationals to "modernize" the economy, and promulgating amnesties to absolve their military cohabitants of terrorist crimes. The working class and the peasants—who fortunately do not read the texts about classless democracy but feel the painful class effects of neoliberal policies—increasingly turn to autonomous forms of class action.

The reemergence of class politics following the application by the electoral regime of its neoliberal doctrines is to be expected—and Chile is no exception to the Latin American pattern. In the period immediately following the retreat of the military and in the euphoria of mass electoral victories, Christian Democratic and Socialist intellectuals were able to live the illusion that the electoral regime represented all classes and embodied democracy for every person. Theory was formulated as an electoral celebration. Class political realities were revealed, however, as the regime's policies and practices unfolded and class cleavages and international conflict sharpened.

The greatest appeal of neoliberalism, in Chile and elsewhere, is in the conjunctural moment just prior to and just after its electoral triumph. The particular conjuncture that allowed the rise of neoliberal conceptions of political change gives way to sharp class cleavages and new popular movements, and the consequent targets are increasingly the civilian regimes and their military guardians. As civilian regimes turn toward the military to solve the problems of ensuing instability, the distinction between "democratic" and authoritarian regimes becomes blurred.

In our analysis of the Chilean transition, the utility of the state and regime distinction will become evident: Chile is clearly a case of regime change accompanied by the continuity of state institutions.

Conclusion:
Democracy and Beyond—The Socioeconomic Pivot

The installation of an elected-civilian regime ushers in a new political period. Freedoms of speech, press, and assembly are established, and some restrictions on labor, peasant, and professional organizations are modified. These basic changes, however, are grafted onto the existing state institutions (the civil and military bureaucracies) inherited from the previous regime. The journey toward democracy thus represents both a rupture with past governments and a continuity of previous state structures.

Basic to the transition, however, are the long-term, large-scale economic obligations inherited by the electoral regime, as well as the restraints these obligations impose on policy. These constraints can be divided into "popular" and "elite" types. Popular constraints include demands by the following groups:

- By labor, for wage increases to compensate for salaries lost during military rule
- By the unemployed, made redundant by economic restructuring and free market strategies, for jobs
- By locally owned indebted enterprises, for low interest loans and credits
- By industrial firms, for protection, subsidies, and increased state spending

In the aftermath of austerity measures imposed by the military, the electorate presses for reactivation of the economy and redistribution of income through an active state role, with increased spending and investment.

Elite constraints include pressuring the regime to maintain the neoliberal model and to specifically pursue the following:

- Elite export sector demands for high and stable exchange rates and flexible and cheap labor
- Debt payments to banks and adherence to prior or impending agreements with the International Monetary Fund (IMF), with all of its restrictive prescriptions and pressures
- Policies to increase exports and maintain international competitiveness
- Maintenance of the access of international capital to financial, service, and productive sectors and measures that guarantee foreign investment

As a result of these elite constraints, the civilian political class, which had been critical of the socioeconomic politics of the military regime, undergoes a veritable political neutering: It endorses the existing socioeconomic order, forswearing political representation of long-repressed popular demands, and commits itself to respect the newly defined boundaries for politico-economic discourse. Yet the stability of civilian political institutions is related to their capacity to deal with the political, economic, and human rights issues inherited from the military. Unlike the previous military regime, the civilian government operating in a competitive electoral setting must subject its political decisions to popular consent. Economic and social measures that adversely affect essential constituents alienate electoral support, weaken the incumbent regime, and polarize the society.

Easy and Hard Choices

The policy choices facing electoral regimes can be analyzed by examining two periods: the initial period of relatively easy choices, and the subsequent period of difficult choices. From the beginning, the new regime's margin of maneuverability is very narrow—although the initial popular euphoria over delegitimization of the military provides the regime with enough substantial political capital to make rapid and deep-going changes with broad popular support, if it possesses the political will. As our previous discussion indicates, however, this is very unlikely given the political compromises and selection processes negotiated prior to the elections. The time frame for universal consensus is quite limited. Popular support in the initial period is sustained (and even increased) through regime measures liberating the press, opening the universities, and legalizing basic freedoms. The easy measures, those that do not evoke any serious resistance and do not have an economic cost, may include an investigation of corrupt practices of the military and its cohorts; an exposure of illegal embezzlement of funds from state enterprises; an initial pay hike; and a proclamation of the intention to reform the old order.

After the initial enthusiasm surrounding these provisions has passed—and given the severity of the socioeconomic problems, it passes quickly—the public turns to the realm of socioeconomic policy. Within six months to a year the legal-political changes have lost their capacity to sustain support and to mute criticism. The moment of truth arrives, in which hard choices have to be made—with all of their political and social costs. These are the choices made between popular and elite constituencies—either allocating resources for socioeconomic improvement of living standards for wage and salary earners and for investment in productive processes, thus ensuring internal political stability, or continuing to promote the interests of the export elites, foreign bankers, and investors.

The High Cost of Continuities

The social and economic content of the nascent democratic regime plays a major role in determining its future stability. Measures that satisfy elite interests but adversely affect substantial electoral supporters can lead to massive disaffection, increased sociopolitical polarization, and political crises. Radicalization of the political process and ascent of more populist regimes can trigger a new cycle of military intervention, popular insurgency, and externally directed destabilization campaigns.

The perspective developed thus far, articulating the topics covered in the following chapters, emphasizes the linkage between political compromises made prior to assumption of power by the elected regime and the choice of socioeconomic policy in the postelectoral period. The critical factor underlying the process of transition is the contrast between the legal-political changes and the socioeconomic and institutional continuities. The critical actors—parties and personalities that lead the return to electoral politics—are those who have passed the screening process in the previous period of negotiation and electoral competition.

The very commitments that enable these groups to gain political office, however, prevent them from initiating new policies, redefining international obligations, and pursuing profound institutional innovations in the state. The result is a new cycle that follows a pattern of democracy; instability; popular disaffection; increasing reliance on the military; and the threat of a return to authoritarian rule. As we argue in the ensuing chapters, the problem is not inherent in Latin American (or any Third World) culture, tradition, or political character, or in any other form of ahistorical or asocial abstract classification. Rather, the cycle is rooted in the continuities of class, gender, and political practices that accept and endorse international and institutional frameworks that operate in opposition to majoritarian popular aspirations.

3

The Pinochet Regime

With the violent overthrow of Salvador Allende's socialist government in 1973, the military regime headed by General Pinochet initiated one of the continent's most radical experiments in social change, halting and reversing a broad trend in socioeconomic development that had been several decades in the making. The regime's clearly stated aim[1] to bring about a profound transformation in Chile was implemented, at the economic level, with a program that (1) opened the Chilean economy to the workings of global capital, removing existing barriers to its free movement in and out of the country, (2) reoriented national production toward the world market and export agriculture, (3) increased the scope of "free enterprise" in the economy through large-scale privatization of the means of production and a drastic cut in state spending, and (4) expanded capitalist production. The experiment yielded annual rates of aggregate growth[2] beyond the norm for the region as a whole, giving rise to talk (especially in Chile, among the regime's apologists) of an "economic miracle."

The 1982–1983 world crisis, which hit Chile harder than any other Latin American country, soon stilled such talk, raising instead the specter of economic collapse—and, with the first political opening in ten years, raised hopes as well for a possible end to the military dictatorship. However, a recovery program, initiated in 1984 by a second generation of Chicago-trained economists, soon dispelled these hopes. Once again, persistent and significant rates of growth in production and exports, a second "boom" under conditions of fiscal "stability" (balanced accounts, low inflation) rare in the region, stimulated dreams (and official rhetoric) of developments that would lead to Chile becoming another Korea or Taiwan, placing it in the vanguard of Latin American success stories.

In 1989 and 1990, in the context of a "democratic transition," the Chilean economy continued to post impressive rates of growth in overall production and exports, under conditions of relative macroeconomic stability and an unprecedented influx of foreign investment, generating, amid plaudits from representatives of global capital, widespread reference to economic policies introduced and pursued by the military regime as the continent's most promising economic model, a showcase for the neoliberal program of structural reforms and free market policies.

The apparent economic success of the Chilean model of export-oriented laissez-faire capitalist development has raised a series of critical questions in Chile and elsewhere. For one thing, the Pinochet regime, in its more than sixteen-year dictatorial control of the state and its repressive apparatus, had imposed the conditions necessary for the implementation of an austerity program of structural adjustments based on an archetypal (and close to ideologically pure) neoliberal model of capitalist development. In terms of these conditions, most notably the destruction and repression of working-class organizations, Chile also presents a challenging instance of an old and recently renewed debate on the relationship between "economic progress" (development) and "political freedom" (liberal democracy) as well as the more academic debate on the relationship between growth and equity.[3] For another thing, in the 1980s and early 1990s socialists the world over have had to confront (and still do) the most diverse regimes that pursue essentially similar neoliberal and monetarist programs of structural adjustments in the national economy to suit the workings of the world market, and have done so with close to intellectual—and political—paralysis, unable to clearly formulate an alternative strategy and development program under conditions prevailing in the world capitalist system. The collapse of the Soviet model of socialist development, occurring around the same time as the return to liberal democracy in Chile, has deepened and broadened this crisis in socialist theory and practice and has strengthened conditions for an emerging Washington-based consensus on an exceedingly "market-friendly" approach to national and global development.[4]

The aim of this chapter is to address some of these issues in the context of developments in Chile, a nation that presents, in a condensed form, sociopolitical processes observed in much of Latin America and elsewhere. To this purpose, we will (1) describe the major conditions of "Project Chile"—the efforts of the Pinochet regime to arrest and reverse Allende's path toward socialism and to radically restructure Chile's economy and society in the interest of "big capital," (2) evaluate the outcomes and impact of the economic model, the key project of the Pinochet regime's counterrevolution. A close look at this model, beyond the macroeconomic indicators that are commonly derived from data aggregated for the population as a whole, reveals an underside to Chile's economic miracle: the growth of social inequalities and the creation of widespread impoverishment and marginality. The all-too-frequent focusing by the regime's apologists and observers on Chile's macroeconomic indicators draws attention away from and masks the fact that although the economy is performing well, most people are not. The benefits of the model have accrued to the few, but the costs have been heavy, borne by a large mass of people, mainly Chile's working class. We will briefly touch on the economic, and on some of the political, conditions for Chile's transformation under Pinochet.

The Pinochet Agenda

The military coup in 1973 against Salvador Allende's Socialist regime was not simply a response to conditions specific to Chile. Similar conditions and developments occurred elsewhere in the Southern Cone of the continent—in Brazil (1964), Bolivia (1971), Argentina (1976), and Uruguay (1978). In each case, a national security regime was installed under prerevolutionary conditions involving a crisis in the existing pact of domination and a growing mobilization of the working classes and popular sectors. In this context, the stated objective of the armed forces in Chile, and elsewhere in the region, was to protect the country's traditions and institutions from the social and political forces of subversion, behind which, according to the U.S.-formulated Doctrine of National Security (DNS), were the expansionist aims of the Soviet Union (USSR).[5] But the real (and sometimes stated) objective of the military rulers was nothing less than the re-foundation of the capitalist system at all levels (economic, social, and political)—to restructure and adapt the system to the new realities of global capital, and, at a different level and as a coincidence of economic and institutional interests, to create the necessary conditions for the ruling classes to reestablish their lost hegemony.[6] In effect, the military coup in Chile, and those elsewhere in Latin America, brought an end to the crisis in the prevailing system of domination and did so in the interest of national and international capital. The capture of the state apparatus by the political Left was totally unacceptable to members of the ruling class. They tolerated it for a time, defending their propertied interests while they prepared for the overthrow of the Allende regime and making their move in September 1973, by which time, and with massive U.S. support, the objective conditions for a counterrevolution had been created. The ensuing counterrevolution smashed the growing mass movement, repressed its organizations and its most advanced cadres, and destroyed popular power in its embryonic appearance.

The Pinochet Regime's "Silent Revolution"

It is difficult to find another case in Latin America where a fraction of the economically dominant ruling class has had as much space and time to effect a series of changes in the economic and political structures of society, in accord with its own long-term interests. Because of the monopoly on political power held by this class—via its pact with the military junta, which with political parties in recess arrogated to itself special powers and ruled Chile with an iron hand for more than sixteen years—a coalition of right-wing economic and political groups within the class managed to create almost laboratory-like conditions for economic and political experimentation. In the process, a major transformation of the country's political and economic structures was effected, creating a veritable (if silent) revolution.[7] Apart from the experiment's social base resting in key sectors of the bourgeoisie (including large and medium industrialists; agro-export capitalists; the traditional oligarchy; the *patria financiera,* a new class of finance capitalists; and sectors of the traditional and new petite bourgeoisie), there were three major conditions for the regime's realization of its goal: (1) the inclusion of the armed forces, united and in absolute control of the state apparatus, (2) the political and ideological support of a right-wing coalition, and (3) the introduction of an economic program designed by a group of young economists with postgraduate training in Chicago, acolytes of Milton Friedman and Arnold Harberger and subscribers to the Friedman-Harberger neoliberal, monetarist model of capitalist development.

The Military Junta

The determinant element in the changes decreed and enforced by the regime in its years of state power, from 1973 to 1989, was the military junta, with its combined command of the three branches of the armed forces, as well as of the carabineros, the militarized police used to maintain internal order. At the beginning, the dominant logic for the "Fuerzas Armadas y del Orden" (Armed Forces and Police) was the prosecution of war against the internal enemy, or forces of "subversion," which, in the military's interpretation of the DNS, involved the coalition of leftist parties that had formed the political base of Allende's 1970–1973 government, and the leaders of the growing labor union movement, together with the mass of supporters and other elements in the population seduced or tainted by "Marxist totalitarian doctrine" (read "socialism," in almost any form). In the wake of the 1973 coup, this war was fought on a number of fronts and involved the violent repression of opposition forces and organizations in Chile's civil society, with the execution, torture, murder, and exile of tens of thousands of political and union activists and supporters. According to Chile's Commission of Human Rights, operations conducted by the state's repressive apparatus (expanded to include Dirección de Inteligencia Nacional [DINA] and the carabineros) during the sixteen and one-half years of military rule included the immediate postcoup execution of at least 1,500 activists; the exile of an estimated 15,000 others; and the imprisonment, torturing, assassination, and "disappearance" (and "false confrontation") of thousands more. In recent calculations by CODEPU (Comite Nacional de Defensa de los Derechos del Pueblo), the military regime was responsible for up to 11,536 human rights violations in the recent postcrisis (1984–1988) period alone, beginning with the resurgence of social protests in 1984.[8] Almost all of these violations, including 163 murders, 446 cases of torture, 1,927 arrests, and a number of celebrated cases of *amedrentamientos* (acts of intimidation) were committed with legal impunity.[9]

The Economic Model

The pillar of the military regime, or, the backbone of the new system of class domination, was a program of economic policies designed by the Chicago Boys, a group of young Chilean economists with postgraduate training at the University of Chicago. The policies, offered to the military regime as early as 1973,[10] were not unique. They were part of a neoliberal program of structural adjustments formulated by the economists at the IMF and the World Bank, adopted by a number of countries in the region in the late 1970s and, in the context of a generalized debt crisis, by virtually all others in the 1980s. Not only was Chile the first country in the region to adopt a neoliberal structural adjustment and stabilization program (deregulation, world-market pricing, and privatization) but nowhere else in Latin America (or elsewhere) was the program adopted so completely and with as much doctrinal purity.

Even today, after a decade of structural adjustment programs (SAP), most countries in Latin America have not fully adopted the policy and institutional changes specified in the doctrine (and this includes regimes that are fully oriented toward the free market ideology, as in Mexico, Brazil, and Colombia, and regimes such as those in Argentina and Peru, which were elected on a populist platform, but upon gaining power have vigorously pursued a neoliberal agenda). In Chile, all of the basic structural reforms envisaged by the IMF and the World Bank, and other proponents of structural adjustment, were already in place in the late 1970s. In fact it was this program of structural reforms and associated policies (see Table 3.1) that is referred to in recent efforts to present the Chilean model as an example, par excellence, for Third World development.

Despite the collapse of this neoliberal experiment with structural adjustment in the early 1980s, the reforms and policies instituted in the 1970s are now seen as having laid the foundation for the more sustainable path of growth and development pursued by a second generation of more pragmatic, and ostensibly less doctrinaire, neoliberals; these neoliberals, according to one of several erstwhile critics-turned-practitioners of the

TABLE 3.1   Basic Structural Reforms

1972–1973	*Post-1973*
Privatization	
State controls more than 500 enterprises and banks	In 1980, 25 enterprises (including one bank) in public sector
Price Regime	
Generalized control of prices	Prices freed from state control (excluding wages, exchange rates)
Trade Regime	
Multiple exchange rates	Unified exchange rate
Barriers and quotas	10% duty
High tariffs (averaging 94%, reaching 220%)	No other trade barriers
Deposits on imports (10,000%)	—
Fiscal Regime	
Sales tax	Value-added tax (20%)
High level public employment	Reduction of public employment
High budget deficit	Budget surplus (1979–81)
Domestic Capital Market	
Control of interest rates	Free interest rates
State control of bank sector credit controls	Re-privatization of banks Liberalization of capital market
Capital Account	
Total control of capital flow	Gradual liberalization of capital flow
Government is principal holder of external debt	Private sector is principal holder of private debt
Labor Regime	
Powerful unions with power	Atomization of unions without power to negotiate
Job tenure law	Right of dismissal
Obligatory wage readjustment	Drastic reduction of real wages
High nonwage labor costs (40% of wages)	

SOURCE: Patricio Meller, "Revisión del Proceso de Ajuste Chileno de Década del 80," *Colección Estudios CIEPLAN* no. 30 (Santiago: CIEPLAN, 1990), p. 7. Reprinted with permission.

military regime's economic policies, have left the present regime a legacy of "growth with macroeconomic stability." The Chilean model has demonstrated (in the view of its apologists) that "prosperity [is] born of pain" and structural adjustment, the costs of which have to be endured in the short run for the sake of the long-term public benefit. Chile's macroeconomic "performance" in the late 1980s has been remarkably successful, it is argued, because the painful but necessary process of adjustment was undertaken so early—in the 1970s.[11] The costs of this adjustment, it could be added, were admittedly high, but they had been largely absorbed by the post-1973 generation of workers and producers in the first phase of Pinochet's plan to transform Chile's political economy.

The policies put into practice by the Pinochet regime, and now proposed as a model for Third World development, were based on a program of structural reforms introduced by the regime in various stages, in response to changing circumstances and as economic and political conditions allowed. Although observers and analysts may, and do, debate the intent and the impact of these policies, their basic elements can be summarized and periodized easily enough.

The Restoration of the Market (September 1973 to April 1975)

On assuming power, the military junta and its hastily constructed cabinet had no blueprint or plan for the changes they were intent on bringing about. The important issues for Pinochet and his colleagues, and for the bourgeoisie, which in the main was supportive of the regime, were to reverse the "transition to socialism" pursued by the Allende regime: to reappropriate property that had been confiscated during a decade of agrarian reform, reprivatize the banks and large economic enterprises, remove both price controls on consumer goods and subsidies of basic foodstuffs, lower wages, and break the political power of labor. To bring about and institute these changes immediate measures were taken to restore market relations in the economy.

The first condition for restoring the market was to make a radical change in the structure of property relations formed in the period of liberal reforms (1967–1973). This change was pursued (and largely achieved) through a policy of (1) privatization of state enterprises and other means of production, (2) liberalization, the freeing of prices, deregulation of trade, and removal of restrictions on the free mobility of capital, and (3) repression of the working class and its organizations, to ensure political conditions for these policies. One of the first measures taken was the privatization of banks and state enterprises, which were transferred to or fell under the control of a cluster of large economic groups that dominated the so-called capital market (and that used the acquired banks to take control of intermediate financial institutions and the shares of privatized state enterprises). As a result of such measures, by 1980 only 27 of the 507 state enterprises set up before or during Allende's tenure were left.[12] The majority of these enterprises fell under the control of los grupos economicós, a small but powerful complex of conglomerates, which by 1981 had taken over much of the country's productive apparatus, controlling more than half of the assets of Chile's major private enterprises (68 percent of the assets of all corporations operating on the stock market) and accounting for 45 percent of all foreign capital borrowed as of 1977. By 1982, the banks that were built or purchased by the two biggest of these conglomerates (Cruzat and Vial) accounted for 42 percent of all banking capital in Chile and 60 percent of all available and extended credit.[13]

In addition to the concentration of investment and loan capital and the appropriation of state assets, measures were adopted to reverse the process of agrarian reform, with many properties being returned to their former owners, and up to 45 percent of the peasants surrendering their property rights.[14] By 1980 at least a third of these properties had been returned to their former owners, the export-oriented agrocapitalists who formed the nucleus of the big economic groups that dominated the private sector.

The second major condition for the restoration of market relations in the Chilean economy was deregulation of economic activity and liberalization of trade and the movement of capital. A number of measures were adopted to create this condition. In the process, the regime practically eliminated all restrictions on foreign direct investment (FDI), creating an "almost irresistible package of guarantees for the foreign investor," with "extraordinarily permissive" treatment.[15] Although FDI did not enter Chile with the alacrity of loan capital (by 1979 only $500 million of the $4,150 million authorized for FDI had, in effect, come in), the influx of FDI funds did result in an important repositioning of foreign capital and the further introduction of branch plant operations, especially in the mining sector. As for loan capital, it literally flooded in, especially with the introduction in 1976 of the Economic Recovery Program (ERP), and in 1978, of a far-reaching modernization program. From 1975 to 1979 Chile experienced an extraordinary expansion of credit from private international banks, over $6,120.9 million, equivalent to five years of copper export earnings or eight years of earnings from nontraditional exports. This volume of capital allowed the regime to service the rapidly growing public debt, at the time the highest in the world on a per capita basis, with accumulated payments of $6,593.6 million, representing 45–50 percent of all export earnings.

The processes of privatization and liberalization restored the primacy of the market in the Chilean economy. By using a simple formula—the free market plus its financial correlate, the capital market—the system of property relations in Chile was transformed without an explicit policy objective having been made. Initial measures included the freeing of prices for all goods and services except for one factor of production, labor power. The freeing of prices, combined with privatization and the concentration of property, provoked a massive transfer of resources to a small cluster of property owners, whereas the prohibition of strikes, the dissolution of unions, and the control of wages brought about a rapid decline in the effective income and purchasing power of workers employed at or above the minimum wage.

As a result of these measures, the average income of workers at the minimum wage fell 50 percent in the first two years of the military regime, rising slowly by 1978 to 61.4 percent of the 1972 level. At the same time, various measures designed to concentrate wealth and income led to a drop in the share of wages in total income, from a high of 62.8 percent in 1972, one of the highest in Latin America, to 41.1 percent in 1976, one of the lowest.[16] This loss of disposable income and the drastic reduction in purchasing power within the popular sectors of society were aggravated by a simultaneous reduction in social expenditures by the state. Hence, during the first four years of the military regime, total per capita social expenditures decreased by 50 percent, going from US$143 in 1972 to US$68 in 1974, leveling off at US$70 in 1978.[17]

These various measures, designed to shrink the state and to strengthen private capital, were accompanied by a strong ideological campaign to deify the market, transforming it into a central economic and political value. The key argument advanced was that the free market, or economic freedom, would create the basis for individual freedom and, indeed, for political freedom or democracy. It was in this context that General Pinochet, commander in chief and head of the military junta, proposed years later (in September 1988) to give the world a lesson in democracy.

The third condition for structural adjustment of the economy was the repression of the working class and the disarticulation of its organizations through suppression of the right to strike, suspension of unions (until 1979, when they were authorized to operate under many restrictions), reform of labor legislation, relaxation of worker dismissal regulations, and a dramatic decrease in social security tax benefits to workers and in other forms of the social wage.

The stated objectives of these measures were to overcome financial imbalance and restore stability, control inflation, and stabilize external accounts. However, they were clearly designed to change the structure of class relations by (1) accelerating the processes of reversion and concentration of property, (2) changing the structure of production by destroying forms of capital associated with traditional sectors of industry and redirecting it toward the agro-export sector privileged by the model, (3) inserting Chile's economy into the world market, and (4) transferring economic resources to the rich and to those disposed to invest, and from labor to capital.[18] The latter was achieved through labor legislation that resulted in a decrease from 40 percent to 3 percent in the social security tax paid by employers and in decreases in other forms of the social wage, the abolition of taxes on wealth and capital gains, and the removal of restrictions on profit remittances by foreign capital. The effort also included a currency devaluation, which, among other things, functioned as a mechanism of internal adjustment, designed to ensure the low wages required of the economic model. Another such mechanism was a high level of effective unemployment. The official rate reached 18.7 percent in 1975 during a major recession, but this high level of joblessness was consciously maintained in subsequent years under improved economic conditions. For the entire decade that followed, the level of joblessness averaged 15.7 percent, easily the highest (and worst) in all Latin America.

Shock Therapy and Crisis (April 1975 to mid-1976)

With Chile's economy integrated into the world market and the major means of production privatized, the attention of the Chicago Boys turned to the problem of inflation, which by 1975 had climbed to 340.7 percent. The stock remedy applied was a drastic cut in both state spending and the supply of money and credit, as well as a further opening of the economy to the world market through a drastic reduction of both import duties (from 100 percent in 1975 to 15 percent in 1978) and controls on profit repatriation. The consequence of this antiinflation, monetarist "shock" policy was a 50 percent reduction in the level of inflation, a significant increase in unemployment (up to 18.7 percent in 1975, from 3.3 percent in 1972, 4.8 percent in 1973, and 9.1 percent in 1974), a sharp drop in output (12.9 percent), and further reduction in an already low level of capital formation and investment (down from 17.7 percent in 1974 to 13.3 percent), as well as in the value of real wages and social program expenditures.[19]

On the political front, having repressed the social and political organizations of the working class and having eliminated various civil liberties, the regime implemented a policy of selective repression that led to a growing number of "disappearances" and a dramatic decline in the number of workers' organizations, weakened by repressive laws and unemployment; this was possibly the regime's most effective form of union repression, as it had, according to a study by Jaime Ruiz-Tagle, a greater impact than raids, imprisonment, or exile.[20]

Recovery (mid-1976 to 1978)

By mid-1976, with macroeconomic stability restored, the economy began a slow recovery, albeit from a very low base, after the most severe recession since the 1930s. By 1981, however, six years into the ERP, and despite record rates of growth for the previous four years, the gross national product (GNP) was still below the level achieved in 1970, with growth rates barely at the historic low level of 4.5 percent (posted on average from 1960 to 1973) and well below the rate achieved by most other countries in the region. Overall, from 1974 to 1981 the growth rate in production averaged 2.1 percent, one of the lowest in Latin America.[21] Most of the recorded growth was in the nontraditional exports sector, specifically in fresh fruits, and lumber and forestry derivatives. From 1971 until 1981 this sector increased production from US$73.5 million to US$807.3 million, increasing its share of total exports from 7.6 percent to 20.5 percent.[22] In the industrial sector, however, accumulated capital was destroyed on a massive scale, especially in metals, the mechanical and electrical sectors, and in machinery, as well as in the capital goods subsector that had been at the center of the industrialization process that had driven economic and social developments in Chile throughout the 1960s and early 1970s. In this capital goods subsector from 1974 to 1987, manufacturing industries suffered not only a relative but also an absolute decline in levels of production and employment.[23] It was not until 1988 that industries with value-added operations recovered levels of output achieved under the Allende regime.

The "Economic Miracle" (1978 to June 1981)

With the productive apparatus geared to exports and the economy adjusted to the world market, the economic model generated impressive rates of growth in overall production, particularly in nontraditional exports. Exports in this sector grew at an annual rate exceeding 10 percent, accounting for much of the overall growth, that is, for 32 percent over four years. However, the economic miracle (high growth, low inflation) was illusory, as it was based on unrealistic economic assumptions, and was, in fact, a fragile edifice of debt, high interest rates, and speculation. Further, the economy had become both highly vulnerable to downturns in the world market and excessively dependent on the fortunes of a few conglomerates. Under these conditions, the high growth rates generated by the model were more apparent than real and could not be sustained.

In the first place, the bulk of this growth was but a recovery of former levels of productive capacity. Although the economy grew at an impressive annual rate from 1976 to 1980, averaging 6.6 percent per annum, if we take into account the high level of idle capacity generated by the 1975 crisis, we have one of the lowest rates of growth in Latin America, where economies over this period expanded at an annual average of 5.6 percent. Only Argentina experienced lower average rates of growth.

Second, the boom was fueled by an extraordinary influx of capital provided by private international banks, which led to an explosive growth in accumulated public and private debt. From 1977 to 1981 the volume of accumulated debt based on foreign capital, contracted by the banks controlled by the big economic groups, tripled. As of December 1980, two of the biggest (Vial and Cruzat) by themselves accounted for 51.9 percent of Chile's foreign debts in the banking sector, for 81.8 percent of mutual funds, and for 57.6 percent of life insurance.[24] Apart from the problems associated with this debt, the heavy reliance on foreign loans contributed to the very low rate of domestic capital formation (12 percent) maintained for over a decade after the coup, too low to sustain solid long-term growth. The mass of capital inflow also masked underlying structural imbalances, as well as the speculative practices of major entrepreneurs seeking to capitalize on the high rates of return on short-term interest.

Third, much of the recorded growth was artificial or fictitious, either deployed in the unproductive sectors of the economy (such as in the marketing of imported products and in financial services, the two most dynamic sectors of the model, with rates of growth in excess of 15 percent from 1974 to 1980) or based on speculative operations. From 1977 to 1981 around 80 percent of recorded growth was in the unproductive sectors of the economy and was based to a considerable degree on speculative forms of capital in search of high interest rates (the highest in the world at the time, at 50.5 percent in 1977 and 45 percent in 1978) on deposits or loans. Fully one-fifth of the per capita "growth" recorded between 1974 and 1981 was used to pay interest on loans and to remit profits abroad. Because of the high spread between interest rates on foreign and domestic capital, 25 points on average in the period from 1975 to 1981, most foreign capital also entered the circuit of speculative activity, contributing substantially to an explosive imbalance between the supply of capital in circulation and the relatively stagnant level of production.[25] Foreign capital was also used to finance agro-exports as well as the massive imports that provided luxury goods for the upper stratum of the bourgeoisie, and it was substituted for national production of industrial durable goods, which declined precipitously over the period. Under these conditions, the regime's technocrats braced themselves for a wave of external shocks (a sharp drop in copper prices, an increase in oil costs, and the raising by the U.S. Federal Reserve Board of the prime lending rate, which sent interest rates skyrocketing in Chile) and for a storm that was working itself through the capitalist system worldwide.

The Automatic Adjustment (June 1981–April 1982)
and the 1982–1983 Crisis

The storm hit Chile in mid-1982, but, in the context of a global crisis in capitalist production, the regime's economic team opted for a policy of "doing nothing," on the assumption that the crisis would be short-lived; that with all basic reforms already in place, the economy was equipped to confront any problems; and most important, that these market reforms would result in an "automatic adjustment."[26] But things turned out otherwise. Having grossly overborrowed, caught by exceedingly high and rising interest rates in an economy that was highly exposed and vulnerable to outside forces at a time when copper prices were plummeting, overseas markets were receding, and sources of new capital had evaporated, the Chilean economy in 1982 and 1983 was devastated like no other in the region, with a fall of 16.7 percent in production, an official unemployment rate that climbed to 26 percent, a proliferation of bankruptcies of enterprises and financial institutions, with the country's biggest economic groups on the brink of financial collapse, saved only by a massive bail-out by the state.[27]

With the Chilean economy in crisis, the IMF imposed draconian conditions in return for new loans, and overseas investors demanded that the regime guarantee the entire external debt (US$7.7 billion) of all state-controlled companies, including the banks of the two biggest conglomerates, whose outstanding liabilities exceeded their assets by a factor of two. The officials of the regime, desperate by then, had no recourse but to meet the IMF's conditions and sign, thus fully protecting the foreign banks while passing on the debt burden to domestic taxpayers. The total cost of the bail-out, including protection of the investment of 10,000 bond- and shareholders, represented 3 percent of the country's GNP for each of three years involved (1983–1985), an effective subsidy to capital twice the amount set aside to compensate 600,000 unemployed (400,000 received nothing).[28] In effect, whereas the economic gains from social production during the boom were privatized, losses on the mass of functioning capital were socialized.

Correction, Adjustment, Recovery (1984–1989)

In March 1983, in the throes of the crisis, the government signed a standby agreement with the IMF based on a mutual understanding concerning diagnosis and remedy vis-à-vis the system's macroeconomic imbalances. The agreement included fiscal action to raise taxes and reduce expenditures, including a major privatization program and monetary restraint; further trade liberalization (tariffs in 1982 had been restored and increased to 35 percent); the use of "neutral" instruments for establishing lending, tariff, and exchange rates; deregulation and adjustment of relative prices for goods and services; and new bank credits of US$1.3 billion, which led to an unprecedented supply of further "new money" from foreign private banks, the IMF, and the World Bank. Also, under conditions of high unemployment, purposefully maintained for a period of four years,[29] real wages were pushed downward, thereby increasing the profitability of the restructured and export-oriented enterprises.

In effect, policies in force up to the 1982 crisis were generally maintained but with a more "structured" macroeconomic program designed to secure external balance, lower inflation, and reactivate growth while reducing the high costs of adjustment. The same policy re-

TABLE 3.2   Evolution of Real Wages, 1980–1987 (in percent)

	Revised Index of Real Wages	Minimum Wage
1980	95.0	97.7
1981	105.0	102.3
1982	110.3	101.2
1983	91.1	79.3
1984	86.5	69.5
1985	80.0	64.7
1986	81.5	60.3
1987	81.2	55.5

SOURCE: Patricio Meller, "Revisión del Proceso de Ajuste Chileno de Década del 80," *Colección Estudios CIEPLAN* no. 30 (Santiago: CIEPLAN, 1990), p. 44. Reprinted with permission.

gime was maintained in subsequent years, implemented under particularly favorable international conditions.[30] The policies, adopted by Minister of Finance Hernán Büchi upon taking office in 1985, were designed to reduce the requirement for external capital and to stimulate exports. But, without question, the major aim of these policies was to reduce wages and keep them low, a condition maintained deliberately for a period of five consecutive years (1983–1987) as a direct result of restrictive monetarist policies, implemented through the abolition of wage indexation (with the wage floor set at 1979 levels), high unemployment, and the slashing of social expenditures. Real wages, in the process, lost 41.4 percent of their purchasing power on average. The minimum wage, applicable to most workers in the service, construction, and commerce sectors of the economy, was reduced by at least 40 percent.[31] By 1987, as a result of this policy, the minimum wage index was only 55 percent of its 1980 level, although that of the average wage had recovered 81 percent of its 1980 level (see Table 3.2).

This policy of shifting the burden of adjustment onto workers was not unique to Chile, although one analyst, economist Joseph Ramos, states "that there is no reason why [such] costs ... should be distributed unequally." It appears, however, that in each case that he studied (Argentina, Uruguay, and Chile) "income was sharply redistributed against wage earners as [reflected in] ... the very sharp fall in real wages," which, he notes, "was much sharper than the decline in the growth of national income. In the case of Chile this cost was further exacerbated by the unprecedented increase in unemployment to levels two to three times above the historic rate."[32] It is interesting that Ramos sees "no reason" why the working classes should bear the brunt of the adjustment process, even while he acknowledges the class bias of the regime's policies and its role in directly controlling and breaking the power of trade unions. Notwithstanding the operation of the state apparatus in the interests of capital, Ramos, like so many other economists, refuses to see what is at issue: the subordination of labor to capital.

Implemented under favorable international conditions, within the framework of an agreement with the IMF, the policies adopted by Büchi and company led (or contributed) to an economic recovery in 1984 and, as of 1985, consistent gross domestic product (GDP) growth.[33] Produced with macroeconomic stability (balanced accounts and low inflation), this record was on par or better than most countries in the region, although consistent with a continentwide trend and far inferior to levels of growth recorded by Cuba under a radically different economic regime.

As in the previous period of expansion (1977–1981) most of the recorded "growth" was based on primary product exports, not only in the traditional sector of copper mining, where growth reflected not so much increased production as higher prices, but also in fish and forest products and in the rapidly expanding fresh fruit industry. In these sectors, called the "new growth poles" of the Chilean economy—and the axis of the new model of capital accumulation—rates of growth in excess of 40 percent were recorded for the years 1985–1989, a veritable boom that pointed to a major expansion of the economy's productive forces as well as to highly favorable (and unsustainable) world market conditions. Similar patterns of growth, however, were recorded in the sectors of manufacturing and construction, the former tied to export agriculture, the latter to low-cost housing provided by social sector public spending. By 1990, exports constituted 30 percent of GDP, versus 12.2 percent in 1960, 11.5 percent in 1970, and 23.7 percent in 1980.[34]

In the favorable context of this expanding export-driven economy, the military regime confronted the requirements of its new constitution of 1980 and took the second step in its plans to institutionalize a "protected democracy." It set up a plebiscite, which was eventually conducted on October 5, 1988, with the aim of confirming General Pinochet as president of the Republic for a further eight years, to ensure continuity of the economic model. As it happened (largely through miscalculation and an overwrought belief in its own Silent Revolution), the government was defeated; another set of more open elections was scheduled and the eventual outcome was the installation of a civilian regime based on a Christian Democratic–led "alliance for democracy."

Evaluating the Pinochet Agenda

Sixteen years of military dictatorship have spawned a considerable number of studies on the process of capital accumulation in Chile and on the political forces mobilized in the process.[35] Most of these studies take a liberal (Social Democratic or Christian Democratic) or Socialist perspective, with a focus on either the expansive dynamics of the system (notwithstanding its fundamentally unjust and antidemocratic nature) or its negative destructive character. With the exception of a short period (1979–1981) that corresponded to the height of an economic boom, the central focus of these studies has been on the destructive character of the accumulation process under the economic model, on its propensity toward crisis and stagnation, and on the gross inequities and social costs involved.

The thesis generally advanced in these studies (a moderate form of the catastrophic scenarios drawn over the years by many leftists) is grounded in an analysis of the system's two major crises (1975–1976, 1982–1983) and is supported by considerable evidence. First, in aggregate terms, from 1970 to 1989, Chile's GDP (a poor but often-used proxy measure of society's productive forces) grew at a slow pace (relative to the 1960s and to other Latin American countries over the same period), with an annual average of 1.8–2.0 percent. On a per capita basis, a tendency toward stagnation was even clearer. Not only did the GDP grow at a rate (0.1–0.2 percent) well below the Latin American average, even taking into account the impact of three crises (a fall of 5.6 percent in 1973, of 2.9 percent in 1975, and of 14.1 percent in 1982), but by 1989 the GDP was still 6.1 percent below the 1981 level, not yet having recovered the level reached in 1970. For the entire period of military rule (1974–1989) only five Latin American countries had a worse record.[36] Some miracle!

There certainly have been some growth poles, with certain sectors exhibiting significant growth in volume and value, but these were generally in a primary resource "export-enclave," with little value added to the production process and with few links to the rest of the economy; in any case, growth in these areas was on a par with that of other countries in the region. Moreover, production gains in this sector were made at the expense of traditional agriculture and industry, especially in the durable goods sector, where from 1977 to 1981 production levels fell sharply, with profits accruing to an increasingly concentrated cluster of enterprises operating in this dynamic agro-export sector. In addition, as noted earlier, fully 80 percent of the recorded growth in the 1976–1981 boom was in the unproductive sectors of the economy (in services and finance) and was based to a considerable degree on highly speculative capital, most of it borrowed from abroad. In the industrial sector, the traditional engine of growth in Chile, growth was virtually nonexistent in the first phase of Chile's economic miracle, at a mere 0.6 percent a year, and collapsed in 1982, falling 28 percent in production and 24 percent in employment, before the mild recovery of 1984, followed by more sustained growth since.

In the broader Latin American context, this development was striking, reflecting a major realignment of the Chilean economy and its axis of accumulation. Throughout the 1960s, the rhythm of industrial growth in Chile was at about 90 percent of the Latin American average. However, in the first period of military rule (1973–1981), whereas developing countries on average had an output 30 percent higher than 1973, Chile showed a decrease of 9 percent.[37] Between 1981 and 1984, when the entire region suffered a severe recession in response to the worldwide recession, Chile was much more severely affected in industrial production and employment levels than anywhere else in the region. Manufacturing production in 1982 fell a staggering 28 percent, contributing in 1983 to a record unemployment rate of 34.6 percent and an average rate of urban unemployment of 22.5 percent for the years 1980–1981, twice that of any other Latin American country, and three times the regional average. In the most recent postcrisis period (1983–1989), industrial production recovered, growing at an average of 6 percent a year, but, as pointed out by the Inter-American Development Bank (IDB) and the United Nations Economic Commission for Latin America and the Caribbean (ECLAC) in their annual reports on Latin America, this growth was based on a disproportionately high level of idle capacity (that is, it reflected a recovery of earlier levels rather than new growth) and particularly favorable international conditions for Chilean exports, especially copper, which still accounted for 49.8 percent of total exports; the recovery also occurred during a period of superior levels of industrial growth in the region as a whole, with countries like Brazil and Cuba outpacing the rest of Latin America by far.

Left Behind by the Boom

A second, even more telling, indicator of stagnation can be found in the material conditions experienced by the majority of the working population that has had to bear the costs of the Chilean model. All of the standard indicators show that the working class in its multitudinous forms was worse off in 1989, at the height of a second boom in capitalist production, than in 1970 or in 1973, preceding the counterrevolution. The high rate of surplus value extracted by a handful of enterprises from a relatively low mass of functioning capital could not disguise the considerable loss of purchasing power by the working population, with a fall of 20 percent in the real value of average wages and a fall of 40 percent in the value of the minimum wage occurring from 1982 to 1983 alone.[38] From 1983 to 1987, the real value of the average wage and the minimum wage, paid to most workers in commerce, construction, and services, continued to fall, to 43.3 percent of the 1982 level, according to one estimate. By 1988, the purchasing power of wages began to recover, but in 1989 it was still well below its 1970 level. This decline in purchasing power reflected the dramatic drop

TABLE 3.3   Consumption by Household Quintiles (percent distribution)

Quintile	1970	1980	1989
1 (poorest 20%)	7.6	5.2	4.4
2	11.8	9.3	8.2
3	15.6	13.6	12.7
4	20.5	20.9	20.1
5 (richest 20%)	44.5	51.0	54.6

SOURCE: Programa de Economía del Trabajo, *Informe Anual* (Santiago: PET, 1990), p. 192.

of 21.6 percent in labor's share of national income (from 52.3 percent to 30.7 percent) over the same period.[39]

This loss of purchasing power in wages and income is reflected in another economic indicator, one that more directly relates to the well-being and standard of living of the "average" citizen: the level of consumption of goods and services produced. According to Instituto Nacional de Estadística (INE) and Central Bank data, this indicator grew at an annual rate of 3.1 percent from 1960 to 1972; fell 57.7 percent in 1975; recovered somewhat in the years of the boom, reaching a level in 1982 that was 9 percent below that of 1972, before falling drastically, and then recovering in 1987, reaching a level that was still 32 percent below that of 1972.[40] And these are averages, made without taking into account the sharp increase in the unequal distribution of income resulting from the regime's policies. Taking this distribution into account (see Table 3.3) indicates that the richest households, in the top, or fifth, quintile, increased their share of consumption from 44.5 percent in 1970, and 51 percent in 1980, to a startling 54.6 percent in 1989.

Over the same period, indications are that at least 60 percent of the population was relatively, if not absolutely, worse off, with an estimated 41.2 percent of the population (five million people) living in a state of poverty, one-third of them indigent or desperately poor, in a state of misery, with a level of income that could barely support existence[41] (see Table 3.3). In fact, in the *poblaciones*, the converted shantytowns on the periphery of Santiago and other major cities, the majority of poor families relied (and still rely) not only on a host of informal activities that often netted each economically active individual barely US$1 a day) but on a network of *ollas comunes* (soup kitchens) for their daily caloric intake.[42] Only the formation of such community-based economic organizations headed off the worst economic effects of Chile's model of capitalist development on the masses of urban poor. And recent statistics prepared by INE suggest that this has not improved after two years under the democratically elected Aylwin regime. The rural population, numbering over 3 million, by all indications has been one of the most impoverished sectors of Chilean society.[43]

TABLE 3.4   Poor and Indigent Households, Greater Santiago (percent distribution)

	1970	1980	1989
Indigent	8.4	11.7	14.9
Poor	20.1	24.3	26.3
Not poor	71.5	64.6	58.8

SOURCE: Programa de Economía del Trabajo, *Informe Anual 1990–1991* (Santiago: PET, 1990), p. 195.

Conclusion:
Poverty in Wealth—Chilean Development

Analysis of economic and social developments under the Pinochet regime supports this proposition: Poverty is the real product of capitalist development. Despite Pinochet's apparent preoccupation with extreme poverty and with government programs targeting indigent households, virtually all independent surveys have found that the military regime's economic policies dramatically increased the incidence and depth of poverty. By conservative estimates (see Table 3.4), the first phase of the military regime saw a 25 percent increase in the relative number of poor households and a 39 percent increase in the percentage of households whose members were desperately poor, unable to meet even their basic needs. A study by the proregime economist Aristedes Torche, based on the ability to meet "basic needs" in food, health, and housing, showed that by 1985 over 45 percent of all Chileans remained poor and that 25 percent of these were indigent. And more recent data suggest that, if anything, the problem worsened from 1985 to 1989, at the height of another boom. Clearly, the fruits of this boom were very unevenly distributed. By the end of the military regime, after five years of "renewed growth," 41 percent of families in Chile, representing 44.4 percent of the population and over half of the rural population, were at or were pushed below the poverty line by economic policy conditions well beyond their control. A revealing datum, an expression of growing impoverishment, was the reduction of 7 percent in the daily caloric intake of the poorest 40 percent of the population over the most recent period of recovery and growth.[44] The daily caloric intake of the poorest 40 percent of the population was reduced from 2,019 in 1970 and 1,751 in 1980 to 1,629 in 1990.[45] Other studies on health and conditions resulting from low income and poverty tell the same story about the grinding struggle to survive the regime's economic policies. The apparent success of the regime in lowering the infant mortality rate and in increasing the literacy rate, two key indicators used by the United Nations Development Program (UNDP) to measure a country's human development, did not change the nature of this struggle.

TABLE 3.5   Concentration in the Export Sector by Main Industry

| | | Participation of Large Firms in the Value of Exports | |
	Number of Large Firms	Industry Share	Value Total Exports
Mining	7	97.1	52.2
Agriculture	8	80.6	6.7
Forest products	5	78.4	2.2
Fish products	6	51.1	4.7
Food	6	67.3	0.4
Wine and beverage	2	70.2	1.1
Wood	7	78.6	5.5
Paper, cellulose	2	90.0	–
Chemical products	2	71.4	0.3

SOURCE: *Análisis* no. 238, August 1–7, 1988, p. 31.

Poverty, however, was clearly but one side—the underside—of the accumulation process under Chile's military regime. Widespread conditions of poverty, in the course of sixteen years of untrammeled capitalist development, express the normal functioning of a system based on the accumulation of wealth, and the concentration and centralization of capital, the conditions of which are equally in abundance in Chile. Indeed, after over sixteen years of military rule, the enrichment of the few and the concentration of productive assets and capital in the major divisions and branches of the economy reached major proportions. For example, in the harvesting and processing of fish, an important sector of Chile's "primary-export" model of capitalist development, the seven largest firms (four belonging to one major economic group, COMPLEJO, controlled by the Angelini family) accounted for 64 percent of fish landings, 65 percent of the production and 68 percent of the export of fish meal, and 32 percent of wage labor in the industry.[46] In the same year (1986), six firms controlled 52 percent of the export of fresh fruit and four firms (three of them belonging to Angelini and another big economic group) accounted for 65 percent of the export of forest products.[47] This concentration of capital in the target sectors of the neoliberal agro-export model (see Table 3.5) parallels the central dynamic of capitalist development—the substitution of capital for labor—and, concomitantly, the growth of an industrial reserve army, that is, a mass of surplus labor subject to the dictates of capital and its structural conditions of unemployment and poverty.[48]

The social formation of the proletariat in its various forms, including the various types of surplus labor that have surfaced in recent years, provides the most telling expression—and indictment—of the functioning of a model of capital accumulation based on the "superexploitation of labor."[49]

The operation of the economic model under the Pinochet regime has transformed the working class in Chile. In the early 1970s, the industrial proletariat constituted an important, even central, component of the working class. In 1972, nonagricultural production workers constituted 27.8 percent of the economically active population. By 1982, as a result of the shift of productive capital into the new growth poles (export agriculture, forestry, fish) and a massive displacement of capital into financial transactions, commerce, and other unproductive activities, this sector of the working class, the industrial proletariat, was decimated—reduced to 11 percent of the labor force.[50] In the years of the first economic boom (1977–1981), "productive" economic activities (agriculture, fishery, industry, and mining) accounted for only 6.9 percent of all new jobs, whereas fully 77 percent of the estimated 632,200 new jobs created were in the unproductive branches of commerce and services. At the same time, up to 40 percent of all jobs generated were in the so-called informal sector, a heterogenous group of unstable professions and enterprises based largely on self-employment. Indications are that, since 1973, most of the workers who were expelled or displaced from the industrial sector, as well as the new entrants in the labor market, were either absorbed by the informal sector of the urban economy or joined the swollen ranks of the unemployed.[51]

A major effect of the large-scale restructuring of capital has been the creation of a large mass of labor power available to capital under conditions of superexploitation, that is, the suppression of wages below the value of labor power. This process can be traced in the evolution of the working class and in its organizational capacity, internal composition, and working conditions—an evolution that has included the expansion of lower-paid jobs, the loss of defensive organizations for the working class, the fall and long-term decline in the purchasing power of wages, and the dramatic reduction in the working class share (vis-à-vis capital) of the national income. As early as 1956, the economist Nicholas Kaldor had traced the economic problems of Chile to the low and falling share of labor (wages) in national income. In 1954, the share in national income was only 20 percent (versus 23 percent for self-employed earnings and 10 percent for rents), which compared to 59 percent for the United States and 41 percent for the United Kingdom.[52] For Kaldor, the "problem" was rooted in the excessive share in national income of the propertied class, which was the weak link in the economic structure because of its high propensity toward personal consumption. This point relates to an old debate, but there is no question that this problem has dramatically worsened as a direct re-sult of the military regime's policies. The "problem," however, is not the low propensity of the capitalist class to save and invest—rather, it is that class's strategy of superexploitation.

This strategy, fully supported by the military regime's economic poli-cies, is reflected in the significant decline of labor's share in both national income and value added in the process of production. But the legacy of ex-ploitation and superexploitation is even greater and more visible in the proportion of the labor force that is either employed or held in reserve in the strategic sector of export agriculture. In this sector, the accumulation of capital has resulted in the drastic reduction of regularly paid perma-nent workers and the corresponding expansion of *temporeros* (workers hired on a seasonal basis), without capital having to bear the reproduction costs of their labor power.

According to these statistics, from 1975 to 1986 the permanent labor force lost 25 percent of its members, whereas the number of temporeros doubled. Of the temporeros surveyed in 1986, 37.4 percent had always been temporeros, 21.8 percent originated in the peasantry, and 33 percent were recruited from the urban centers, or were workers, or self-employed, or students in the cities or small towns. As for residence, which is a better indicator of the superexploitation conditions under which the labor power of the temporeros was and is being reproduced, 40.4 percent lived in the peasant communities, 39.7 percent in the urbanized villages and small towns, and 12.9 percent in urban shantytowns.[53] The conditions of this superexploitation, the economic basis of Chile's export-led boom in capitalist production, are reflected in a clear—and drastic—deterioration in the level of pay and other conditions of existence among the rural prole-tariat and the peasantry. As noted by Comisión Económica para América Latina (CEPAL) economist Joseph Ramos, the high incidence of rural pov-erty resulted in large measure from successful efforts by capitalists man-aging their farm enterprises to offset increases in the nonlabor components of their production costs and to keep profit levels stable and preserve "production vitality" by reducing their overall wage bill. Condi-tions for this wage reduction, as pointed out by another CEPAL econo-mist, include the "existence of a backward sector … of small holders (about 80,000 properties), who receive little or no attention from the gov-ernment … a large mass of farm workers without permanent jobs living in very precarious conditions."[54]

The depression of wages well below the value of labor power has been the economic model's principal mechanism of internal adjustment. Major effects of this adjustment have been the dramatic growth of social inequal-ities in income and widespread conditions of poverty, conditions that both broadened and deepened in the process of recovery and economic expansion. The statistics are startling. In 1979–1980 the richest 10 percent of households accounted for 36.5 percent of the national income. Ten years later, in 1989, their share rose to 46.8 percent. At the other extreme, the share in national income of the bottom 50 percent of income earners fell from 20.4 percent to 16.8 percent.[55]

The social costs of the structural adjustments made by the regime are reflected to some extent in the decline in state expenditures, that is, in the consumption by government of goods and services, particularly as it relates to social programs that address the basic needs of the working class and the poor. In comparing various countries in terms of levels of government consumption as a percentage of GDP, Chile showed the greatest decline relative to other countries for which data are available—a real overall decline of 2.2 percent from 1973 to 1981, and another decline of 2.6 percent from 1982 to 1987, reflecting a reduction of 10 percent in per capita spending on social programs over this period (12.5 percent reduction for health, 6.4 percent for education, and 7.1 percent for housing).[56] Over this period, in eight of the other ten countries the level of government consumption actually rose.

A reduction in the government's share of national income indirectly creates or exacerbates conditions of poverty and lowers the social wage that sets the floor for required income levels. A more direct, albeit very general, measure of the level of exploitation is the share of wages in national income, which, as we have seen, declined dramatically. Another indicator is employee earnings as a percentage of value added in manufacturing. Data using this measure are available for ten countries, seven of which suffered declines.[57] However, in terms of these data, Chile had by far the lowest level (16.7 percent) in 1973–1981, compared to 37.1 percent in Mexico, 33.8 percent in Uruguay, 29.1 percent in Venezuela, 25.9 percent in Argentina, 38.1 percent in Bolivia, and 28.4 percent in Brazil, the one other country that had drastically restructured the position of labor in the 1970s. In a subsequent period (1982–1985), when most countries followed Chile's lead in reducing the share of labor in national income, seven out of ten countries experienced further declines (especially Mexico, which went from 37.1 percent to 26.2 percent), whereas Chile, at 17.7 percent, continued to have the highest level of exploitation, as measured by the share of value added in manufacturing. Such superexploitation is critical to Chile's economic model and to its superior "performance" in posting solid rates of growth in output under conditions of macroeconomic stability. The relative "success" of the military regime's policies remains a subject of debate, although the current regime has clearly chosen to build on and to continue the same policies in all important respects, as it is determined, above all and at all costs, to secure conditions of macroeconomic equilibrium. But in the last resort, it cannot be denied or ignored that military rule, and the machinery of a national security state, did provide the essential conditions for economic growth—the other side of Chile's "economic miracle." For one thing, major economic conditions, such as those relating to the postplebiscite flurry of privatizations, were all created by decree, subject neither to consultation nor to discussion. In addition, the economic conditions thus created would never have been tolerated by civil societies of "democratic" regimes that did not dispose of the same repressive instruments. Further, the laws enacted by the military junta, which had arrogated to itself all legislative and executive powers, were predicated on a right-wing ideology, the sectarian interests of the bourgeoisie, and a regime of military force and political terror.

In its efforts to restructure Chilean society and politics, the Pinochet regime all but destroyed the power of organized labor, as well as the organizations of the urban poor formed in the protest movement of the early 1970s. This repression permitted the regime to impose a level of austerity on the working population that other governments in the region were incapable of—and to keep the lid on the simmering discontent of the many the boom left behind. But the result has been a form of repressed stability, resembling steam bottled up in a kettle, that not even a second political opening in 1989 and a subsequent return to an elected-civilian regime has been able to release.

Notes

1. The military regime defined its initial objectives in General Pinochet's pronouncement of September 11, 1973, shortly before Allende was deposed.

2. In terms of its GDP, Chile's economy grew at the following rates: 9.9 percent (1977), 8.2 percent (1978), 8.3 percent (1979), 7.8 percent (1980), and 5.7 percent (1981).

3. On the development versus democracy debate, see, inter alia, Orlando Letelier, "The Chicago Boys in Chile," *The Nation*, August 28, 1976. On the growth versus equity debate, in the context of recent developments in Chile and Latin America, see the special issue of Corporación de Investigaciones Económicas para América Latina (CIEPLAN) 31 (March 1991) and CEPAL, *Transformación Productiva con Equidad* (Santiago: Naciones Unidas, 1990).

4. The economic model implemented in Chile by the military government as of 1973 is an extreme and archetypal case of structural adjustment and monetarist policies—a neoliberal program of laissez-faire capitalist development that has been introduced widely and rapidly all over Latin America in the 1980s in response to the need for international capital to insure the capacity of debtor countries to service their mounting external debts *and* to restore growth. The free market model pioneered by the economic team of the military regime and implemented under almost ideal political conditions (i.e., a total free hand and a concentration of armed force) involved a reform package based on a neoclassical

theory of growth, a theoretical model formulated, inter alia, by Ronald McKinnon, Edward Shaw, Anne O. Krueger, and the staff of the World Bank. See John Williamson, "What Washington Means by Policy Reform" (paper for conference, Latin American Adjustment: How Much Has Happened?) (Washington, D.C.: Institute for International Economics, 1989). For an example of the "Washington consensus" about policy reform see Bela Balassa et al., *Towards Renewed Economic Growth in Latin America* (Washington, D.C.: Institute for International Economics, 1986). This model, however, has little to say about how to stabilize an economy in the short run. Thus, in practice, the model is appended to a traditional IMF recipe and provides the basis of the IMF proposals for structural reform or institutional changes that have been implemented to varying degrees in the 1980s in almost all countries in Latin America. Chile, in effect, pioneered these proposals.

5. It is widely recognized that the military regimes that took power in South America in the 1960s and 1970s (Brazil in 1964, Bolivia in 1971, Chile in 1973, Argentina in 1976, Uruguay in 1978) represented a new and distinct type of dictatorship based on the DNS elaborated in the United States and subscribed to by the armed forces of most countries in the region.

6. The strategy of ISI (import-substitution industrialization) in force in most of South America from the 1930s until the 1970s was geared toward expansion of the domestic market, providing the basis of the populist, nationalist politics that mobilized and incorporated the growing middle class and, increasingly (in the 1960s), diverse segments of the working and popular classes. By the end of the 1960s this democratizing process, together with the process of land reform all over the continent, had eroded the economic privileges and political power of the traditional oligarchy and the agrarian bourgeoisie, producing both a crisis in the pact of domination and conditions (of class war) that pitted a resolute and increasingly militant working class against a class that was struggling to resolve its hegemony ("order").

7. In 1987, Joaquin L. Lavin, vice-president of the right-wing Unión Demócrata Independiente (UDI), which provided the Pinochet regime with most of its civilian functionaries over the years, published a best-selling book, *Chile: Revolución Silenciosa* (Santiago: Zig-Zag, 1987). The book summarizes the transformations realized by the regime, with major focus on the modernization of capitalist enterprises and on the incorporation of new technologies in the major branches of industry and economic sectors. Lavin's conception of a "Silent Revolution" caused considerable repercussions within Chile. He not only captured the regime's sense of its accomplishments but in doing so inadvertently raised the issue of the many people for whom the revolutionary process has been silent to the point of being quite invisible, marginalizing them completely from its "benefits," about which more below.

8. *Fortin*, September 23, 1988.

9. *La Epoca*, September 20, 1988.

10. On the night of the coup, September 11, 1973, a publishing house owned by Augustín Edwards was churning out a document known to insiders as "the brick," a 500-page blueprint for reversing Allende's economic policies—the product of months of study by opposition economists under the sponsorship of the Society to Promote Manufacturing (SOFOFA) and its president, Orlando Saenz. This

document was the basis of the program eventually accepted by Pinochet and his colleagues. On the process involved, see Pamela Constable and Arturo Valenzuela, *Chile Under Pinochet: A Nation of Enemies* (New York: Norton, 1991), pp. 166ff.

11. As Andrés Fontaine, a leading economist at the Central Bank, Santiago, comments in a 1977 mimeo, the one fundamental element distinguishing Chile from the rest of Latin America is that in Chile "we began structural reforms and tackling the fiscal deficit in the mid-70s (with an Economic Recovery Program that initiated large-scale privatization, a currency devaluation, a near uniform 10 percent import tariff, and a drastic cut in state spending) a full ten years before most other countries in the region."

12. Fernando Dahse, *Mapa de la Extrema Riqueza* (Santiago: Editorial Aconcagua, 1979), pp. 175–179.

13. Ibid., pp. 140–147, 159.

14. Sergio Bitar, *Chile: Liberalismo, Económico y Dictadura Política* (Lima: Instituto de Estudios Peruanos, 1980), p. 130.

15. *Business Latin America*, March 30, 1977, p. 103.

16. Bitar, op. cit., p. 44.

17. *Revista Hoy*, September 6, 1978, p. 8.

18. "Who would be more efficient in spending money? The poor? The ignorant? By no means: the rich, he who ... has success in other areas." See Milton Friedman, *Chile: Bases para un Desarrollo Económico*, Fundación de Estudios Económicos/Banco Hipotecario de Chile (Santiago: Editorial Universitaria, 1975).

19. José P. Arellano, *Politicas Sociales y Desarrollo: Chile, 1924–1984* (Santiago: CIEPLAN, 1988), p. 19.

20. See Jaime Ruiz-Tagle, *El Sindicalismo Chileno Despues del Plan Laboral* (Santiago: Programa de Economía del Trabajo, 1985).

21. Ricardo Ffrench-Davis, "The Monetarist Experiment in Chile: A Critical Survey," *World Development* 11, 1 (1983), p. 916.

22. Andrés Sanfuentes, "Chile: Effects of the Adjustment Policies on the Agriculture and Forestry Sector," *CEPAL Review* no. 3 (December) (Santiago: United Nations, 1987), p. 119.

23. *Colección Estudios CIEPLAN* no. 28 (June) (Santiago: CIEPLAN, 1990).

24. Andrés Sanfuentes, "Los Grupos Económicos: Control y Políticas," *Colección Estudios CIEPLAN* no. 15 (December) (Santiago: CIEPLAN, 1984), p. 142.

25. Oscar Muñoz, *Chile y su Industrialización* (Santiago: CIEPLAN, 1986), p. 259.

26. Patricio Meller, "Revisión del Proceso de Ajuste Chileno de la de Década del 80," *Colección Estudios CIEPLAN* no. 30 (December) (Santiago: CIEPLAN, 1990), p. 17.

27. There is voluminous literature on the 1982–1983 crisis, resulting, according to most analysts, from both the external "shock" and serious policy errors. See, in particular, Arellano, op. cit.; Sebastián Edwards and Alejandra Edwards, *Monetarism and Liberalization* (Cambridge: Ballinger, 1987); Alejandro Foxley, "Experimentos Neoliberales en América Latina," *Colección Estudios CIEPLAN* no. 7 (March) (Santiago: CIEPLAN, 1982); Ffrench-Davis, op. cit.; and Meller, op. cit.

28. Meller, op. cit., p. 42.

29. Sanfuentes, 1987, op. cit., p. 123.

30. Both Banco Interamericano de Desarrollo (BID) and CEPAL in their 1988 reports on the economic performance of Latin American countries highlighted the particularly favorable external conditions for Chile (terms of trade, copper prices, U.S. and world demand for forest and fruit products, and so on). See CEPAL, *Panorama Económico de América Latina 1988* (Santiago: Naciones Unidas, 1988), p. 39. In addition to these favorable conditions, growth was also based on considerable idle capacity arising from the 1982–1983 recession.

31. Meller, op. cit., p. 43.

32. Joseph Ramos, "Stabilization and Adjustment Policies in the Southern Cone, 1974–1983," *CEPAL Review* no. 25 (April) (Santiago: United Nations, 1985), p. 106.

33. Rates of growth for these years exceeded the Latin American average.

34. Alvaro Diaz, *El Capitalismo Chileno en Los 90: Crecimiento Económico y Desigualdad Social* (Santiago: Ediciones PAS, 1991), p. 58.

35. Many of these studies have been conducted by researchers connected with various research centers concerned with social change (CIEPLAN, AHC [Academia de Humanismo Cristiano], CEP [Centro de Estudios Públicos], SUR [SUR Profesionales], FLACSO [Facultad Latinoamericana de Ciencias Sociales], ILET [Instituto Latinoamericano de Estudios Transnacionales], GIA [Grupo de Investigaciones Agrarias], GEA [Grupo de Estudios Agro-Regionales], ICAL [Instituto de Ciencias Alejandro Lipschutz]). See, in particular, Ricardo Ffrench-Davis and Oscar Muñoz, "Desarrollo Económico, Inestablidad y Desequilibrios Políticos en Chile: 1950–89," *Colección Estudios CIEPLAN* no. 28 (June) (Santiago: CIEPLAN, 1990), pp. 121–156.

36. Ricardo Ffrench-Davis, *The Impact of Global Recession and National Policies on Living Standards: Chile, 1973–87* (Santiago: CIEPLAN, 1988), pp. 13–33.

37. Ibid., 17.

38. Meller, op. cit., pp. 43–44.

39. According to the economists of ICAL, workers lost 56.7 percent of their purchasing power from 1983 to 1987 (*Fortin*, September 14, 1988, p. 7). This average loss was further broken down as follows: skilled operators (-42.8 percent); unskilled operators (-56.4 percent); and personal service workers (-71.0 percent). Calculations of purchasing power differ markedly. According to ICAL calculations, the index of real wages in 1989 stood at 65 percent of the 1970 level, while INE places it at 92 percent; the Central Bank, using December 1982 as 100.0, has it at 101.9 for 1989, compared to 81.7 for 1970. Notwithstanding the fact that these latter figures were used by visiting economists such as Ritter (A.R.M. Ritter, "Development Strategy and Structural Adjustment in Chile 1973–1990," *Canadian Journal of Latin American and Caribbean Studies*, 15, 30 [1990]) in their positive or sanguine evaluation of the Chilean model, it is very likely that the truth—an accurate representation of reality—lies somewhere between the alternative figures presented by ICAL and INE.

40. See Table 10, "Availability of Goods" in PET, *Series de Indicadores Económico-Sociales: Series Anuales, 1960–1980* (Santiago: PET, 1990), p. 24.

41. The matter of definition and measurement of Chile's poor is the subject of considerable controversy. By the government's calculations, advertised in the plebiscite campaign, the proportion of total families living in poverty had been reduced by one-third, moving from 21 percent in 1970 to 14 percent in 1982 (see

Alejandro Rojas, *Mapa de la Extrema Pobreza en Chile: 1982*. [Santiago: Universidad Católica de Chile, Instituto de Economía, 1988]). But as numerous studies (see, especially, Mariana Schkolnik and Berta Teitelboim, *Pobreza y Desempleo en Poblaciones: La Otra Cara del Modelo Neoliberal* [Santiago: Academia de Humanismo Cristiano-Programa de Economía del Trabajo, 1988]; Eugenio Ortega and Ernesto Tironi, *Pobreza en Chile* [Santiago: Centro de Estudios del Desarrollo, 1988]; and Raúl Urzua and Patricio Dooner, eds., *La Opción Preferencial por los Pobres* [Santiago: CISOC-Centro Bellarmino, 1987]) have demonstrated, the government's measure of poverty (families living in substandard housing) is highly suspect. The government measure can be compared to the reasonable measure used in a variety of other studies, where the measure is most generally based on family income in relation to the value of a basic food basket. Using this definition, a recent study by Programa Regional de Empleo para América Latina y el Caribe (PREALC) (*La Epoca*, September 17, 1988) calculated that the number of families living in poverty rose from 29 percent in 1969 to 45 percent in 1985 and that, out of all the families, the proportion of indigent or desperately poor rose from 8.4 percent to 19 percent. More recent studies commissioned by PET (Programa de Economía del Trabajo, AHC) in 1988 show a similar situation, leading to the much-used and debated calculation of 5 million poor (out of a total population of 12.4 million). By one calculation (*El Siglo*, September 1988), the total daily income received on average by these 5 million people is less than the daily profits (US$411 million) generated by two of Chile's richest families, the Angelini and Matte families.

42. Recent studies (Schkolnik and Teitelboim, op. cit.) show that over 50 percent of the Chilean population consumes less than 1,600 calories a day per capita, in relation to the 2,310 minimum recommended by the World Health Organization.

43. See Sanfuentes, 1987, op. cit.

44. Diaz, op. cit., p. 20.

45. Ibid., statistical appendix.

46. Jacqueline Weinstein, "Pesca Industrial: Ganancias Privadas Versus Beneficios Sociales," *Coyuntura Económica* no. 15 (June) (Santiago: PET, 1988), pp. 92–93.

47. Jorge Echeñique, *Evolución Reciente de la Agricultura y Sus Incógnitas Futuras* (Santiago: Confederación Nacional de Cooperativas Campesinas, 1987), pp. 20–21.

48. See Henry Veltmeyer, "Surplus Labor and Class Formation on the Latin American Periphery" in Ronald Chilcote and Dale Johnson, eds., *Theories of Development* (Newbury: Sage, 1983) on the various forms taken by the relative surplus populations in Chile and Latin America.

49. "Superexploitation" here refers to the capacity of the system to draw on labor power at below its value, that is, without capital having to bear the full costs of its reproduction (see Veltmeyer, op. cit.). The conditions of superexploitation in Chilean agriculture are brought into focus in a study by CEPAL, "El Desarrollo Frutícola y Forestal en Chile y Sus Derivaciones Sociales," *Estudio e Informes* no. 57 (Santiago: Naciones Unidas, 1986), p. 64, which notes that "in its semi-proletarian character the peasant offers his surplus family labor to the agricultural temporary labor markets, the result of which is the depression of wages ... since he is disposed to work for less money than needed for his family reproduction [because of]

access to a piece of land that guarantees a minimum of subsistence" (Veltmeyer's translation).

50. See Javier Martínez and Arturo León, *Clases y Clasificaciones Sociales: Investigaciones Sobre la Estructura Social Chilena 1970–1983* (Santiago: Centro de Estudios del Desarrollo, 1987).

51. "El Desempeño Empleador de la Economía Chilena Bajo el Gobierno Militar," *Coyuntura Económica* no. 14 (April) (Santiago: PET, 1987), p. 70.

52. Gabriel Palma and Mario Marcel, "Kaldor y el 'Discreto Encanto' de la Burguesía Chilena," *Colección Estudios CIEPLAN* no. 28 (June) (Santiago: CIEPLAN, 1990), p. 91. These figures include workers in government make-work projects (Programa de Empleo Mínimo [PEM] and Programa Ocupacional para Jefes de Hogar [POJH]) and in various forms of self-employment (work on one's own account) who are normally paid 30 percent to 60 percent of the minimum wage. Fully 40 percent (34.4 percent exclusive of PEM) of the economically active population in 1981 just prior to the 1982–1983 recession was defined by CEPAL and other sources as "underemployed" and by Urzua and Dooner, op. cit., as "excluded categories."

53. Sergio Gomez and Jorge Echeñique, *La Agricultura Chilena: Los Dos Caras de la Modernización* (Santiago: FLACSO-Agraria, 1988), p. 197.

54. Sanfuentes, 1987, op. cit., p. 120.

55. Diaz, op. cit., pp. 58–59.

56. Meller, op. cit., p. 49.

57. See Manuel Pastor and Gary Dymski, "Debt Crisis and Class Conflict in Latin America," *Capital and Class,* 43 (Spring 1991).

4

From Critics to Celebrants

During that luncheon, which took place six months before the elections, they (Aylwin and Foxley) gave us all sort of guarantees that economic policy would continue to be the same as what we had known before: an open market, favorable investment terms, in sum, all the good things that we inherited from the military government. And a year later, there is no doubt in my mind that the grand warranty that this country has, in fact, is precisely Alejandro Foxley as Minister of Finance.*

—Eduardo Matte,
President of Cape Horn Methanol[1]

Pinochet's Opponents:
Politico-Economic Conversion

The convoluted process by which Christian Democratic and Socialist intellectuals converted from being critics of Pinochet's economic model to becoming architects of its continuity constitutes a crucial but heretofore insufficiently examined aspect of the Chilean transition. In fact, the scope and swiftness of their intellectual conversion had a decisive political impact on the transition process. The modifications introduced into their conceptual matrix and economic discourse were sufficiently genuine, substantive, and exhaustive to win the confidence of transnational and local corporate elites. Hence, in March of 1991, as the elected government completed its first year in office, Jaime Guzmán, chief ideologue of the Pinochet dictatorship, expressed his satisfaction that Aylwin's economic team had preserved "the central lines of the development strategy supported by the previous government ... and persevered in following serious and orthodox macroeconomic management."[2] Six months later, Andrés Allamand, president of the right-wing organization Renovación Nacional, could gloat that Christian Democratic Finance Minister Alejandro Foxley and Socialist Economics Minister Carlos Ominami "could perfectly well have been members of Pinochet's cabinet."[3]

---

* *All quotations originally in Spanish have been translated by Fernando Ignacio Leiva.*

46

This chapter examines the intellectual trajectory of the principal economic policymakers of the Concertación de Partidos por la Democracia (Concertación) coalition and Aylwin administration of the early 1990s: the Christian Democrats, Alejandro Foxley (finance), Edgardo Boeninger (presidential staff), René Cortázar (labor), and Juan Pablo Arellano (budget), as well as the Socialists, Carlos Ominami (economics) and Eugenio Tironi (information). By mapping the evolution of their economic discourse as they ascend in status from harassed oppositionists to elite negotiators with the military, and then to occupants of ministerial posts, this chapter seeks to answer two groups of related questions: (1) why Christian Democratic and Socialist economists converted from critics to defenders of the project of capitalist restructuring initiated by Pinochet, and (2) which of the politico-economic premises defended by neoliberals under Pinochet were explicitly internalized by convergent Socialist and Christian Democratic economists. A holistic understanding of the Chilean transition is impossible without explaining how those who had been adamant critics of neoliberalism during the 1970s and early 1980s could reach the 1990s embracing neoliberalism's historic project of structurally transforming the Chilean economy by fully integrating it into the global market.

Itinerary of a Realignment

Tracing this intellectual conversion is necessary for a number of other reasons. First, and above all, members of Aylwin's economic team and their supporters justify continuing with Pinochet's economic model by claiming that their hands are tied. Aylwin policymakers contend that they are hamstrung by "authoritarian enclaves" embedded in the inherited institutional framework. This chapter demonstrates, however, that current socioeconomic and macropolicy continuities are better explained by the profound theoretical realignment of Christian Democratic and Socialist intellectuals, rather than by any inherited budgetary or institutional constraints.

This study of the Christian Democratic and Socialist intellectual transformation highlights the neglected socioeconomic dimension of the negotiated transition because, as we will argue, appropriate assurances about the continuity of basic class and power structures had to be offered well in advance of electoral contests. In the case of Chile, these assurances took the form of a comprehensive modification in the economic discourse of the majority of Pinochet's opponents. Behind this conversion lies a series of seminars, which proliferated after 1983, attended by Socialist, Christian Democratic, and neoliberal intellectuals. These encounters led to a systematic process of consensus building on the nature of the relationship between the resource-intensive export-oriented economic model and the post-Pinochet political system.

A final reason for exploring this conversion is that Foxley and Ominami's receptiveness to the neoliberal legacy reflects a broader, continentwide shift in Latin American economic development thinking. The increasing convergence between monetarism and structuralism on macroeconomic policies and long-run development strategies has led to the rise of Latin American neostructuralism.[4] Wielding this new discourse, many elected-civilian regimes (for example, in Chile and Mexico), as well as regional development agencies, such as the United Nations ECLAC and the International Labor Organization's Regional Employment Program (known as PREALC), have constructed a politico-economic prescription that couches support for the process of capitalist restructuring and globalization in the language of *concertación* (concerted action). Thus, the study of the intellectual conversion of the Chilean opposition intellectuals during the late 1980s can provide valuable insight into the origins of the neodevelopmental discourse emerging in the 1990s.[5]

Interaction Between Theory and Society

The reason for choosing one set of policies, or a particular development strategy, and abandoning another has to do with the complex interaction of economic, political, and cultural forces. That people change their minds over time as the reality around them is changing is a constituent element of any historical process; that Christian Democratic and Socialist economists converted from being erstwhile critics to current celebrants of the neoliberal model is not, therefore, censurable per se. What needs to be determined is the societal impact of their newly adopted beliefs. What social forces were unleashed or inhibited by these newly embraced ideas? What social practices were legitimized or repressed by these ideas? We will argue that by adopting a new conceptual matrix Pinochet's former critics ensured the continuity of the neoliberal economic model and contributed to the political legitimation of the drastic process of capitalist restructuring carried out under Pinochet.[6]

The Conversion from Critics to Celebrants

During the late 1970s, economists, such as Foxley and Ominami, produced a wealth of documented critiques of the neoliberal economic policies ruthlessly enforced under Pinochet. Foxley and his collaborators at CIEPLAN, for example, became widely known in development circles as promoters of alternative policies and development strategies. Ominami, during his exile in France, joined the Socialist party and became a follower of the Parisian wing of the French Regulationist school. Upon his return to Chile in the mid-1980s, in direct opposition to the prevailing neoliberal strategy of the Pinochet regime, Ominami actively defended the need for a national industrial policy and for international competitiveness based on endogenous technological innovation.[7]

The technical consistency and broad range of Foxley and Ominami's work earned them widespread acclaim among academic and international institutions. By the end of the 1980s, however, both Foxley and Ominami had completed a spectacular intellectual about-face, radically retreating from their earlier critical posture vis-à-vis Pinochet's economic model and its export-oriented accumulation strategy. Thus, the 1980s came to an end in Chile with a profound conceptual and political reorientation of opposition intellectuals.

This conceptual turnaround can best be understood as the outcome of three separate but intersecting processes consummated during the 1983–1989 period:

1. The shift from initial condemnation of the Chicago Boys' economic policies to acknowledgement of their success in structurally "modernizing" the Chilean economy.
2. The shift from intransigent criticism of the military dictatorship to acceptance of the principles of a "protected democracy" embodied in Pinochet's 1980 constitution.
3. The shift from the transformative zeal of 1950s structuralism to the status quo–conscious Latin American neostructuralism of the 1990s.

By hastening a comprehensive recasting of previous ideals of redistribution into molds more congruent with the prevalent neoliberal economic model, these shifts contributed toward creating the necessary conditions for a negotiated transition.[8]

Well in advance of the October 1988 plebiscite, these three shifts had radically altered the conceptual framework and politico-economic discourse of Pinochet's opponents. The societal political impact of this realignment was considerable. It provided transnational and local corporate elites with adequate assurances that (1) private property would remain sacrosanct, (2) the resource-intensive export-oriented pattern of capital accumulation would be maintained, (3) the massive transfer of assets and property carried out under state terrorism would remain unchallenged, and (4) no major innovations in macroeconomic management would be introduced by a post-Pinochet elected-civilian government.

To fully grasp the magnitude, scope, and significance of this conceptual realignment, we proceed to review each of these three shifts separately.

From Condemnation to Admiration of the Chicago Boys

We, who as opposition economists were very critical of the military regime's economic management ... have also mastered the positive lessons offered by that management in its more recent phase.

—Alejandro Foxley, 1988[9]

The first of these movements is best illustrated by the waning critique of neoliberal policies on the part of CIEPLAN, the Christian Democratic economic think tank founded in 1975, which served as the base of operations for the economists who were to design Aylwin's economic strategy and eventually fill the key economic posts of his administration.

CIEPLAN's critique of neoliberal macroeconomic management, short-term stabilization policies, and long-term structural reforms was closely correlated to the cyclical movement of the Chilean economy during the 1975–1989 period. Hence, CIEPLAN's critique reached maximum intensity in the middle of the 1982–1983 economic crisis, when its analysts envisioned the imminent collapse of the neoliberal model. After 1983, however, as growth rates recovered under Büchi's more pragmatic policies, CIEPLAN's critique began to lose vigor, diminishing in content and scope. This tendency continued until 1989, by which time Foxley and his closest collaborators had moved toward accepting Pinochet's economic model, had acknowledged the success of the capitalist restructuring carried out under his rule, and, finally, had "mastered the positive lessons" offered by the Chicago Boys' export-oriented strategy of economic development.

The Pre-1983 Critique

During the 1977–1980 period, while the Chicago Boys were boasting that by ruthlessly applying the principles taught to them by Milton Friedman they had engineered a veritable "Chilean economic miracle," CIEPLAN researchers were arriving at an altogether different conclusion. Up until 1978, they indicated, increases in production had barely allowed for recuperation from the 13 percent drop in GDP registered in 1975; a lower inflation rate had been achieved at the expense of creating other imbalances; and, given the persistence of low investment rates, increases in GDP could not be sustained. In addition, they called attention to the inherent inequality generated by the model, warning that it seemed unlikely that " ... the concentration in income distribution observed in what has transpired of the present economic experiment will be modified as a result of the spontaneous functioning of the market."[10] Thus, even though surface events could suggest economic success, a more profound analysis revealed that claims to an economic miracle were nothing more than "a very exaggerated wave of optimism without sufficient basis in reality."[11]

It was during this phase of their critique that Foxley and his CIEPLAN colleagues enhanced their reputation as resolute critics of neoliberalism. In their bid to demystify the "economic miracle," they were forced to challenge head-on the lavish praise bestowed by the IMF and World Bank upon the Chicago Boys' handling of the economy. In this debate, Foxley argued that depending on which macroeconomic indicators were chosen, two very different and opposing conclusions about the 1974–1980 period could be reached. International lending institutions, such as the IMF, as well as private international banks, judged the dictatorship's economic policies as a success by preferentially looking at the following indicators: (1) inflation, (2) rate of GDP growth, (3) fiscal deficit, and (4) dynamism of nontraditional exports. But by only considering these indicators, the IMF and the World Bank were overlooking the concomitant deterioration in living conditions and "the more striking features of Chile's economic experience" of the 1974–1980 period: "the simultaneous deterioration of the employment rate, real wages, per capita consumption and other social indicators that measure the population's access to housing education and health, as well as the skewed distribution of consumption depending on the range of income."[12]

In purely macroeconomic terms, Chile could not be presented as an example of successfully applied neoliberal economics, if one considered that (1) the growth rate during the years 1974–1980 was well below the 1960–1970 average, (2) the average growth rate of the goods producing sector was also below the average rate of the preceding decade, (3) most of the GDP growth rate could be explained by the expansion of the service sector, (4) the potential for future growth remained weak, given the low investment rate of 11 percent yearly, and (5) the level of employment grew very slowly, whereas the unemployment rate remained fixed at an extraordinarily high level.[13] Foxley remained highly critical of the processes of privatization and market liberalization implemented before 1983. He attacked the neoliberals' claim that such policies had neutral distributive effects. In Foxley's view, privatization and market liberalization had "implied a massive transference of resources to the private sector, particularly towards financial entities and large industrial concerns."[14]

In sum, during the first decade of dictatorial rule, Foxley's, as well as CIEPLAN's, critique not only challenged the effectiveness of neoliberal macroeconomic management but also denounced the severe social bias of the stabilization process carried out by the Chicago Boys. Additionally, serious misgivings were also expressed regarding the structural reforms being implemented: privatization of state enterprises, the opening of the economy to international trade and financial flows, and the changes brought about in the productive structure and in income distribution.

In the midst of the 1982 crisis, the disastrous legacy of "global monetarism" could be succinctly summarized as "paralysis of the productive structure, wasted and unused human and material resources, and an all-encompassing financial crisis."[15] At the time of the 1982–1983 crisis, CIEPLAN's critique of neoliberalism incorporated three central components: (1) Pinochet's economic model was judged to be a failure, (2) emphasis was placed on distributional aspects and the class bias of neoliberal policies, challenging the Chicago Boys' claim to "technical neutrality," and (3) the need was recognized for an alternative model of development that could confront neoliberalism's devastating aftermath. The course followed by events after 1983, however, was to progressively erode each one of these components. By 1988, the model had been judged a success, distributional indicators had been forgotten in lieu of economic growth indicators, and continuity, rather than replacement of the model, had become the dominant element in Foxley's new economic discourse.

One reasonable explanation for such transformation was that, as the crisis deepened, Foxley astutely noticed a new factor entering the political scene: The more dynamic sectors of the capitalist class began to express dissatisfaction with the "rigid" application of neoliberal doctrine. Seizing the opportunity, Foxley launched a strategy to win entrepreneurial support for his critique, stressing the economic model's incapacity to service adequately the needs of the financial and exporting sectors. He adamantly denounced the "permanent damage" done to the economy, the "weakening of the productive structure, the growing difficulties for firms to fully realize their export potential, and the undermining of entrepreneurial credibility on economic policy, along with increasing social and psychological damage to more than one-third of the labor force."[16]

As tens of thousands of urban poor took to the streets during the 1983–1986 national protests, offering through their mobilization efforts a "practical" evaluation of the neoliberal model, Foxley's search for entrepreneurial support eclipsed the social content of his own intellectual critique of the model.

Recognition of Neoliberal Success

After 1983, Foxley's assessment of Chile's "neoconservative experiment" shifted radically. By 1989, the magnitude of this change was so evident that Foxley himself felt obliged to account for it. He did so by publicly recognizing the transformative power of the neoliberal project:

The 1982–83 crisis was a disaster of great proportions. ... At the time, some of us wrote different articles that obviously contained a very harsh critique of the economic policies that had led to the crisis. Now, if one abruptly jumps forward and situates oneself at the end of the year 1989, one has no choice but to recognize that as an outcome of that deep crisis, there finally took place what—I believe—the authors of the profound structural change envisioned in 1974 were hoping would happen: a fundamental recomposition of the mode of functioning of the Chilean economy, with a reorientation of the productive structure towards the external sector, with a strong incentive and adequate response on the part of a significant portion of the private sector, whose animal spirits were finally awakened, and who, in the pain and heat of the crisis, were able to initiate a process of investment, a process of productive modernization, and an increase in exports, *which I would dare to assess as extraordinarily successful* [emphasis added].[17]

By 1989, Foxley explicitly recognized that, as a result of the crisis induced by the policies of the Chicago Boys, the Chilean economy successfully completed the structural transformation "originally envisioned in 1974." Thus, by the late 1980s, Foxley was certifying success on the basis of those selective criteria that in his earlier works he had branded as dearer to the IMF and the private international banks than to the requirements of a comprehensive analysis. In the face of two indicators brandished as proof of an "extraordinarily successful" model—the increase in exports and the recuperation of investment levels—Foxley's pre-1983 misgivings quickly evaporated. Evaluative criteria emphasizing social and distributional indicators were discarded; the biting criticism of the pre-1983 period had completely disappeared.[18]

From Converts to Crusaders for the Model

Under closer scrutiny, the centrist opposition's intellectual conversion entailed acknowledging not only the successes of neoliberal policy under Pinochet but also the active commitment to preserve and support the structural transformation of Chilean capitalism carried out by the military regime. A new language and cadence, very different from that voiced in the 1982–1983 period appears. In his converted condition, Foxley's new credo eerily echoed the Chicago Boys at the height of their fanaticism under Sergio de Castro, Pinochet's minister of finance from the 1970s until 1982, as shows in Foxley's remarks:

First, and above all, we [Aylwin's economic team] are putting all our chips behind an open economy; we are putting our stakes on the modernizing process of the Chilean economy, and on its integration, as fully as is possible, in world markets; we are wagering that increases in productivity will become the motor of the process of modernization; that, to a significant extent, the process of modernization will rest on the capacity of Chilean entrepreneurs to successfully confront the challenge, going beyond those obvious sectors in which it is easy to make a profit. We are betting on the ability of our entrepreneurs to introduce more sophisticated processes and phases, becoming competitive also in the manufacturing sector. We are betting on ... implementing all those measures that comprise a modern economy that is successful in world markets at the end of the twentieth century. We bet on our capacity to establish a better relationship between entrepreneurs and workers, so that through the principle of cooperation, the endogenous increase in productivity can be stimulated within each enterprise.[19]

All of the essential components of the neoliberal creed under Pinochet—support for the capitalist class and the expansion of its export activities, intensified internationalization and integration into world markets, control of labor conflicts for the sake of export-competitiveness—were also explicitly assumed by Christian Democratic and Socialist policymakers. Convergence with neoliberalism at the end of the 1980s could take place in Chile only by ignoring (aside from perfunctory lip service) the impoverishment of an ever-larger number of Chileans accompanying the purported modernization taking place during the pivotal years 1983–1989.[20] In the end, it seems that Foxley and his collaborators were seduced by the sweeping force of the capitalist restructuring process set in motion by the victorious alliance between Pinochet's state terror and Friedman's unencumbered market forces.

An intellectual retreat of such magnitude cannot be explained solely on the basis of the allure cast by selective positive economic indicators. Such an interpretation fails to consider simultaneous political and ideological processes that also influenced and reshaped the conceptual paradigm and discourse current in Chile's reemerging political class. It is toward these two other factors—the reconceptualization of democracy and the reformulation of a long-term development strategy—that we now turn our attention in order to better comprehend the conversion of Pinochet's former critics.

From Critique to Acceptance of a Protected Political System

The Price of Democracy

If the post-1983 rapid growth in exports persuaded Christian Democratic and Socialist leaders that neoliberal economic policies had been successful, then the massive and combative popular protests of the 1983–1986 period convinced them of the need to reappraise the authoritarian regime's conception of a protected political system. If the price of democracy (i.e., the transfer of power to a civilian regime) was to be the adoption of the postulates and foundations of the political system erected by the military dictatorship, Chile's centrist forces were more than willing to pay it.

Consequently, the pivotal realignment of intellectual and political forces during the years 1982–1989 also entailed the progressive abandonment of the principles and institutions embodied in Chile's 1925 constitution and in its democratic liberal traditions. Such action was passed off as "an extraordinary effort at political convergence," as Christian Democratic and Socialist leaders progressively remodeled their own conception of political democracy until it became compatible with the notion of "protected democracy" embodied in Pinochet's 1980 constitution.[21]

Concerted Action, Economic Order, Feasible Democracy

Leading Christian Democratic and Socialist intellectuals focused their attention on two major political concerns at the beginning of the 1980s, asking: What institutions could safely replace Pinochet's iron rule in a highly polarized society such as Chile's? How could transition from military dictatorship to civilian rule be facilitated? To solve the complex political problems posed by both of these questions, a select group of Christian Democratic and Socialist economists and intellectuals began to study and elaborate two central concepts: (1) the possibility of social and political concerted action, or "concertación," and (2) the relationship between "democracy and economic order" in the post-Pinochet era.[22]

The evolution of their thinking regarding these two notions between 1982 and 1989 reveals the extent to which capitalist restructuring under the military regime exacted major modifications in the political principles upheld by Pinochet's opponents. As we shall see below, these modifications committed centrist political parties to defending both the "social market economy" and a political system that, in the name of democracy, had been expressly designed to prevent social actors from tampering with private property rights and the free functioning of market forces.

"Concertación"—a Disciplining Mechanism

Writing during the height of the 1982 crisis, at a time when opposition economists considered the neoliberal economic model to be close to collapse and a change in political regime to be imminent, Foxley appeared troubled by the implications of a sudden end to Pinochet's rule. He felt that the replacement of the military dictatorship by an elected-civilian regime presupposed major changes in the political realm:

The essential problem can be summed up as follows: the consolidation of democracy in a postauthoritarian setting simultaneously demands the development of civil society, implying greater autonomy for social organizations, and the development of participation and consensus building mechanisms [concertación] at the level of those public decisions that directly affect the living and working conditions of the population, that is, regarding economic policies.[23]

Foxley further stated that the strengthening of autonomous social organizations, which necessarily follow the return to democracy, could lead to serious destabilizing consequences.

Once the autonomy of social organizations expands—a prerequisite for strengthening civil society vis-à-vis the state—these organizations do nothing more than reproduce the main conflicts in society. If these conflicts involve class contradictions or antagonistic ideological currents, each autonomous organization will but passively mirror such conflict. As a result, these conflicts will be strengthened and amplified, increasing society's polarization instead of reducing it. The system becomes more unstable.[24]

Recognizing this danger, Foxley and his colleagues focused their energies on answering the following question: "Is it possible to reduce the variance of the probable outcomes of the democratizing process, eliminating those alternatives that directly threaten important social actors?"[25]

The answer suggested by Foxley in 1982 was to recognize that these social conflicts existed and to establish the existence of a *prior agreement*, or concertación, among social and political actors regarding the boundaries of actions considered to be legitimate. In this manner, he argued, the mechanism of concertación would impede the danger of democratization of civil society and subsequent expression of unmet popular demands, which might eventually escalate out of government control. If the primary conflict could somehow be wrested away from the autonomous social organizations and be taken up and encased by the political system, then it could effectively be regulated by a global and societywide type of agreement. Political instability could thus be avoided if those entrusted with representing the "main conflict"—the postauthoritarian political parties and political class—vowed to circumscribe these antagonisms within previously agreed-upon boundaries. In this manner, the capitalist elites would not feel threatened and the military could return to its barracks. Hence, in a scenario where the economic model would be challenged by intensifying popular demands, Foxley conceptualized concertación as a mechanism for disciplining social organizations and subordinating them to the "higher needs" of stabilizing the postauthoritarian political system.

The Shrinking Scope of Concertación

Given that in 1982 the demise of the military regime seemed imminent, Foxley envisioned this mechanism of consensus as constituting the stable foundation for a new political regime. To play this role effectively, however, this consensus, or concertación, had to cover a broad spectrum of both political and economic topics, including (1) the rules of coexistence, namely, the constitutional norms regulating the electoral system and political parties that would guarantee both "pluralism" and respect for the "agreed-upon boundaries" to avoid the destabilization of democracy, (2) full citizen rights, "including economic rights guaranteeing the evolution of the economy towards greater equity," (3) the structure of property, and, finally, (4) the mechanisms through which workers participate in economic decisions.[26]

But important changes had transpired by 1988. Pinochet and the military regime had successfully weathered the 1982–1983 crisis, and Foxley had become a convert to the neoliberal export-oriented model. Pinochet, far from losing power, was dictating the conditions and rhythm of the transition. These changes forced an extensive redefinition of the scope and character of the much-sought-after concertación.

After 1983, the concept of concertación was compressed dramatically: It was reduced from being the basis of a new political regime to a mechanism to "decongest the state" and improve the efficiency of the economic system. By 1987, speaking at the tenth session of the Annual National Assembly of Private Enterprise (ENADE), Foxley had effectively downgraded the concept of concertación to a functional—not a foundational—mechanism.[27]

> If one wants to decongest the state apparatus of a host of decisions traditionally falling on its shoulders ... because everyone appealed to the political system in order to solve problems not necessarily belonging to the political system ... then the way to achieve this objective is to seek spaces conducive to the building of agreements between entrepreneurs and workers without the intervention of the state, or in any case, where state interference is much less than in the past.
>
> This is "concertación social," understood as a careful and incremental, yet permanent, exercise; as the space where workers and the private sector discuss their problems duly supported by technical teams with proven capacity for dialogue and understanding among themselves. If such is the case, then the process of concertación can, in fact, enormously relieve the state; it can reduce the levels of tension and social conflict and can contribute to the overall efficiency of the economic system.[28]

By early 1990, the concept of concertación had been further whittled down to a mere tool for negotiating minor modifications in Pinochet's labor legislation. Addressing a meeting of international academics and officials from international organizations supportive of CIEPLAN's work, René Cortázar, the incoming minister of labor, clarified that the concept of concertación was circumscribed by the necessity of generating an agreement on the fundamental rules of the game; specifically, "concertación is linked to the issue of labor reforms and the issue of social policy."[29] Cortázar made sure to stress the point that the existence of a weak trade union movement representing less than 10 percent of the labor force in no way undermined the prospects of concertación. The feebleness of the labor movement

> would naturally be a very serious problem if, with such a structure of mediation of interests, one were attempting to establish a consensus related to the issue of income policies. ... However, the requirements from a structure of interest mediation are very different if one wants to use it to generate certain consensuses regarding labor and economic institutions *which rest upon a legal foundation*. The purpose here is to *provide, through the means of concertación, a basis of legitimacy for a legal institution* [emphasis added].[30]

In the time span from 1982 to 1989, therefore, the concept of concertación was reduced from a broad social pact conceived as the foundation for a democratic system replacing an authoritarian regime in crisis (1982) to an instrument for improving the efficiency of a successful economic model (1988), and hence to a tool for legitimizing the need to make labor-capital relations flexible, as codified by Pinochet's repressive labor legislation of 1990. The progressive contraction of one of the leading concepts in the discourse of the convergent Christian Democratic and Socialist forces only mirrored the parallel acceptance of the military regime's 1980 constitution and its vision of a political system subordinate to the requirements of the export-oriented model of capital accumulation.

Democracy Subordinate to Economic Order

The acceptance of Pinochet's restrictive political system and the shrinking scope of the concept of concertación can be linked to the regular seminars among leading neoliberal, Socialist, and Christian Democratic intellectuals that began to take place after 1983. A key site for these encounters was the Centro de Estudios del Desarrollo (CED). Under the direction of Edgardo Boeninger, and heavily funded by U.S. and European governments and foundations, CED hammered out a common research agenda for opposition intellectuals who, up until then, found themselves dispersed in numerous externally funded private research institutes.[31]

These meetings enabled a select group of politically influential opposition intellectuals to achieve important objectives. First, in close consultation with neoliberal ideologues and advisors to Pinochet, Christian Democratic and Socialist intellectuals were able to identify and clearly understand the guarantees demanded by international banks, the local corporate elites, and the officer corps of the armed forces before acquiescing in a negotiated transition. Second, through these seminars, Christian Democratic and Socialist economists were able to refashion their economic discourse and formulate policies securely circumscribed and firmly encased within politico-economic parameters acceptable to the bloc in power. Third, these seminars developed the embryo of a new political class, one with a common historical perspective and platform—a political class able to negotiate with the dictatorship and elaborate a strategy capable of winning entrepreneurial acceptance, while maintaining sufficient democratic credentials to win broad electoral support and ascendency over the democratic social movements.

The "Theory of Change Under Democracy"

A central focus of these meetings was the nature of the relationship between economic order and democracy. In 1984, Edgardo Boeninger attempted to summarize the lessons drawn from these neoliberal, Socialist, and Christian Democratic encounters in what he called the "theory of change under democracy."[32]

According to Boeninger, the first pillar of this theory was the recognition that "the viability of alternation in political power through the holding of periodic elections is conditioned by the participants not feeling in the extreme situation of threat or risk in light of the possible outcome of such political competition."[33] Allende and the Popular Unity coalition had clearly violated this precept, and any new attempts at structural transformation through peaceful and constitutional means would neither be acceptable nor be supported by this theory.

A second pillar of the theory synthesized by Boeninger acknowledged the existence of a permanent tension between the will of the majority and a "national consensus." The overwhelming majority in society might desire major socioeconomic reforms, such as a national health system, but this violated national consensus because there would always exist a minority opposed to it. A theory of change under democracy must avoid the "devastating consequences of attempts to impose the will of the majority." In this regard, Boeninger advised that "a confrontational strategy that is detrimental to the political Right and to property owning and military sectors produces behaviors in the economic agents that can create serious upheavals in the economy, such as capital flight and stoppage of investments."[34] Democracy, therefore, implies not only majority rule but also conscientious respect for the rights of the capitalist minority.

The major conclusions of this theory are as follows: (1) the principle of majority rule "must not have unrestricted application," and (2) in order to successfully carry out changes under democracy, a previous "solid social and political consensus" is necessary.[35] Remarkably, the two pillars of this theory of change under democracy discovered by Boeninger and the Christian Democrats in 1984 were also the supporting structures of Pinochet's 1980 constitution.

Democratic Procedures—Not Enough

These two general principles for the postauthoritarian political order obviously have as a cornerstone the existing socioeconomic order. Boeninger acknowledged this and advanced the crucial axiom for the political operation that, under his general coordination, was to culminate half a decade later in Aylwin's election:

> It is neither sufficient nor possible for democracy to be consolidated only on the basis of respect for democratic procedures, if there does not exist a degree of substantial agreement (agreement on fundamentals) specifically regarding the economic order; this is particularly the case in Chile, where this has historically constituted the area of greatest political and social strife.[36]

However, after articulating the theory, a major question remained unresolved: How could this "agreement on fundamentals" be reached? Socialists, as well as Christian Democrats, had been major actors in polarizing any discussions on economic matters in the past. Historically, the two parties' respective political platforms had raised contentious issues, such as property rights, the role of the state, the structure of economic power, wealth and income distribution, popular participation in decisionmaking and economic control, and finally, the role of the market and planning. The seminars among neoliberal, Christian Democratic, and Socialist intellectuals concluded with agreement that the best way to move forward was "to identify the vital interests and values of the diverse social sectors and classes in order to find formulas of consensus concerning respect and mutual and simultaneous acceptance of such interests and values by all actors involved."[37] "Vital interests" had to be clearly identified so that a political system of mutual guarantees could be designed. Such a system had to ensure the security and satisfaction of the minority—the decisive minority constituted by large property owners and the armed forces, the same minority that after September 11, 1973, had successfully and brutally imposed its will on the majority of Chileans.

Economic Order and the Political System

Boeninger summarized the five basic guidelines that should govern the relationship between the political system and the existing economic order. These would ensure the successful transition to, and the subsequent consolidation necessary for, a correctly conceived democracy. The five points put forth by Boeninger were:

1. A minimum convergence on socioeconomic programs envisioned by the different political parties competing for power is necessary. These parties must explicitly recognize the need for substantive agreements on fundamentals so that any possible change in the government coalition "is not perceived as an intolerable threat by those sectors who make up the minority."
2. An explicit recognition of traditional private property over the means of production is also a basic precondition.
3. Gradualism in social and economic change must be maintained so that any change can be accepted by the capitalist elites, the armed forces, and international investors. Efforts at "overcoming poverty and at achieving a progressive diminution of inequality must not undercut freedom's economic dimension [i.e., private property]."
4. Priority must be given to economic growth; distributive concerns must be clearly subordinated to the needs of economic growth to avoid a situation where, "the problem of distribution becomes a zero-sum game inevitably leading to confrontation among classes."
5. Simultaneity must exist between economic growth and improvement in the distribution of its results to ensure political legitimacy and long-run stability.

It is both symbolic and bitterly ironic that Boeninger's master blueprint was originally written in 1984. For, not only does his theory of change under democracy remind one of Orwellian doublespeak, but, as Boeninger was writing his theory, tens of thousands of soldiers were storming Santiago streets, repressing the massive protests by thousands of Chile's dispossessed. These victims of Pinochet's economic model were fighting for both change *and* democracy, finding no need to carefully calculate their actions according to Boeninger's "new" theory. But the five principles outlined by Boeninger in 1984 turned out to be of crucial importance for the subsequent evolution of political events. On the one hand, these five principles defined the strategic direction followed in the construction of a centrist political coalition capable of replacing Pinochet.[38] On the other hand, these five principles also became the key parameters defining Aylwin's economic program of government.

Neoliberal Hegemony in Politics and Economics

It is striking to observe the extent to which, during the period 1983–1989, neoliberal ideologues gained hegemony over centrist and leftist intellectuals. Friedman's disciples were finally able to subordinate Pinochet's opponents ideologically in the economic, as well as political, spheres. In one respect, the opposition intelligentsia was forced to accept that it had been the Chicago Boys—and not they—who had successfully carried out the structural reforms that "modernized" Chile; in another respect, it had been neoliberal thinkers—and not the occurrence of social movements—who taught them the appropriate "democratic theory" capable of bringing an end to the "state of exception" (a term meaning the state has assumed some exceptional form, such as fascism or dictatorship) and generating those institutions for political normalization after Pinochet.

This novel theory of change under democracy spread from a small and select group of intellectuals to a broader group of party leaders. After 1984, the political leadership began a vast revision of what Boeninger called the scope and opportunity contained in programmatic proposals for change. The Democratic Alliance, formed in 1983 by six anti-Pinochet political parties—the precursor to Concertación—quickly toned down its demand for Pinochet's removal and retracted its call to convene a Constitutional Assembly. Joint action with the more militant social organizations and leftist parties was denounced as counterproductive. Confrontational social mobilization by hundreds or thousands of Chileans was frowned upon and was successfully subordinated to the "political mobilization" carefully dosed out by the cognoscenti of Boeninger's theory.

The politics of confrontation at the grass roots was increasingly replaced by the politics of concerted action on the part of political elites. The 1980 constitution, as well as Pinochet's conditions and timetable, was finally accepted. However, behind these developments, later touted as examples of pragmatism and political realism, one finds the hidden presence of the socioeconomic pivot of the Chilean transition: the explicit acceptance of the legitimacy of the capitalists' veto power and commitment to protect the preexisting configuration of class power.

After 1983, the "success" of the economic model led Christian Democratic and Socialist intellectuals to revise their overall historical assessment of the military regime. Their attitude shifted as, grudgingly at first and with growing admiration later, they came to see Pinochet and the Chicago Boys in a very different historical light. No longer could they be anathematized as "uncivilized" tyrants or "prehistoric" political specimens—rather, they were acknowledged as historically modernizing forces.

From the Eurocentric perspective of Chilean elite intellectuals, Pinochet's regime was credited with succeeding where all previous governments and earlier generations of technocrats had failed: The regime had managed to introduce a small backwater country into the global mainstream. Eugenio Tironi, Eurocentrist, Socialist ideologue, and Aylwin's minister of information as of 1993, typifies the more avid reinterpreters of Pinochet as a "modernizer."

> Under Pinochet, particularly after the 1983–1985 crisis, Chile experienced a modernizing thrust of a very different nature than those unfolding before 1973—one that corresponds closely to modernization tendencies at the international level, including reduction of the state's role; efforts to induce flexiblity, specialization, and internationalization of productive structures; abandonment of the goal of full employment; privatization of public enterprises and services; multiplication of atypical employment and reduction of the mass of waged workers; public assistance of a minimalist and discretionary character (in opposition to the universalism of the welfare state); and liberalization and new flexibility for labor markets. This has been the purpose of the Pinochet revolution in Chile; with different modes and intensities, this has also been the purpose of modernizing processes in all of the contemporary world, whether countries are developed or undeveloped, capitalist or socialist.[39]

The sudden realization that the wheels of history were spinning in the direction claimed all along by Pinochet and his neoliberal ideologues contributed to pushing the ideological conversion of Christian Democratic and Socialist opponents into high gear. Tironi and other Socialist converts exalted the "Pinochet revolution" for contributing toward having reduced "society's dependency on the state, having propelled a process of individualization and diversification [that] has accentuated the gap between private and public life, which forces a lesser politicization of social organizations ... and fosters a more pragmatic, secular, and individualist culture."[40] Thus Pinochet not only was credited with revolutionizing the forces of production (the economy), but also was exalted—book burnings and concentration camps aside—for modernizing culture.

Chile's opposition intelligentsia discerned that if state terror and unencumbered market forces had made it possible for Chile to take decisive steps down the coveted and universal "path to modernization," then it became utopian—nay, foolish—to resist the dictatorship. In light of their classless and pragmatic historical analysis, they concluded that, instead of opposing an authoritarian regime that had successfully engendered Chile's modernization, they should join ranks with the modernizing crusade, giving it a more "human face." These commitments on the part of Pinochet's former critics were to define (1) the course of subsequent events, (2) the nature of the Chilean transition, and (3) the characteristics of the post-Pinochet political system.

Status Quo–Conscious Neostructuralism

Another factor entering into the intellectual conversion of Pinochet's critics concerns changes in Latin American economic development theory over the past decade. The demise of structuralism, given the onslaught of neoliberalism and the subsequent emergence of Latin American neostructuralist thinking, also facilitated the intellectual conversion of Christian Democratic and Socialist economists. The major components of the structuralist, neoliberal, and neostructuralist schools are schematically presented in Table 4.1. In the Latin American case, neostructuralism's long-term strategy of "dynamic entry into the world economy"[41] condoned convergence with the strategic objectives of neoliberalism, opening the economy to international flows, privatizing publicly owned enterprises, and liberating market forces from state regulation. By embracing neostructuralism, Chilean opposition policymakers were drastically breaking with their intellectual past; they were publicly renouncing state intervention and economic planning, repudiating the style of macroeconomic management and policy tools that in previous decades they had used when seeking to achieve modernization through industrialization.[42]

The passage from structuralism[43] to neostructuralism in the case of Latin American economists involved much more than a remixing and reapportionment of structuralism's traditional policy ingredients. The crucial distinction between structuralism and Latin American neostructuralism rested on "the awareness that proposals for long-term transformation cannot be made without taking into account the probable chain reaction set off during the transitional moments of attempted structural change."[44] The emergence of Latin American neostructuralism was definitive proof that this lesson had been thoroughly understood and uncompromisingly internalized.

In the eyes of the Chilean ruling classes, the ISI strategy and related policies had been partially responsible for the societal crisis from which they had barely extricated themselves, thanks to the timely intervention of the military. With Latin American neostructuralism's declared reverence for macroeconomic balances, elites felt assured that the transition from an authoritarian to an elected-civilian regime would not significantly modify the previous patterns of macroeconomic management. To the satisfaction of elites, the major schools of development theory—monetarism and structuralism, which had waged memorable confrontations in previous decades, polarizing political debates and dividing the loyalties of technocrats and administrators—had converged, in the form

TABLE 4.1 Structuralism, Neoliberalism, and Latin American Neostructuralism Compared

Paradigm	Structuralism	Neoliberalism	Neostructuralism
Motto	Structural reforms	Structural adjustment	Structural change; "productive transformation with social equity"
Purpose	Modernization through industrialization	Modernization through privatization	Modernization through internationalization
Vision of development	Requires explicit political will and state intervention rationalized through the planning process	Spontaneous outcome of market forces	A deliberate process in which social and political energies are focused in support of a societywide agreed upon project
Key agent of development	The state	The market	Insertion in world economy; technical change
Obstacles to overcome	Historical power relations and institutions that erode efficiency of price system; international market that reproduces center-periphery differentiation	Mistaken domestic policies and institutions: inward-looking growth, overvalued currency, protectionist policies, suffocating state role	Pattern of external insertion; uncoordinated productive apparatus; concentrated income distribution
Role of the state	Structural reforms Steer capital accumulation Develop key industrial sectors Protect economy from external fluctuations	Provide minimum conditions for market to function: private property, enforce contracts, maintain order, collect data, provide limited social services	Generate social and political consensus Complement the market Increase competitiveness of exports Eradicate poverty
Social conflict	State absorbs pressure from conflicting social groups to politically regulate economic variables	Repression to disarticulate collective social actors "Trickle-down" effect Targeted subsidies	Social conflict should be channeled/subordinated to "common goal" of competitive insertion in the world economy Poor must develop their own "entrepreneurial spirit" "Informal sector" must be linked to the export drive
	Economy is subordinate to politics/democracy	Politics is subordinate to the economy	Political space is determined by requirements of export drive

of Latin American neostructuralism. Due to this convergence, Latin American neostructuralists could cling to the axiomatic and philosophical heritage of 1950s structuralism, while espousing a long-run development strategy and macroeconomic policies perfectly compatible with neoliberal doctrine, the needs of international finance capital, and the requirements of local corporate capitalists.

It would be incorrect to describe Aylwin's economic team as neostructuralist, but it is undeniable that the reigning intellectual climate in the late 1980s facilitated Christian Democratic and Socialist economists' embrace of neoliberal prescriptions. It is not surprising to find a close correlation between structuralism's conceptual transformation and the intellectual metamorphosis of Pinochet's opponents from critics to celebrants of the export-oriented model. Both processes involved a conscious abandonment of attempts to reform the existing configuration of class power by relying on state intervention and the exaltation of social cohesion and political stability; both processes involved the discovery of the alleged omnipotence of international market forces and the modernizing vigor of global capital.[45]

To fully appreciate how emergent Latin American neostructuralist thinking reinforced the intellectual conversion of Pinochet's critics, as well as how it provided the technico-ideological foundation for the Concertación coalition's government program, let us briefly review the passage from structuralism to neostructuralism.

From Structuralism to Neostructuralism

The metamorphosis of Latin American structuralists into neostructuralists occurred in four stages: (1) realization that the banners of structural reform had been taken up by monetarists, (2) public mea culpa for theoretical and policy shortcomings of the ISI strategy, (3) reformulation of assumptions and redefinition of a long-term development strategy, and (4) political competition with neoliberals over who was best equipped to "manage" the internationalization of the continent's productive and sociopolitical structures. Each one of these stages represents the progressive undermining of the transformative zeal of 1950s structuralism and a step toward convergence with the dominant neoliberal paradigm.

A number of authors (Nora Lustig, Osvaldo Rosales, Sergio Bitar, Osvaldo Sunkel, and Gustavo Zuleta) have identified the set of critical issues that formed the corpus of the structuralists' self-criticism. A common theme raised by these authors is that insufficient attention was paid to financial variables, as well as to appropriate short-term policy instruments.[46] More important, however, the critical retrospective also targeted the core of structuralist beliefs. Previously held views about the ineffectiveness of the price system and the negative consequences of entering the international market, concepts that underpinned the structuralists' long-run development strategy, were criticized. Along with overestimation of state interventionism, structuralists also had to atone for "an exaggerated and overly prolonged pessimism about external markets."[47] The Keynesian strategy for growth also had to be repudiated because "it consisted mainly in ensuring the demand and integration of the domestic market, but it ignored productive efficiency. In fact, the security of the market deadened innovation, giving rise to a business attitude only concerned with profits."[48]

In spite of attenuating factors, structuralists had to bear responsibility for promoting erroneous economic conceptions that had led to what one of the penitents dubbed "the Greek tragedy of social change."[49] A composite list of the erroneous conceptions admitted to by structuralists is as follows: (1) weak handling of short-term macroeconomic policies, (2) faulty understanding of monetary and financial aspects, (3) excessive confidence in the value of economic interventionism, (4) complacent attitude toward inflation and the fiscal deficit, (5) utilization of prices as a redistributive mechanism, (6) underestimation of the market's role, (7) omission of external constraint considerations, (8) utilization of income distribution measures based on the demand-side, ignoring the supply-side aspects, (9) ignoring the impact of expectations on the evolution of macroeconomic aggregates, and (10) allowing feudal or political management of state enterprises.[50]

Requiring little more to become an outright declaration of theoretical surrender, the above inventory of acknowledged errors effectively dissolved the core of Latin American structuralist thinking. The compilation of past and misguided ideas became the founding document for Latin American neostructuralism. But the above listing also cleared the way for the repentant structuralists to adopt the key planks of the neoliberal economic program: (1) reorienting economic activity toward exterior markets, (2) increasing and improving allocation of domestic savings, (3) reforming the role of the state in the economy, and (4) obtaining international capitalist support for the development strategy.

The structuralists' mea culpa, with its recognition of having promoted mistaken ideas and incorrect policies, successfully buried Latin American middle class aspirations for national and sovereign economic development, side by side with the spent remains of the "first original body of development theory to emanate from the Third World."[51]

Latin American Neostructuralism

Convergence with Neoliberalism

The conceptual soul of Latin American neostructuralism is not to be found in its structuralist past, but in its recent cuddling up to neoliberalism. The similarities with neoliberalism are numerous and substantial, and center around issues that are critical to the continuity of preexisting class power, as shown below.

Acceleration of Export Growth. Like neoliberalist strategy, the neostructuralist variety prioritizes accelerating economic growth through increasing exports, both in quantum and value terms. Efficiency and international competitiveness of economic units are both the ends and means for economic success. Given that exports are the engine of economic growth, appropriate policies, such as low tariffs and high, stable exchange rates, must be adopted. It is export-led growth, and not redistributive reforms, that ultimately allows the reduction of poverty, the maintenance of political stability, and the attainment of social harmony.

Changing Productive Structures. There is agreement that changing the structure of Latin America's external trade should be the central goal of a long-term development strategy and that competitiveness in international markets is the predominant factor governing the direction and necessary transformation of a country's productive structure.[52]

Foreign Direct Investment. Neostructuralism, like neoliberalism, considers foreign direct investment channeled through multinational corporations to be a constructive and dynamic force in regional economic development.

Macroeconomic Balances. Draconian stabilization programs initially carried out by neoliberals to control inflation, balance the fiscal budget, and bring exports and imports in line led to a fall in the value of labor power through massive impoverishment and reduction in the standard of living. Neostructuralists adhere to maintaining these achievements, rejecting popular demands that might endanger the fluid operation of markets.

Flexible Labor Markets. There is agreement that flexible labor markets are a condition for transforming productive structures. For neoliberals, the liberalization of labor markets and the need to induce flexibility of real wages is defended as a necessity for increased employment levels. Latin American neostructuralists claim that liberalization of labor markets and making real wages flexible are requirements for export competitiveness. Neostructuralism designs specific actions to increase "the flexibility of the labor market to adapt itself to the required changes, and [to facilitate] greater mobility of labor. The objective is to facilitate the reallocation of labor and prevent the labor market from becoming an obstacle to productive transformation."[53]

Poverty. Neostructuralism's "growth with equity" is but an updated version of the "trickle-down theory." As in neoliberalism, it contends that economic growth and exposure of the poor to market forces are the best strategies to deal with poverty. Since the elimination of poverty is a medium- and long-run result, targeting the extremely poor for subsidies and better-focused poverty alleviation programs are necessary.

Superiority over Neoliberalism

Neostructuralism does not advocate a different development strategy or a different class project from that defended by neoliberalism: both converge on a celebration of an "open economy" development strategy.[54] But beyond key similarities, the ways in which neostructuralism differs from neoliberalism, in the context of the 1990s, give neostructuralism greater political appeal for ruling class purposes.

Neostructuralism offers significant advantages over neoliberalism concerning the likely attainment of two crucial goals for successful restructuring: promoting export competitiveness and maintaining social harmony. Latin American neostructuralists argue that, given the frenzied pace of technological innovation and international competition, delays in achieving a dynamic entry into world markets, whether due to strictly economic or political causes, can have crippling consequences. In vying for entrepreneurial support, neostructuralists emphasize their superiority over neoliberals in understanding the sociological and political factors that accompany structural change. Not properly taking these factors into account can mean either underutilizing existing possibilities or being bogged down by unforeseen social resistance to the desired structural change. Neostructuralists argue that neoliberalism attempts to achieve a broad set of objectives with a limited number of tools since "it restricts the scope of what is possible to certain inspirational 'principles' established a priori. It tends, therefore, to reject the use of different measures of regulation and public sector involvement to orchestrate structure change."[55]

Accordingly, it is this broader vision that makes neostructuralists feel they are superior managers of the state apparatus and more successful administrators of macroeconomic balances. Although they share the same long-term strategy as neoliberals, neostructuralists have the advantage of using political and ideological ascendancy to generate consent and acceptance on the part of civil society, thus reducing social resistance and, therefore, the economic costs of a process of structural change. In the case of Chile, given the neoliberals' close association with the military dictatorship, neostructuralists offer the discourse that can manage to win the active consent of the governed, at the same time that it ensures strengthening the export model.[56]

Neostructuralism's Program

The agenda of Latin American neostructuralism includes four key components that dovetail with the current political and economic interests of the ruling classes:

Promoting Structural Change. The state and the political system must play an active role in creating the ideological conditions necessary for a dynamic entry into international markets. The replacement of a culture of conflict with one of cooperation can significantly facilitate the necessary structural transformations required. In this sense,

> the question is not so much the size of the State as its capacity for management and concerted action. Its main economic function can be defined as follows: It must formulate a strategic vision of the development process; it must reorder and maintain economic incentives and relative prices in a manner coherent with this strategy; and through constructive dialogue and concerted action, *it must ensure that all social and political sectors are committed to this strategy* [emphasis added].[57]

The state's role as manufacturer of broad consent and of an accepted "national agenda" is of key importance, since the "road to development demands a consensus between the public and the private sector, between worker and employer organizations, and between enterprises of the same sector, to guarantee the flexibility and the capacity to adapt to the speed of technological change."[58]

Systemic Competitiveness. Neostructuralism claims that societies, not commodities, compete in international markets. Failure to penetrate world markets does not reflect failure of a particular exporting firm but rather a shortcoming of the exporting society as a whole. Competitiveness is systemic; and therefore a holistic, societywide effort is required to ensure the competitiveness of "our" exports. The systemic character of competitiveness is illustrated by the fact that an exporting firm is enmeshed in a broad network of linkages that determine its capacity to export—linkages to the educational system; to technological, energy, and transport infrastructure; to a particular set of institutions governing worker-employer relations; to a mode of interface between public and private institutions.

From Resource-intensive to Manufactured Exports. Left to the exclusive forces of the market, Latin American countries will augment exports of basically resource-intensive goods, the least dynamic niche of world trade. Export of manufactured goods requires medium- and long-range investment plans, technological development, training, and organizational development for external trade. Neostructuralists are open to a broader range of policy instruments to accomplish the dynamic entry into world markets.

Social Conflict. Neostructuralists think that social conflicts, instead of being repressed, should be reduced and subordinated to the requirements of a "shared goal." Neoliberals accept social unrest as an inevitable aspect of adjustment and handle social unrest through repression. Neostructuralists, however, place greater emphasis on co-optation and acquiescence through the subordination of social conflicts to the "common goal."

Neoliberalism became the theory necessary for draconian stabilization programs and for the profound structural transformations that massively privatized social assets and, under the cover of state terror, unleashed upon society the unregulated forces of the market. Neostructuralism is the theoretical construct more appropriate to the consolidation and legitimation of such restructuring. In the case of Chile, it is neostructuralism, not neoliberalism, that ensures better conditions for the expansion of capital in the 1990s; it combines measures that promote the expansion of capital and the increase of export competitiveness with the call for concerted action and the coalescing of social consensus around such an agenda. Whereas the class bias of neoliberalism was starkly clear, the neostructuralist discourse *has the advantage of promoting the same class interests and the same long-run development strategy, though enrobed in the discourse of social harmony.* It has, therefore, a better chance of being able to generate a broader political, and social, base of support for capitalist rule.

Breaking with Structuralism: Societal Impact

In the context of the 1990s, in which international finance capital and a transnationalized capitalist class dominates Latin American societies, an economic theory that aims to avoid fracturing "minimum social agreements" must present a total and absolute, irreversible distancing from key tenets of the structuralist, Keynesian approach. Latin American neostructuralism achieves this by reversing some of the founding propositions of structuralist thought.

1. Rather than being the root and propagating mechanism for economic backwardness, internationalization of productive and commercial structures is now welcomed and seen as the only route to modernization. Foreign capital and multinational corporations, previously considered as mechanisms for deepening dependency, have become indispensable promoters of productive modernization.

2. The logic of distribution, in theory, is now independent from the logic of capitalist accumulation. Greater economic justice and equity is reachable in the medium and long term, while maintaining present modes of accumulation and ensuring that economic growth accelerates and the volume of exports increases. Equality is not the result of social reforms but is the end product of economic growth.

3. Private capitalists and the market, not the state, are key, efficient actors in economic development. The role assigned to the state is to ensure the conservation of macrobalances and levels of governability so that markets can operate competently; the state is not expected to engage in productive or planning activities.

To be able to create compatibility between the internationalization of socioeconomic structures and electoral or representative political forms, the neostructuralist paradigm is forced to completely break with Latin American structuralism's commitment to social change, its reshaping of power relations, and its redrawing of private property rights. As one Chilean economist states,

> The experience of Southern Cone countries led a number of social scientists and political leaders to explain the crumbling of democratic systems at least partially in terms of the rupture of certain minimum social agreements and the unleashing of a struggle over the appropriation of state surplus. ... These experiences have influenced the neostructuralist paradigm, promoting the search for a modality of consensuses, concerted action, and participation that makes it possible to either reduce conflicts, or at least subordinate them to the attainments of a common goal.[59]

Thus, Latin American neostructuralism's clean rupture with its precursor is reflected in its new conception of social change. In the 1990s, social change has to be redefined as the participation of social actors in the process of capitalist restructuring and privatization of common goods, not as altering the relations of power in society.

After more than a decade and one-half in which authoritarianism and state terrorism had been the tools of choice for promoting capitalist restructuring, a new discourse emphasizing social harmony and concerted action entered the politico-ideological stage under the watchful eyes of the military and transnational capital. To the satisfaction of the bloc in power, the promoters of this discourse firmly believed that social harmony and "national reconciliation" could be achieved only on the basis of refining the neoliberal agenda. Only "a more efficient insertion in the world economy would provide the space so that a shared national effort could translate into benefits for all."[60]

The emergence of Latin American neostructuralism helped articulate and solidify the discourse wielded by the Chilean intelligentsia as they broke with their intellectual past, becoming active supporters of internationalization of the Latin American economies along the lines dictated by global capital. This latter path came to be seen not only as the easiest road to modernization, but also as the only one capable of generating the longed-for social harmony. By embracing key aspects of the neostructuralist discourse, Chilean opposition policymakers drastically broke with their intellectual past. By publicly renouncing state intervention and economic planning, opposition intellectuals were also renouncing any intention to ever again raise the issue of modifying private property rights and seriously regulate the operation of the market.

Conclusion

Christian Democratic and Socialist intellectuals underwent a profound conceptual realignment during the years 1982–1989. Their conversion from critics of Pinochet to celebrants of the neoliberal economic model was the result of intersecting and mutually reinforcing economic, political, and ideological processes. By guaranteeing basic socioeconomic and class continuities, such a conversion facilitated ruling class and military acquiescence in a negotiated transition. Because adequate safeguards were provided during the transition, the outcome of such economic, political, and conceptual shifts also furnished an acceptable technico-ideological foundation for the political strategy of Chile's centrist opposition, as well as for the development strategy of the current Aylwin administration.

Before the 1982–1983 crisis, opposition economists forcefully denounced the social costs and economic failure of the neoliberal model. The ensuing recomposition of Chilean capitalism—evidenced in climbing growth rates, expanding exports, and rising investment levels—convinced the opposition of the benefits of an export-oriented model of accumulation. In spite of earlier criticisms, capitalist restructuring carried out by Pinochet and the Chicago Boys came to be seen as a uniquely potent and successful approach to modernization.

On a political level, the search for institutional mechanisms that could insure political stability under a postauthoritarian civilian regime encouraged Christian Democratic and Socialist leaders to reconceptualize the relationship between economic order and the political system. These efforts, made in close consultation with neoliberal ideologues and advisers to the military regime, led to the formulation of the theory of change under democracy and the subsequent acceptance of Pinochet's 1980 constitution. The idea that mechanisms of political representation should be subordinate to the requirements of the economic model encouraged progressive reduction in the scope of social and political concertación. In 1983 it had societywide and regime-founding dimensions encompassing political and economic aspects, but by 1989 it had shrunk to being an instrument useful for legitimizing Pinochet's labor legislation; originally conceived as a mechanism to promote workers' socioeconomic rights, it was transformed into a means to thwart the possibility that wage demands undercut the competitiveness of Chile's resource-intensive exports based on cheap labor.

On the level of development theory, the emergence of Latin American neostructuralism made the intellectual transformation of Pinochet's critics irreversible. By renouncing the heritage of Latin American structuralism, Christian Democratic and Socialist economists embraced macroeconomic management principles and a long-run open economy development strategy, which sought to perfect, not undermine, the neoliberal model.

The overview presented in this chapter has also revealed three distinctive features of the intellectual transformation of Chilean opposition intellectuals.

First of all, this conversion was not a passive process by which Christian Democratic and Socialist intellectuals were forced to compress their political economic conceptions under the threat of military reaction and retrenchment. On the contrary, they were active protagonists in the reinterpretation of history and in the construction of a "new" discourse. Their commitment to preserve the neoliberal economic model should not be seen as a "tactical" maneuver, but as a new long-term factor of Chilean political reality. Precisely because it was an active and creative process, a real and not a feigned change, this conversion allowed a response to the material needs of the dominant classes and generated massive electoral support as well.

A second feature of the passage from critics to celebrants was the highly centralized and elitist character of this operation. The embryo for this conceptually renovated and trustworthy political class was generated in externally funded think tanks and thence its influence extended progressively—to specialized party commissions, to elected party positions, to public relations firms and image makers for electoral contests, and on to occupation of key positions in the state apparatus. The small group of individuals that in 1983 spearheaded the conceptual turnaround described in this chapter (Christian Democrats Foxley, Boeninger, Cortázar; and Socialists Correa, Ominami, and Tironi, among others) occupy key governmental posts in the 1990s.

A third critical feature of this conversion is the contradictory character of the resulting discourse. On the one hand, it must evoke favorable responses from international and local investors ("macroeconomic balances," "productive efficiency," "export-competitiveness"); on the other, it must elicit support from the working class and the popular classes ("social equity," "la alegría ya viene" [happiness is coming], "invertir en la gente" [investing in people]).

When considered in toto, the dramatic conceptual realignment accomplished by Christian Democratic and Socialist intellectuals attests more to their sensitivity to the needs of capital than to the integrity of their democratic ideals. Before 1973, while under the influences of the structuralist, Keynesian paradigm, they strove for a political democracy in which the state would absorb the pressure from conflicting social groups in order to politically regulate basic economic variables. During this period, they sought to subordinate, with different degrees of success, the market forces to the perceived needs of the middle class, the proletariat, and the popular sectors. After their intellectual conversion, they became unequivocal supporters of the opening of the Chilean economy to the world market and of its accelerated internationalization under the conditions dictated by international capital.

In the 1990s era of "modernization through internationalization," Christian Democratic and Socialist intellectuals argue that the magnitude of national political space and the dimensions of democracy are defined by the requirements of the economic system and the open economy development strategy. By championing export competitiveness, they have committed themselves to reestablishing the hegemony of *the market over the political process*. For the post-Pinochet political class, the primary concern seems to be not the democratization of society but the diffusion of the submissive values and compliant behavior patterns required by the subordination of politics to the dictates of the international market.

If Chile under Pinochet became a test site for neoliberal doctrine, under Aylwin it has become a laboratory for continuation of neoliberal policies under the discourse of concerted action and social harmony. If in the past the Chilean disciples of Milton Friedman came to be seen as the standardbearers of capitalist restructuring, Chile's Christian Democratic and Socialist intellectuals in the 1990s occupy the continent's "cutting edge" in terms of executing a coherent politico-economic effort to legitimize and consolidate such restructuring. Their task has been made easier thus far by a combination of political vision, economic boom, social quietude, and absence of a popular alternative.

Notes

1. See *Revista Caras*, no. 74, February 11, 1991, p. 30. This interview with Eduardo Matte, president of one of the largest transnationals operating in Chile in association with the Matte conglomerate, provides glimpses of the behind-the-

scenes negotiations between the incoming Aylwin government and representatives of Chile's powerful economic groups.

2. *El Mercurio*, March 10, 1990, p. C-3.

3. Statement by Andrés Allamand, president of the right-wing party, Renovación Nacional, at the International Symposium on the Transition to Democracy, held in Santiago, Chile, September 1991.

4. The distinction between Latin American neostructuralism (i.e., the recent work of the United Nations Economic Commission for Latin America and the Caribbean [ECLAC]) and U.S. neostructuralists such as Lance Taylor, must be emphasized. Whereas U.S. neostructuralists exhibit specific concern for redistributive efforts and model building, Latin American neostructuralists seem primarily concerned with convincing the economic elites that they will be better administrators than the dogmatic neoliberals of the past. The emergence, characteristics, and consequences of Latin American neostructuralism in the Chilean case are analyzed later on in this chapter.

5. A good example of policies legitimizing and complementing the process of capitalist restructuring imposed by neoliberalism is to be found in the recent publications of ECLAC and the International Labor Organization's Regional Program for Employment in Latin America and the Caribbean, better known by its Spanish acronym, PREALC. See ECLAC, *Changing Productive Relations with Social Equity: The Prime Task of Latin America and the Caribbean Development in the 1990s* (Santiago: United Nations, 1991) and PREALC, "Empleo y Equidad: Desafíos de los 90," *Documentos de Trabajo* no. 354 (October) (Santiago: Organización Internacional del Trabajo, 1990).

6. The societal impact of this conceptual realignment is explored later on in Chap. 6.

7. See Carlos Ominami, "Desindustrialización y Reestructuración Industrial en América Latina: Los Ejemplos de Argentina, Brasil y Chile," *Colección de Estudios CIEPLAN* no. 23 (March) (Santiago: CIEPLAN, 1988), pp. 87–115. Also see Carlos Ominami and Roberto Madrid, "Chile: Elementos para la Evaluación del Desarrollo Exportador," *Proposiciones* no. 18 (January) (Santiago: Ediciones SUR, 1991), pp. 120–158.

8. For a discussion on the nature of economic guarantees being requested by the dominant classes, see James Petras and Fernando Ignacio Leiva, "Chile: The Authoritarian Transition to Electoral Politics: A Critique," *Latin American Perspectives*, 15, 3 (Summer 1988), pp. 97–114.

9. See Alejandro Foxley, "Bases para el Desarrollo de la Economía Chilena: Una Visión Alternativa," *Colección Estudios CIEPLAN* no. 26 (June) (Santiago: CIEPLAN, 1989), pp. 175–185.

10. José P. Arellano and René Cortázar, "Del Milagro a la Crisis: Algunas Reflexiones Sobre el Momento Económico," *Colección Estudios CIEPLAN* no. 8 (July) (Santiago: CIEPLAN, 1982), p. 59.

11. Ibid., p. 45.

12. Alejandro Foxley, "Experimentos Neoliberales en América Latina," *Colección Estudios CIEPLAN* no. 7 (March) (Santiago: CIEPLAN, 1982), p. 41.

13. See Foxley, 1982, pp. 39 and 40.

14. Ibid., p. 57.

15. See Alejandro Foxley, "Cinco Lecciones de la Crisis Actual," *Colección Estudios CIEPLAN* no. 8 (July) (Santiago: CIEPLAN, 1982), p. 163.

16. The new economic management approach advocated by Foxley in 1982 rests on five lessons drawn from the crisis that demonstrate the need to: (1) overcome the passivity of the state, (2) generate a more stable environment for exports, (3) pursue the creation of jobs through public policy since industry cannot waste its resources, (4) overcome totalizing ideological constructs, and (5) emphasize the need for a democratic system so that "erroneous approaches" can be replaced by an economic policy that "permanently considers the needs of all, not only of those who have greater power or influence over the market." After 1983, each of these lessons will be forgotten, due not only to Foxley's emergent pragmatism but also, fundamentally, to admiration for the structural changes successfully brought about by the disciples of Milton Friedman.

17. See Alejandro Foxley, "La Política Económica para la Transición," in Oscar Muñoz, comp., *Transición a la Democracia: Marco Político y Económico* (Santiago: CIEPLAN, 1990), p. 104.

18. In his 1989 assessment, Foxley recognizes the persistence of two limitations in the Pinochet-neoliberal economic model: (1) the "disassociation between the modernizing process and the delay in the trickle down" of benefits to the general population and (2) the still weak long-term basis for the "sustained and continuous increase in productivity." Whereas in his pre-1983 thinking Foxley attributed these to the existence of the neoliberal economic model itself, in his new stance he sees them only as side effects to be remedied by maintaining the model and applying the appropriate corrective measures.

19. See Foxley, 1990, op. cit., pp. 111–112.

20. That this conversion is based on ideological components rather than on a concrete analysis of the situation is illustrated by two sets of facts. On the one hand, during the time of their conversion, inequality in income distribution increased. Thus, according to the Instituto Nacional de Estadísticas, the poorest 40 percent of households lowered its share of national income from 14.10 percent in 1978 to 11.77 percent in 1988. Hence, no basis existed for eliminating distributive concerns from the assessment of the model. On the other hand, the alleged modernization of the productive structure is of a disputable character. An Inter-American Development Bank–funded study carried out by three PET economists finds no evidence of technical innovation in the manufacturing sector attributable to the opening of the economy. See Rafael Agacino, Gonzalo Rivas, and Enrique Román, "Apertura y Eficiencia Productiva: La Experiencia Chilena 1975–1989" (Santiago, Chile: PET, 1992, Mimeographed).

21. For a self-congratulatory interpretation of this process, see Joseph S. Tulchin and Augusto Varas, eds., *From Dictatorship to Democracy: Rebuilding Political Consensus in Chile* (Washington, D.C.: Woodrow Wilson Center for Current Studies on Latin America, 1991).

22. The exploration of these concepts forced Foxley and the economists at CIEPLAN to shed their initial technocratic identity and impelled them to venture

onto terrain that they recognized as being more in line with the interests of political economy and overt political activity than with strictly technical concerns.

23. See Alejandro Foxley, "Algunas Condiciones para una Democratización Estable: El Caso de Chile," *Colección Estudios CIEPLAN* no. 9 (December) (Santiago: CIEPLAN, 1982), pp. 159–160.

24. Ibid., p. 161.

25. Ibid., p. 148.

26. Ibid., p. 164.

27. For a fuller history of the process of social concertación and its participants, see Mario Albuquerque and Eugenio Rivera, "El Debate en Torno a la Concertación Social y Económica," *Proposiciones* no. 18 (January) (Santiago: Ediciones SUR, 1990). These authors were the first to notice the shrinking scope of the concept of social concertación, which we have expanded in this chapter.

28. See Foxley, 1989, op. cit., pp. 184–185.

29. See René Cortázar, "El Proceso de Cambio y la Concertación Social," in Muñoz, op. cit., pp. 69–70.

30. Ibid., p. 79.

31. Edgardo Boeninger, current general secretary of the Aylwin cabinet, is credited with being a calculating political operator and the éminence grise behind the negotiated transition. He is often credited with the political success of the Concertación coalition. Each party and ideological camp controlled a private research center: the neoliberals had CEP; the Socialists were at FLACSO and SUR; the Christian Democrats were based at CIEPLAN and at the Instituto Chileno de Estudios Humanistas (IChEH). The National Endowment for Democracy (NED), a funding agency of the U.S. Congress, and major U.S. and European foundations were the principal funders of CED as well as of the other research centers.

32. See Edgardo Boeninger, "Desafíos Económicos para la Construcción de la Democracia," in *Orden Económico y Democracia* (Santiago: CED, 1985), pp. 9–90.

33. Ibid., p. 18.

34. Ibid., p. 20.

35. Ibid., p. 22.

36. Ibid., p. 20.

37. Ibid., p. 22.

38. In August 1985, a majority of political organizations (with the exception of the pro-Pinochet Unión Demócrata Independiente [UDI] and the leftist Movimiento Democrático Popular [MDP]) signed the document, Acuerdo Nacional. In September 1986, parties, including those belonging to the crumbling MDP, signed the Bases de Sustentación del Régimen Democrático. Both documents have these five principles at their core.

39. See Eugenio Tironi, "Crisis, Desintegración y Modernización," *Proposiciones* no. 18 (January) (Santiago: Ediciones SUR, 1990), p. 29.

40. Ibid., p. 32.

41. See ECLAC, *Changing Productive Relations with Social Equity*, op. cit.

42. In this vein, Ricardo Ffrench-Davis, a prominent member of CIEPLAN, stipulated that Latin American neostructuralism had to be seen as "the effort to renew

the structuralist tradition, incorporating into it a systematic preoccupation with the design of economic policy ... macroeconomic balance, coordination between short- and long-term concerted action between the public and private sectors." See Ricardo Ffrench-Davis, "Esbozo de un Planteamiento Neoestructuralista," *Revista de la CEPAL* no. 34 (April) (Santiago: Naciones Unidas, 1988), p. 39.

43. For an excellent discussion of structuralism, see chap. 2, "The Structuralist School of Development," in Cristóbal Kay, *Latin American Theories of Development and Underdevelopment* (London and New York: Routledge, 1989).

44. Nora Lustig, "Del Estructuralismo al Neoestructuralismo: La Búsqueda de un Paradigma Heterodójo," *Colección Estudios CIEPLAN* no. 23 (March) (Santiago: CIEPLAN, 1988), p. 47.

45. Significantly, the sites for structuralism's conceptual revision were the international development agencies with headquarters in Chile's capital, Santiago. After 1973, ECLAC, and to a lesser extent, PREALC, had provided many Socialist and Christian Democratic economists and social scientists with employment as researchers and consultants. These agencies had become important intellectual and institutional havens for them during the Pinochet regime. Thus the solid intellectual link arose between the revision of structuralism's basic assumptions and the renewal of Christian Democratic and Socialist leaders and intellectuals.

46. See Osvaldo Rosales, "Balance y Renovación en el Paradigma Estructuralista del Desarrollo Latinoamericano," *Revista de la CEPAL* no. 34 (April) (Santiago: Naciones Unidas, 1988). Also see Nora Lustig, op. cit., p. 47; and Sergio Bitar, "Neoliberalismo Versus Neoestructuralismo en América Latina," *Revista de la CEPAL* no. 34 (April) (Santiago: Naciones Unidas, 1988), p. 47.

47. See Osvaldo Sunkel and Gustavo Zuleta, "Neo-structuralism Versus Neoliberalism in the 1990s," *CEPAL Review* no. 42 (December) (Santiago: United Nations, 1990), p. 48.

48. Ibid., p. 44.

49. See Osvaldo Rosales, "Posibilidades y Desafíos de una Estrategia de Desarrollo Alternativa," *Chile: Problemas y Perspectivas del Actual Modelo de Desarrollo. Segunda Parte* (Santiago: Sociedad Chilena de Economía Política [SOCHEP], 1991), p. 5.

50. Ibid., p. 20.

51. See Kay, op. cit.

52. See ECLAC, *Changing Productive Relations with Social Equity*, op. cit.

53. See PREALC, "Empleo y Equidad,"op. cit., p. 80.

54. For a useful, though somewhat dated, discussion of the open economy development strategy see chap. 4, "The Open Economy," in Keith Griffin, *Alternative Strategies for Economic Development* (London: Macmillan, 1989).

55. See Bitar, op. cit., p. 49.

56. The intellectual antecedents to this effort to make capitalist restructuring compatible with the manufacturing of consent can be traced to a three-year study carried out by the Consejo Latinoamericano de Ciencias Sociales; the United Nations Educational, Scientific, and Cultural Organization; and UNDP (CLACSO-UNESCO-UNDP). A summary of this program is presented in Fernando Calderón

and Mario R. Dos Santos, *Hacia un Nuevo Orden Estatal en América Latina: Veinte Tesis Sociopolíticas y un Corolario* (Santiago: Consejo Latinoamericano de Ciencias Sociales/Fondo de Cultura Económica, 1991).

57. See Sunkel and Zuleta, op. cit., p. 45.
58. Ibid.
59. See Bitar, op. cit., p. 60.
60. Ibid.

5

Democracy and Poverty or the Poverty of Democracy?

The transition from a military dictatorship to an electoral regime is best understood by sorting out the events and facts essential to the change. In order to isolate the pertinent facts, however, one needs to identify the major sociopolitical forces acting in each specific context. Through an analysis of their roles, strategies, successes, and failures, the groundwork can be established for an evaluation of the nature of the transition and of its consequences for the future evolution of Chilean politics.

The major sociopolitical forces acting in the transition included (1) the left-wing parties, the autonomous social movements, and the guerrilla groups, (2) the center-right to center-left political parties, trade unions, and civic associations, (3) the armed forces, and the business and financial elites, and (4) the U.S. government and the international banks and financial agencies that it influences. Each of these political groups had a distinct set of interests, strategies, and visions concerning what the transition to electoral politics entailed. The transition is a result of the failure of one bloc's strategy and the success of another's—a success that is tempered by the conditions and compromises within which it was undertaken.

The transition to the post-Pinochet regime can be dated to 1986—a year in which major political battles were engaged and realignments and political pacts consummated that subsequently played themselves out in the years to follow.[1] Several key events and developments came to a head in 1986, a year that culminated in displacement of the Left and of social movements, electoral victory by a coalition of centrist political parties, and continuity in the strategic political and economic features of the Pinochet era.[2]

The most significant event in 1986 was the defeat of the Left, its political repression and subsequent isolation, and the reemergence of the centrist political coalition as the decisive force of the opposition.[3] The defeat took several forms: the guerrillas' failed attempt to assassinate Pinochet and the discovery of the site of their major military arsenal, from which they had hoped to launch a national insurrection; the incapacity to sustain the mass social movements, particularly after the breakup of the Civic Assembly in the aftermath of the general strike of July 1986, and the subsequent repression of the Left by the military regime (following the failed assassination attempt); and the center-right de facto renunciation of mass movement politics. The move toward the center-right included mainly the Christian Democratic, Socialist, and Radical parties. The Left parties included the Communist parties, the Movimiento de Izquierda Revolucionaria (MIR) and fractions of the Movimiento de Acción Popular Unitario (MAPU), and the Socialists. The defeat thus affected the guerrillas and their strategy of "popular rebellion" and the upward trajectory of the social movements, and thus it undermined the growing hegemony of the Left within the opposition. The Pinochet regime combined a dual strategy of encirclement and occupation of the rebellious popular neighborhoods, while opening up negotiations and opportunities for the center-right electoral parties.[4] The failure of the guerrilla assault and the repression and split in the social movements were compounded by the incapacity of the Left to formulate a counterstrategy to Pinochet's turn toward electoral politics for the political class and repression of the social movements. The social movements, however, continued their activity, but the focus turned from national to local issues.[5] And, as the electoral calendar began to unfold, the supporters of the social movements were increasingly subjected to a barrage of pressure from the newly legalized electoral parties, whereas the leftist parties were increasingly divided between those forces attempting to sustain the armed struggle, those seeking to insert themselves into the electoral legal arena and the majority, and those seeking to appease both sides.[6] The defeat of the Left in 1986 was in many ways as serious as that of 1973: It had the same extreme effect of disarticulating the mass organizations, derailing the process of reconstituting social alliances, and calling into question basic strategies. Whereas the loss of lives in 1986 was not in any way comparable to the 1973 loss, the strategic realignment of political forces was in some ways more significant: the Socialists definitively opted for an alliance with the Christian Democrats and redefined their policies to incorporate the neoliberal socioeconomic model. Further, the defeat of 1973 reflected a profound and continuing split of the Chilean population, whereas the defeat of 1986 led to a shift to the right in the entire political spectrum, a realignment that skewed politics toward the professional political class and toward predominance of the permanent institutions of the state at the expense of the social movements in civil society. The electoral transition thus begins with the defeat of the Left, on the terrain established by the Pinochet regime.

The second essential factor shaping the transition was the negotiations and "pact" between the Christian Democratic and Socialist parties and elites and the military high command. The essential element in this process was the preconditions for the pact. The Christian Democratic and So-cialist parties made a major shift in relation to the mass movements, di-recting their followers to eschew mass mobilization, social confrontation, and even strikes, and in particular to reject unified activities with the Left.[7] Two factors weighed heavily in this decision. The first was the grow-ing fear, particularly in early 1986, that the Christian Democratic and So-cialist parties were losing hegemony over the mass movements, that the movements' demands and struggles were exceeding the political and so-cial boundaries of their politics. The attempted assault on Pinochet was both the pretext and the final cause for the political rupture with the Left. The second factor that influenced the center-right to break with the Left and pursue a pact with Pinochet was the increasing "appreciation" of the new socioeconomic model in place and the eagerness to secure political positions, even in the restricted space allocated by the Pinochet dictator-ship.[8] Through its negotiations and pact with Pinochet, the centrist coali-tion gained legality, projected a political strategy with an immediate tar-get (the defeat of Pinochet), and had access to the mass media of a sort that completely marginalized the Left. Thus, what the centrist coalition gave away in terms of institutional power to the Pinochet Right, it gained in electoral organizational influence at the expense of the Left. The negotia-tions with the military legitimated the Pinochet constitution, the armed forces as a political interlocutor, and the rules of the political transition laid down by Pinochet. By circumscribing the activities in civil society and increasing the role of the professional political elites, the issues of the tran-sition were largely redefined into problems of "governability": the capac-ity of the new political elites to sustain the confidence of the established economic investors, the allegiance of the military, and the containment of the pent-up social demands of the popular classes.[9]

The politics of the "negotiated transition" was a preconfiguration of the political style and socioeconomic substance of the electoral regime that was to result. A premium was placed on demobilizing social movements, refocusing political debate on a narrow set of legal-political changes, and centralizing politics in the hands of a professional political elite willing to compromise with the established institutional powers of the state.

The emergence of the pact between the centrist political coalition and the military was accompanied by a new political discourse that eliminated the politics of structural change and rationalized the new accommo-dationist and conformist politics of the opposition parties with the rheto-ric of "realism" and "pragmatism."[10] The transition presented a paradox in which greater electoral freedom was accompanied by a shrinking of the acceptable politico-economic spectrum of views and policies. More im-portant, the negotiating process, involving mutual recognition on the in-stitutional and constitutional terrain of the military regime, provided the model for the construction of the reformed political system: the cohabitation of the electoral regime and the authoritarian state. The success of the center-right in wresting temporary hegemonic influence over the mass movement from the Left was secured by paying a steep price to the military: conceding strategic positions in the state, the economy, and the constitutional framework.

The third factor influencing the transition was the role played by the U.S. government and the international banks it influences. U.S. policy has been based on the practice of sacrificing dictators to save the state.[11] Washington has consistently distinguished between defending its permanent and its transitory interests and has always sought to adapt to social challenges through political changes. For Washington, the defense of the capitalist system, maintenance of international alignments, and policy integration with U.S.-centered military-economic regional organizations are permanent interests defended by strategic institutions in the state. Washington is very rigid in its insistence that state institutions defend strategic interests, though it is flexible in its policy toward regime changes that affect transitory interests.

In the Chilean context, Washington supported the Pinochet coup that overthrew Allende, and it provided economic assistance and promoted trade with the Pinochet regime until the end. However, with the reemergence of the mass social movements from 1983 onward and with the radicalizing of the forms of struggle and leadership from 1985 to 1986, Washington moved increasingly toward political change, that is, toward a regime change based on a negotiated transition that would divide the opposition and preserve the state. Washington sought to facilitate the ascendancy of the center-right "anti-regime" forces over and against the leftist "antisystem" movements, while minimizing the changes in the socioeconomic model and state institutions. Financial and political support extended by the United States and its NATO allies to the centrist civilian coalition was conditional, hinging on breaking ties with the Left and participating in the electoral calendar outlined by the dictatorship.[12] Washington, in turn, agreed to pressure Pinochet to comply with his electoral timetable and accept the outcome. Washington achieved maximum success: a regime change that disarticulated the social mobilization challenging strategic state allies and that legitimized and (temporarily) stabilized state institutions and the socioeconomic model proposed by the new electoral regime. Whereas the social movements forced the issue of regime change, it was Washington that "brokered" the negotiation process that produced the hybrid political system—a popularly elected regime inserted into military-constructed state institutions. Washington sacrificed the Pinochet regime to save the neoliberal state and, in the process, took credit for promoting democracy.

The fourth characteristic of the transition follows from above: The defeat of the Left, the primacy of the military-civil negotiations, and the crucial role of the United States as political broker led to a transformation in the relation of forces between the regime-centered political party machines and professional politicians and the social movements in civil society. The rise of "political society" to prominence (exiled politicians, lawyers, institutional intellectuals, economic consultants, nongovernmental organization [NGO] promoters, and so on) was accompanied by the displacement of the militant grass-roots leaders. The transition reflected the circulation of elites. Electoral party elites replaced the technocratic-military elites. The transitional process thus was marked by an intensification of the politics of elite pacts and maneuvers oriented toward political reconciliation at the top and the displacement of movement leaders involved in mass confrontations and popular mobilizations from below. At the ideological-cultural level, the new, ascending elites developed a double discourse. The discourse directed toward the electorate favored the issues of popular representation; the discourse directed toward the institutions of the state, the economic elite, and Washington spoke the language of accommodation with the armed forces, investors, and overseas bankers. The double discourse captured the ambiguity of the political change—a limited transfer of power, combined with strategic strength vested in the powers of nonelected officials.

In summary, the essential features of the transition were marked by the defeat of the Left and the social movements and the organization of an electoral process on the terrain of the authoritarian Right. The electoral victory of the center-right, and the subsequent regime, was thus limited by the authoritarian parameters and rules of the game determined by the preceding regime.

Institutional Continuities and Their Consequences

The most striking feature of the post-Pinochet electoral regime is the vast range of institutional continuities in the political, legal, and socioeconomic spheres. Once the electoral campaigns ended and the euphoria generated by the electoral parties and leaders subsided, it was clear that the armed forces and the investor classes backing them had secured the better part of the political bargain. At the theoretical level, these continuities call into question the notion of a "transition to democracy" and even raise serious doubts about whether one can even speak of a "democratization" process, except in a very partial, one-sided manner.

The most important structures of the political system—the institutions of the state—have, to an extraordinary degree, remained intact from the previous authoritarian period. An examination of five institutions of crucial importance to any concept of a transition to democracy is illustrative. The armed forces and police, the courts, the civil bureaucracy, the central bank, and the universities all retain the same personnel, in many cases with the same top officials and under the same ideological-political rules as under the previous regime.

Examining the armed forces provides the most noteworthy example: The commander-in-chief is Pinochet and the commanders of all the military branches are holdovers from the dictatorship.[13] Moreover, the military retains control over all policies regarding training, recruitment, and indoctrination; thus it is in a position to reproduce itself in its current mold, retain cohesion, and withstand any civilian-democratic influences in the future. More important, although the secret political police Central Nacional de Informaciones (CNI) was formally dissolved by the civilian president, it was absorbed and reconstituted within the intelligence branches of the military.

Equally important, the military has marked out narrow boundaries for the emerging political class, limiting its capacity to apply the law of the land to crimes by military officials (tortures, assassinations during the dictatorship). It has imposed a constitution that skews congressional representation toward the right and includes a minority of nonelected senators capable of blocking any constitutional amendment that trespasses on the power and prerogatives of the military and propertied classes. Moreover, military officials frequently project their views into the political system and are perceived as an important political branch of the government by both legislators and the executives who hasten to hear their views and court their support.[14]

As a result, in the post-Pinochet period, the military has far greater political weight in the state (and in the political system) than in the period preceding the dictatorship. The military has already put the newly elected politicians on notice that their governance is conditioned by the maintenance of stability and order, which sends a clear message that social disorder would result in a self-determined invitation to take over the reins of government.[15] This directive from the armed forces has clearly negative implications for the capacity of the electoral regime to carry out consequent socioeconomic reforms, which inevitably provoke the ire of the upper classes and require the mobilization of the popular classes.

Just prior to leaving office, the dictatorship offered handsome pensions for early retirement of Supreme Court justices and, subsequently, replaced them with even more subservient unconditional loyalists.[16] The immobility agreements signed by the electoral politicians and the dictator thus freeze the judicial system in the mold left by the authoritarian system. Moreover, given the composition of the legislature, the power of the military, and the discretionary power of the incumbent judges, there is the narrowest of margins for utilizing the legal system to modify the existing concentration of political and economic power. The continuity of the judicial and legal system, reflective of the compromises between the military and electoral politicians in the transition, thus reinforces the immobility of the new electoral regime.

Similar constraints on political and social change exist in the civil bureaucracy.[17] The Pinochet-civilian pact included the immobility of the army of civil appointees of the dictatorship. In most cases, they were appointed because of their loyalty to the dictatorship rather than their competence. They are now entrusted to implement policies that in many cases they oppose. Using their discretionary powers, they are capable of delaying, distorting, or undermining policies of the new administration. Moreover, the new administration has been obliged to add to the bureaucracy to circumvent existing administrative units and to supply a minimum number of jobs as political patronage. In all the ministries, from foreign affairs to economics, the opposition is in a strategic position to influence policy and to secure internal information and documentation as to regime strategy—and plan countermeasures. In many ways, the senior officials are captives of Pinochet's appointed functionaries. And with the immobility agreements there are few prospects for any democratic renovation of the civil service or even for rehiring officials arbitrarily fired by the dictatorship. It is not surprising that the military and the right-wing defense of "legality" overlooks the violent crimes around which the current legal norms were constructed. It is a tragedy that the civilian electoral politicians accept the legitimacy of those claims as the basis for the new political order.

Before leaving office, Pinochet decreed that the director of the Central Bank would possess power independent of elected officials; in addition, he extended his tenure for the greater part of the following decade and increased his decisionmaking power over the economy.[18] By appointing a staunch neoliberal—in agreement with the incoming president—Pinochet ensured that the main contours of the neoliberal model and its main beneficiaries, the export-oriented elites, would have a strategic ally in the state. The electoral regime's submission to this appointment and to the restructuring of state economic decisionmaking reflected both their conversion to Pinochet-style economics and their impotence, as they posed no alternatives in the negotiating process.

The extremely narrow political bounds within which the centrist civilian coalition chose to consummate its agreements with the dictatorship are evident in the university system as well. Here, as in other spheres of civil society, the dictatorship engaged in a savage purge of progressive professors and dissidents, replacing them with political toadies, timeservers, and neoliberal ideologues. One would have expected, with the advent of the electoral regime, a sustained effort to reinstate the professors purged by the dictatorship, or at least an effort to open all positions to public competition. Nothing of the sort happened. A proposal to that effect presented by the head of the Chilean Sociological Association was rejected by the Socialist party as too risky "for the stability of democracy."[19]

What is striking about the new regime is not only the continuities with the past but also the rigidity and tenacity with which it upholds the existing legal and institutional order. It is apparent that the electoral political class is not merely reflecting external pressures; it represents a new political orientation, a long-term conversion to neoliberal strategies. The political forms and organizational structures (the "Socialist" and "Christian Democratic" parties) within which this new political class operates bear no resemblance to the parties of the past. The rupture with the past is total and enduring, involving a basic shift in ideology, programs, development strategy, international orientation, and relationship to the class structure. The terms "reformist" or "populist" no longer apply in the context of supply-side economics, export-oriented strategies, and the embrace of Washington's free market proposal.[20] In present day Chile, no leaders of the two major governmental parties speak of agrarian reform: "That is the dead language of the past," as one "renovating socialist" commented, echoing the editorial pages of the conservative daily, *El Mercurio*.[21] Today in the economic ministries, "modernity" and "realism" speak to the same technocratic growth-oriented discourse as Pinochet's economic advisers.[22] The electoral regime shares with the Pinochet Right the need to maintain and promote "efficient farmers," i.e., the agro-export elite, with the proviso that together they improve housing conditions and wages for "their" workers.[23]

The electoral regime has entered into the logic of the new pattern of accumulation, and from its government position, it hopes to convince investors that an electoral administration is more likely to avoid large-scale conflict and provide better crisis management than a rightist regime could. The regime does not propose any socioeconomic changes that may hinder in the least the consolidation of the new pattern of export growth. As to the audience composed of the armed forces High Command, the electoral politicians argue that political legitimacy and a better international image is more effective in extending access to markets, credit, and military aid than the continuity of the Pinochet military regime.[24]

The clearest expression of the continuity of the Pinochet agro-mineral export model is found in Finance Minister Foxley's assertion that his main job is to "manage the macroeconomic" indicators.[25] The new economic team headed by Foxley (Christian Democrat) and Ominami (Socialist) has set itself the task of deepening and extending the free market model put in place by former Minister of Finance Büchi. This explains Foxley's immediate embrace of Bush's proposal for a Latin American free market and Ominami's boasting that the inflow of foreign investment in his first six months of office has exceeded that of his predecessor.[26] The efforts by the Christian Democrats and Socialists to outflank the Right through ultraliberal policies reveal the distance that separates these parties from their roots in the pre-Pinochet period.[27]

The new electoral regime's policies are firmly directed toward expanding the export and financial sector in the Chilean economy and sustaining the leading economic groups that control the international circuits; the regime is opposed to any changes—even at the margins—in the rules of the game under which the multinationals plunder Chilean natural resources and labor.[28] On the contrary, multinational corporations and their Chilean counterparts are described as crucial actors by the managers of the "macroeconomic indicators." Within the top echelons of the capitalist class, the financial and banking sector—both domestically and overseas—plays a decisive role, as evidenced in the primary role the finance minister has given to inflation and fiscal balances.[29]

In summary, the continuities of the political, economic, social, and ideological system parameters shape the policies of the electoral regime and, in turn, are reinforced by inclusion of the regime in that system. These parameters provide the substantive power framework within which policy debates, electoral campaigns, and ideological and cultural production of the electoral parties takes place.

Discontinuities: The Electoral Regime

The basic change in Chilean politics has taken place at the level of the political regime. There have been three important changes within the political system: a new political base for the regime has emerged; political space for public expression, political organization, and electoral competition has been substantially enlarged; and new forms of political legitimation have been elaborated.

The electoral regime has enlarged the base for political appeal beyond the limited electorate that characterized the previous regime.[30] The new regime, in form at least, is obligated to appeal to and cajole a broad array of classes to vote for its candidates. Furthermore, the electoral parties seek to legitimate their policies in terms of the interests of the "electorate." Nevertheless, there is an increasingly growing gap between the formal freedom of the electorate to choose and the diminishing ability to choose alternative development strategies. Since the centrist regime and the right-wing opposition both favor the current neoliberal model and both accept working within the Pinochet constitutional and political structures, the freedom to choose is sharply restricted, not by repressive powers of the dictatorship, but by the less formal mechanisms of political control over the media and the monopoly on party finances held by the major electoral actors.

In the sphere of public expression there is a greater degree of freedom to publish, speak, and work than under the dictatorship, though the military courts still punish critics of the dictatorship. In addition, various spokespersons of the electoral regime have indicated a desire to restrict speech that "destabilizes" democracy.[31] Mass media access is, for all intents and purposes, controlled by the supporters of the neoliberal model and the civil-military *conviviencia* (coexistence), thus restricting alternative critical perspectives by allowing only marginal access to the larger public. Opinions critical of the current regime are branded as "ultraleftist" and their proponents are disqualified as "extremist ideologues."

Moreover, the carabineros, the paramilitary forces, and the military still exercise their power when they feel that democratic expression conflicts with their conceptions of law and order. During recent human rights demonstrations, the Ministry of Interior's promise to permit peaceful demonstrations without violence was countermanded by the police, and several dissidents were beaten.[32] Likewise, generals in the armed forces have made pronouncements on a whole range of political issues that are theoretically in the province of the civilian government, ranging from Chilean-Bolivian relations and human rights to issues affecting Chilean-German relations.[33]

Political space for party, trade union, and electoral competition has expanded substantially. And there are signs that trade union organization is growing, along with strike activity.[34] The biggest area of growth, however, has been in electoral organizations, which have mushroomed throughout the country. Nevertheless, the initial opening has not been followed by any consequential legislation to "level the playing field" between labor and capital. The labor law proposed by the government does not provide an organizational or financial framework that would facilitate unionization.[35] More important, in keeping with the neoliberal economic policy of having a "flexible labor force," the law hardly restricts the employer's power to fire workers.[36] As a result, during the first six months of the electoral regime, there was actually an increase in firings by employers, while the regime ignored trade union protests.[37] Likewise, in the agro-export sector the regime has taken the side of owners opposing municipal unions (in comparison to enterprise unions) and strikes during harvest (the only time they would have any effect).[38]

In the larger urban context, the electoral regime has been actively displacing locally led social movements through a system of party-controlled electoral organizations that are responsive to the national government.

Through the so-called "solidarity fund," the new regime has instituted a program of state-funded and state-controlled organizations to distribute milk and foodstuffs to the poor.

Although the transition from the dictatorship to an electoral regime represents a substantial qualitative shift in political opportunities for the intellectual and political class, the shift in political forms has not led to similar increases in political participation, power, and independent organization for rural labor and the urban poor and has produced only marginal increases of the sort for urban labor. The contradiction between the increase in formal political space and the continuing constraints imposed by existing state structures and the neoliberal model is already beginning to manifest itself. The contest between social movements and the regime is precisely over the efforts by social movements to provide a substantial popular alternative to elite-controlled political forms.

Democratic Discourse and Elite Circulation

The new electoral elites and their ideologues, most of whom were recruited from externally funded research institutes, have been instrumental in facilitating the transition from social movement to party politics.[39] The electoral elites have combined their democratic discourse on "popular representation" with a practice in which power is consolidated by the party machine. Within the party machine, the electoral elite, linked to the executive and congressional leadership, controls strategic policies as negotiated with the nonelected leaders in the state and economy and the ultra-right-wing parties.

Chile's transition to electoral politics has been a process of "substitution" and concentration of power—meaning the displacement of self-organized movements by atomized party voters, the subordination of voters to party leaders, the fusion of party elites with congressional leaders, and the subordination of the latter to the executive elites. The elections have changed the process of elite selection, the channels of ascent, and the forms of legitimation, but not the process of centralization of political power and the subordination of civil society to the party-state apparatus.

The language of democracy was necessary for the electoral elite to mobilize the populace and to present a credible threat to the ruling military regime and their U.S. backers. From this position, it was able to negotiate power-sharing agreements. Now that it is in power, the electoral elite justifies its subordination of civil society to the state in the name of "stabilizing democracy"—a euphemism for elite rule over the autonomous movements in society. The elitist and "monopolizing" tendencies of the electoral political class explain their strategic effort to displace social movement leadership, an effort that was at least partially successful in advance of the elections and in the immediate postelectoral period. There is an inverse relationship between social movement and electoral politics. The decline of one is accompanied by the ascent of the other. Electoral politicians and sociopolitical grass-roots movements represent not only different styles and forms of politics but also fundamental differences in the substance of power, representation, and class interest.

In social movement vocabulary, democracy starts with the autonomy of civil society and moves toward the subordination of the state to its interests. For the electoral elite, democracy begins with the capturing of the regime and the subordination of civil society to its dictates. Social movements reflect the emergence of natural leaders, self-educated practitioners of direct democracy in assemblies of equals. The electoral elite is made up of a new class of state managers and ideologues funded by the NGOs.

Intellectuals in Uniform

The Chilean intelligentsia represents a classic case of conversion from "critical outsider" to conformist functionary: talking to the people, working for the investors. The conversion is evident in the manipulation of political language. When in opposition, members of the intelligentsia attacked the armed forces' human rights abuses; when in power, they seek to reconcile victims with executioners. In opposition, institutional intellectuals criticized the "neoliberal" market doctrines; in power as functionaries, they celebrate the market and denigrate redistributive policies and popular control of the past.[40] The intellectuals-turned-functionaries' claims to originality ("renovated thinking") are in fact imitations of the commonplace pronouncements of their previous adversaries.

The intellectuals' conversion from critics to celebrants of neoliberal policies reflects the influence of impersonal institutional powers and private social ambitions. At the institutional level, the Chilean intellectuals in opposition lived a perpetual contradiction: their institutes and publications and research opportunities were almost totally dependent upon links with foreign donors, with foundations backed by corporations, and with states favorable to neoliberal politics; at the same time, their writing criticized the Pinochet regime's neoliberal socioeconomic policy. As the end of the Pinochet regime approached, the overseas institutional linkage came increasingly into play. The parallelism between the "internationalization" of intellectual institutions and the neoliberal economy fostered by the military regime begot a converging outlook: the practices of externally financed institutes dependent on an "external market" were excellent training for occupying ministerial posts and administering an economy based on the same principles. The seemingly abrupt reversals of politico-economic positions was thus rooted in the common structural positions that the opposition intellectuals and the Pinochet technocrats occupied. In brief, past linkages shaped contemporary accommodations. From this perspective, it is no surprise to discover that the Ford Foundation funded the "CIEPLAN Boys," who welcomed the Bush initiative for a Latin American free market.

The conversion of the intellectuals to neoliberal doctrines is not a response merely to institutional imperatives. There are also "personal imperatives." Social and political ambitions of the upwardly mobile professionals are divorced from the major economic sources of prestige, power, and wealth (controlled by the multinational corporation in minerals, by the banks, and by local capital, in agriculture). Unable to ascend through these economic routes, and unwilling to challenge the power holders, the upwardly mobile intellectuals can only hope to imitate the elite life-style by managing their interests (Foxley's felicitous term, "managing the macroeconomic indicators"). The intellectuals' unwillingness to transcend the current socioeconomic order, therefore, is not only a failure of the imagination but a celebration of impotence passed off as "pragmatism." What the intellectual functionaries describe as "realism" is service and subordination of the electoral regime to the power of nondemocratic, nonelected social forces and institutions.

Upward mobility, servicing the elite, and the new managerial power, as well as the prerogatives of the intellectuals in power, are all rationalized as "modernization."[41] The discourse of "modernity" so popular among the intellectuals is the universalization of personal success, the ideology of upwardly mobile professionals linked to the export elites. This is particularly offensive to the majority of the poor, as the "modernity" to which the regime intellectuals refer has as its immediate corollary massive marginality and socioeconomic inequalities unparalleled since the turn of the century. The class modernity of the ruling intellectuals is the source of human bondage in Chile: the hundreds of thousands of powerless, exploited, and unorganized farm workers exist in what the intellectuals praise as the "modern," "efficient," and "competitive" agro-export industries. The "dynamic" forestry and paper industry, which the regime intellectuals promote, is based on a captive labor force, reminiscent of the indentured serfs of the past century.[42] The pursuit of professional careers by the celebrants of the new democracy is exercised through the domestic slavery of hundreds of thousands of household servants driven by the immense poverty in the countryside and cities.

The intellectuals-turned-functionaries' dream is to achieve the material life of the neoliberal economic elite: to enter into the world of computerized wealth, replete with stylized homes in the foothills of the *cordillera* (the Andes Mountains), a summer home by the sea, private schools for the children, conferences in the United States and Europe. Under the electoral regime, modernization for the few is the condition for the continued impoverishment of the many. The rebels and dissidents of yesterday are the conformist managers and promoters of foreign capital today. Foxley, Ffrench-Davis, Cortázar, and the CIEPLAN Boys, who began their careers as virulent critics of Pinochet's neoliberal model, are today its staunchest defenders. Former MIR militant and current Economic Minister Ominami, a former fervent opponent of imperialism, is today an enthusiastic supporter of unrestricted foreign investment. Former SUR professionals Tironi and Guillermo Campero, onetime promoters of social movements, have joined the new class of state managers designing policies to limit popular demands within the established order.[43] Presidential spokesperson Enrique Correa—a onetime supporter of armed resistance—is now actively promoting policies facilitating amnesty for the generals under the slogan of "truth and reconciliation," while his former resistance comrades languish in jail. The list of dissident intellectuals converted to conformist functionaries would fill a provincial telephone directory. The point is that a substantial number of former leftist intellectuals have reneged on their responsibilities to the popular movement. They have resolved the tension between a commitment to the popular struggle and the seductions of bourgeois life-style by unequivocally choosing the latter. And they have gone further. Whether out of bad conscience or not, they have attempted to blot out their radical past by systematically falsifying the nature of past struggles, positive changes, and heroic sacrifices, in order to justify their current accommodation with their former adversaries.[44] In effect, the former leftists argue that in their struggles the popular movements committed serious errors and pursued "utopian" sociopolitical goals, whereas the elites who repressed them were realistic pragmatists and architects of a successful economic model. In order to "sell" this rewriting of history, the former leftist intellectuals use their position as former "insiders" to bolster their confessions of past errors, claims of utopian "excesses," and their "discovery" of the "virtues" of the marketplace and of elite-managed electoral politics.[45] These rather obsequious confessions serve the purpose of securing certificates of respectability from agents of the right-wing power structure (*El Mercurio*, the army, and, most of all, the foreign and domestic investors).

It is not as if the former leftists will be totally accepted by the Pinochet Right. There is residual rancor; there are patronage rivalries and fundamentally different electoral constituencies.[46] Still, the debates and differences take place on common institutional and economic terrain and the former leftists have shown an almost infinite capacity to compromise with the Right on all issues of strategic concern to the latter—and these compromises have consistently taken place at the expense of what the former leftist functionaries describe as the "postponed social necessities of the popular classes." Under the aegis of former leftists, it appears that these social necessities will be further postponed in the name of "democracy," "stability," "governability," and, of course, the "macroeconomic indicators." Indeed, people's needs are "micro" (small) and investor confidence is "macro" (large) in the eyes of the Foxley-Ominami economic team.

There is an emerging credibility gap between the discourse of the intellectual and electoral regime, on the one hand, and its popular electoral constituency, on the other. It is manifested in a multiplicity of areas where ideological claims clash with practical realities. The issue of modernity is central to the dispute. The claim of modernity's universalism is belied by the reality of continuing class polarity; claims of the centrality of democratic values clash with the practice of state-promoted elite appropriation of wealth; the claim of a mobile life-style is belied by the constraints of poverty. Further, claims of the efficiency of market allocations are undermined by the reality of the concentration and centralization of economic power, and claims of popular participation are contradicted by the politics of elite decisionmaking.

"Modernity" in Chile is a series of unsubstantiated claims—vicarious symbolism for the many and substantive rewards for the few. "Modernization" ideology is the mechanism by which former leftist intellectuals fit into the matrix of power. Modernization discourse seeks to secure the confidence of the elites by demonstrating the former leftists' willingness to make unpopular decisions (contain labor demands and retain regressive tax, income, and social policies). Modernization discourse focuses on increasing the technological and productive capacities of the existing owners of the means of production. It focuses on providing economic incentives and allocating state resources toward these goals. Finally, the modernization discourse serves as a pretext to dump the populist past and embrace the neoliberal present.

In summary, the leftist intellectual-political class has evolved in three stages. In the early stages of opposition, isolated from the levers of government and dependent on the popular movement, it adopted a populist-redistributive discourse highly critical of both those in power and their neoliberal model and attempted to attach itself to the social movements. In the second stage, as the leftist intellectual-political class approached power, it adopted a double discourse: confidence-building concessions at the top and moderate reforms at the bottom, all rationalized as the new realism. The leftist political class increasingly sought to attach itself to the state and to transform social movements into an electoral base. In the latest (the present) period in government, the now-former leftists pursue policies designed to manage the status quo, speak the language of limited resources, engage in the politics of delayed gratification, and adopt the policies of trickle-down economics. The goals, of course, are stability and adjustments within the system.

Justice and Human Rights

The regime's decision to abdicate its reformist mission in favor of a managerial style will not strengthen the stability of democracy but will empty it of its popular content. The most striking area in which the electoral-civilian regime has taken a stand contrary to the interests of popular democratic development is on the issue of human rights.

Throughout 1990 scores of skeletons and mutilated corpses have been discovered in several mass graves in Chile.[47] They show that the victims were executed, frequently after torture. Trade union and peasant activists and leaders, elected local and state officials, students and professionals, political party leaders and managers of public enterprises have been among those identified. They were victims of the terror unleashed by Pinochet's military regime, which violently seized power in 1973 from the democratically elected Allende government. The military officials responsible for many of these mass executions are known and have been identified by witnesses and human rights groups.[48]

The major issue in Chile is what to do about these crimes against humanity. The "unofficial" position of the newly elected Aylwin government, as well as that of the Socialist and Christian Democratic parties, has been to seek out the victims, exhume them, identify the cause of death, and pay an indemnification to the families.[49] This is described as "truth and reconciliation," a phrase that also makes up the name of an official commission assigned the task of investigating the political murders of the Pinochet period.

The rationale for absolving military commanders of homicide is put in terms of either "consolidating democracy" or "closing the wounds of society."[50] Stability and political democracy, in this view, can be achieved only by avoiding confrontation with the armed forces and its political backers.

Hence, it is deemed necessary to ignore demands for justice from the families of the victims. These demands are described as "retribution," a phrase used by the Pinochet press, some electoral politicians, and most overseas journalists.[51] Justice is seen as a monetary payoff rather than as equity before the law.

But stability, democracy, and justice are not served by "reconciliation." First, absolving the military from capital crimes places it above the law; its members are exempted from punishment for what would be crimes, had they been committed by civilians. This double standard in law enforcement cripples the basic principle underlying democracy: equality before the law.

Second, exoneration of the military for past crimes creates a precedent for the commission of future crimes: Impunity encourages recidivism. The "pragmatic" argument made by some spokesmen for the government—that the application of law against the military could endanger democracy—is an argument against democracy. It presumes that a nonelected, authoritarian institution, and not the popularly elected government, has the final say in applying the law of the land. Insofar as the armed forces continue to determine when and where and against whom laws will apply, Chile does not measure up to any internationally accepted standard of democracy.

The stability of a democracy is not built by granting concessions to the military on issues pertaining to its violent intrusion into democratic politics. The example of Argentina is instructive: Each concession to military demands has simply encouraged new demands, which have escalated to the point where President Carlos Menem, the incumbent, has announced plans to free the remaining generals accused of committing genocide (30,000 killed or disappeared) during the decade of the "dirty war."

Finally, the exoneration of the military perpetuates the culture of fear and intimidation that prevailed during the military period. As one human rights leader remarked when interviewed, "The Truth and Reconciliation Commission encourages some to speak up, but others fear that truth without justice puts the witnesses in danger." Fear of military retribution is real; the military and police courts are still prosecuting their critics in the press, and their paramilitary counterparts have been active in threatening potential witnesses of crimes committed by the military.[52]

With the recent discoveries of mass graves, a substantial majority of Chileans favors bringing those responsible to trial. If ever the Aylwin government had a mandate to begin the process of democratizing the Chilean political system, it is now, in the early 1990s, before citizen indignation dissipates and future discoveries of mass graves become a bureaucratic routine assimilated into a political culture that prizes selective amnesia.

The moral perversity of keeping the antidictatorial resistance fighters in jail, while the regime joins in celebratory banquets and lunches with the high military officials responsible for almost seventeen years of bloody purges, escapes even the most concerned members of the governing coalition. During lunch with the president's brother—the congressperson most concerned with the plight of the prisoners—James Petras compared post-Pinochet Chile with France in the aftermath of World War II.[53] Could one imagine de Gaulle embracing and promoting the officials of the collaborator Vichy regime, while keeping the anti-Fascist Resistance fighters in jail, freeing only those who were "prisoners of conscience" and retaining those who had committed "crimes of blood" (killed Nazis)? In this moral swamp, spokespersons for the electoral regime propose an "amnesty" for both the torturers and their opponents, which would amalgamate executioners and their victims in what could become the most bizarre concept of "evenhanded justice" in history. Of course, the resistance prisoners reject this deal; however, it has found acceptance among renovated Socialists, Christian Democrats, and pro-Pinochet members of congress.

In the human rights and socioeconomic spheres, the major concern of the regime is to accommodate the Right and gain its confidence, in order to manage the system more smoothly. Halfway through the new regime's first year of governing, there were 263 political prisoners from the Pinochet era still in jail.

Members of the electoral political class use their collective "historical" amnesia as a convenient excuse for pursuing their incremental politics: They want to forgive and forget the crimes of the military in order to bargain for greater acceptability; they want to denigrate the successful structural reforms and popular power experiments of the 1960s and early 1970s in order to forge alliances with the investor classes of the 1990s. Recovering the collective memory of the popular struggles, which contain the seeds of a critique and an alternative to the contemporary neoliberal ruling alliance, will be the work of young historians.

Those elements that are not presently part of the political class's political agenda are as important as the regime's failure to implement its electoral program. One is reminded of Sherlock Holmes's solution to the crime in which the pertinent clue was the fact that the watchdog did not bark. The relative cooperation of the far Right with the regime is based on issues that remain unarticulated—the nonissues—that affect land tenure, power, income inequalities, privatizations, and the debt. The moderation of the Right's opposition is based on the decision of the electoral regime to accept Pinochet's wholesale privatizations at below-market prices, to continue debt payments incurred by the previous regime, and to continue subsidizing agrobusiness enterprises (based on violent land seizures of cooperatives). The absence of right-wing confrontations is rooted in the complicity between the new regime and the Right—in continuing Pinochet's rightist policies.

Instead of referring to the hegemony of a democratic political class, it is more appropriate to describe the ascendancy of a new ideology (neoliberalism) and a new class (the agromineral export sector). The electoral regime has appropriated the symbols and substance of the right-wing-constructed configuration of power and has provided a democratic legitimacy. It remains to be seen how long the regime can continue to channel popular demands into incrementalist channels, and how much it will have to concede to consolidate the confidence of the investor class.

Conclusion

This discussion of political change in Chile and the critique of the new electoral regime can be extended to apply to other Latin American cases. The basic issue that is raised concerns the essential difference between "regime" and "state" change. Thus far, our analysis and description has demonstrated, here and in previous chapters, that electoral regimes are not always democratic. Essentially, there are three components of democracy, and they are cultural, political, and organizational. First, in a democracy, there is a civic culture within which decisions are freely made without fear of state terror; in Chile, there is a pervasive culture of fear, cultivated by the political parties and elites that control the legitimate demands of the electorate through constant reference to the danger of "provoking a return of the military." A culture of fear is incompatible with democratic practice. Second, in a democracy, elected national officials create policy on important issues. Today, in Chile, nonelected officials, both foreign and national, shape the basic trade, investment, and debt payment policies. Military officials define the parameters of government action and pronounce on vital issues of human rights, violating the notion of "equal protection under the law." Pinochet-appointed judicial and Central Bank officials define crucial legal and economic policies. Finally, democracy involves an active, organized, and independent civil society based on social movements responsive to popular needs. In Chile, as in nondemocracies elsewhere, electoral machines attempt to subordinate and disarticulate social movements, in order to atomize the electorate and shrink its political vision. The new electoral regime has, in the best of cases, only taken the first tentative legal steps toward opening up the Chilean political system. Substantive democracy will require a different political alignment combined with a different relationship between the state and civil society.

Notes

1. For a detailed discussion, see James Petras and Fernando Ignacio Leiva, "Chile: The Authoritarian Transition to Electoral Politics: A Critique," *Latin American Perspectives*, 15, 3 (Summer 1988), pp. 97–114. See also Fernando Paulsen, "La Política Despues de los Arsenales," *Revista Análisis*, no. 157 (1986).

2. The decisive organizational change was the decision of the Alianza Democratica (the coalition of seven opposition parties from center-right to Social Democratic) to break with the left-wing coalition, Movimiento Democrático Popular, and to engage in a "fruitful dialogue."

3. Interview with Augusto Samaniego, one of the early proponents of the Communist strategy of "popular rebellion," July 24, 1990. Also, Manuel Fernando

Contreras, "La Actual Situación Política y sus Proyecciones," *Crítica y Socialismo* (Santiago: Ediciones CISPO, 1989), pp. 116–122.

4. During 1986–1987, over 100,000 people between 14 and 60 years old were arrested (most temporarily) on operations against 40 shantytowns (*poblaciones*). See Fernando Leiva and James Petras, "Chile: New Urban Movements and the Transition to Democracy," *Monthly Review* 39, 3 (July–August 1987), p. 122.

5. James Petras, "The New Class Basis of Chilean Politics," in Petras and Morris Morley, *U.S. Hegemony Under Siege* (London: Verso, 1990), pp. 241–242. Local activities in the neighborhoods continued, but the electoral leftist press began to ignore them in its news coverage.

6. Interview with Communist leaders, Santiago, Chile, March 1987.

7. See the interviews with J. J. Brunner in *La Segunda*, September 26, 1986. Brunner is the chief ideologue of the Nuñez faction of the Socialist party. For the Christian Democrats, see the interview in *La Segunda*, September 8, 1986. Nuñez's explicit acceptance of the Pinochet constitution is found in *La Tercera*, October 5, 1986.

8. Eugenio Tironi, "Crisis, Desintegración y Modernización," in *Proposiciones* no. 18 (January) (Santiago: Ediciones SUR, 1990), pp. 16–42.

9. The main architect of the governability thesis was Manuel Antonio Garretón. See *The Chilean Political Process* (Boston: Unwin Hyman, 1989).

10. This rhetoric pervades the publications of all the self-styled renovated Socialists (Brunner, Tironi, Garretón, and their political mentors (Nuñez, Arrate, and Lagos) in the leadership of the Socialist party.

11. Under Secretary of State for Inter-American Affairs Robert Gelbard flew to Chile after the July 2–3 general strike and bluntly told the renovated Socialists and Christian Democrats that the Reagan administration opposed the tactics of "social mobilization" and alliances with the Left. Immediately thereafter, the alliances broke apart and the center alliance rejected mobilization politics. See Petras and Leiva, op. cit., pp. 99–100.

12. The National Endowment for Democracy, the Reaganite political interventionary arm, provided hundreds of thousands of dollars for several Chilean research institutions run by right-wing Social Democrats and Christian Democrats, many of them former leftists from the 1960s who were eager recipients of these funds for a "political education" in conformity.

13. On the continuities of military privilege, see "Militares Gastan Mucho y Quieren Más," *Página Abierta*, July 23–August 5, 1990, pp. 18–19.

14. See the interview with Admiral Jorge Martinez Busch, *El Mercurio*, July 22, 1990, pp. D–1 and D–3. On many strategic issues, such as the border dispute with Bolivian military officials, Chilean military officials pronounce their position without consulting the regime. On the issue of human rights, Pinochet has let the government know that the armed forces still stands beyond the law. On September 17, 1990, Pinochet virtually declared the military's independence from civil authority. The regime did nothing to assert its primacy.

15. This threat from the military, in turn, has been transmitted by the regime to its electoral supporters, thus inhibiting the free expression of the Popular Democrats and creating a culture of fear.

16. It was estimated that Pinochet spent several million dollars to secure the "early retirement" of several judges to facilitate his packing the courts.

17. Pinochet's pact with Aylwin on securing tenure for his followers closely resembles the same pact that the Christian Democrats imposed on Allende as a condition for allowing him to take office in 1970. Dissident Socialists complained bitterly about the lack of patronage jobs for the party faithful after the elections. These comments come from an interview with a leader of the Regional Central (Santiago) Socialist Party, July 24, 1990.

18. Andres Bianchi, a long-standing neoliberal opponent of redistributionist politics, was approved by both Pinochet and the Christian Democrats and Socialists, which is symbolic of the new neoliberal concord.

19. Interview with Manuel Barrera, July 19, 1990.

20. On privatization of the electric power-generating companies, see *El Mercurio*, July 13, 1990, pp. 13–14; on foreign investment, *El Mercurio*, July 12, 1990, p. B–1. On Minister of Finance Foxley's support of the Bush free market plan, see *Fortin Mapocho*, July 26, 1990, p. 9.

21. *El Mercurio* gave prominent coverage to right-wing Social Democrat José J. Brunner's messianic promarket message. He described the market as "one of the most powerful mechanisms of coordination [sic] of the economy and society that civilization has perfected over the length of its history," *El Mercurio*, July 20, 1990, p. C–5. The full article appeared in the new ideological vehicle of the renovated Socialists, *Crítica Social* no. 1 (May 1990).

22. See the special issue of *Proposiciones* no. 18 (January) (Santiago: Ediciones SUR, 1990).

23. "Policies, Mechanisms and Organization of International Cooperation," "Concertación de los Partidos para la Democracia," October 1989. Even this minimalist pre-electoral reform program has been abandoned.

24. President Aylwin's regime has been pressuring the U.S. Congress to reopen military aid to Chile in the hope of demonstrating to the Chilean military the utility of better working relations.

25. "Los Cien Días de Aylwin," *Análisis*, June 25–July 1, 1990; *Análisis*, July 16–22, 1990; see also Alvaro Diaz, "Interrogantes Sobre el Rumbo Económico del Gobierno," *Análisis y Perspectivas* no. 2 (May 1990), pp. 49–53.

26. *El Mercurio*, July 13, 1990, p. B–1 and July 12, 1990, p. B–1.

27. On the pre-1973 Socialist and Christian Democratic parties, see James Petras, *Politics and Social Forces in Chilean Development* (Berkeley: University of California Press, 1968).

28. President Aylwin defended the existing Pinochet-established rules for foreign investment by citing the needs of foreign capital for "stable norms"—thus rejecting trade union demands for tax reforms affecting the mining multinationals. See *El Mercurio*, July 19, 1990, p. A–1.

29. See *El Mercurio*, July 21, 1990, p. B–1.

30. The mass appeal of the Aylwin campaign was evident in its sweep of almost all of the urban centers except for two in Santiago, and it covered the range of social classes, from the affluent professionals to the marginal neighborhoods. The two most affluent areas of Santiago, Providencia and Las Condes, retained their loyalties to the dictator.

31. When Enrique Correa, the general secretary of the government, made his pronouncement against "excess liberty" of the press, he was supported by pro-Pinochet Congressman Juan Antonio Coloma, *Fortin Mapocho,* July 16, 1990, p. 2.

32. We observed the peaceful demonstrations of the human rights demonstrators, heard the accords discussed between the government official present and the lawyer from the human rights group, and then watched the police beat the demonstrators on July 25, 1990. On police repression, see *Fortin Mapocho,* July 21, 1990.

33. On Aylwin consulting with the armed forces, see *El Mercurio,* July 20, 1990, p. 1. During September 1990, Pinochet characterized the armed forces of the German Federal Republic as betraying tradition and being a collection of homosexuals and misfits. The Aylwin government merely apologized to the Germans. Pinochet remained commander in chief of the armed forces.

34. *Punto Final,* June 1990, p. 5.

35. Interviews with executive committee members of the Comisión Nacional de Campesina (CNC), July 19, 1990. For a detailed critique, see Emilio Bustos, "Reformas Laborales Cambios de Forma o de Fondo?" *Análisis y Perspectivas* no. 2 (May 1990), pp. 29–48.

36. Ibid.

37. "La Ofensiva de los Despidos," *Punto Final* (June 1990), p. 6.

38. Interview with CNC members, July 19, 1990.

39. James Petras, "La Metamorfosis de los Intelectuales Latinoamericanos," *Estudios Latinoamericanos Mexico* no. 5 (July–December 1988), pp. 81–86.

40. See *El Mercurio,* July 20, 1990, p. C–5, and July 14, 1990, p. C–5.

41. See Tironi, op. cit., and Brunner, op. cit.

42. Gonzalo Falabella, "Trabajo Temporal y Desorganizacion Social, *Proposiciones* no. 18 (January) (Santiago: Ediciones SUR, 1990), pp. 25 and 268.

43. In his early pre-electoral "incarnation," Guillermo Campero championed the militancy and autonomy of the social movements. See his *Entre la Sobrevivencia y la Accion Política* (Santiago: ILET, 1987).

44. See Arrate's "confessions" of popular excesses and "utopian" thought in *El Mercurio,* July 14, 1990, p. C–5.

45. Ibid.

46. General Pinochet's followers were active throughout September 1990, mobilizing demonstrations of support for the military authorities and calling into question the electoral regime's authority.

47. *Análisis,* July 25, 1990, lists locations of several of the mass graves throughout the country.

48. See Patricia Verdugo, *Los Zarpazos del Puma* (Santiago: Ediciones Chile América, 1989). *Fortin Mapocho,* July 14, 1990, p. 14. Extensive documentation is present in the archives of the Agrupación de Familiares de Ejecutados Políticos. Three hundred eight trade union leaders were killed as well as 190 children and adolescents, among the over 2,000 disappeared. See *Fortin Mapocho,* July 20, 1990, pp. 8 and 12 and the special issue of *El Siglo,* July 8–14, 1990.

49. The regime's "forgive and forget" position on military assassinations was most clearly stated by the president of the congress, José Antonio Viera-Gallo, who stated, "We should end polemics about past facts," *El Mercurio,* July 20, 1990, pp. C–3 and D–8.

50. Ibid. Viera-Gallo argued that it was much more important to "develop common tasks with the armed forces, rather than engage in polemics that are harmful to them." Mass murder and torture have become "polemics"; the demands for equal justice before the law are obstacles to pursuing the common neoliberal economic project.

51. *El Mercurio,* a longtime apologist for Pinochet and the military dictatorship, is the primary proponent of this position in Chile. Anthony Lewis and Shirley Christian of the *New York Times* have followed suit.

52. Interviews with Rosa Silva and Berta Ugarte of the Agrupación de Familiares de Ejecutados Políticos de Chile, July 25, 1990. See also *Presos Políticos del Régimen Militar: Nóminas y Cuadros Estadísticos al 30 de Junio* (Santiago: FASIC, 1990).

53. Interview with Andrés Aylwin, deputy in congress and brother of the president. The most bizarre aspect of the Chilean political scene was presented in the newspaper, where photos of the uncovering of the mass graves appeared on one page and photos of President Aylwin meeting and socializing with the military officials appeared on the next. See *El Mercurio,* July 13 and 20, 1990, p. 1. Even the president of the European Parliament, Enrique Baron Crespo, supported the full prosecution of the military, much to the surprise of the Chilean Social and Christian Democrats. See *El Mercurio,* July 26, 1990, p. C–4. One of the most moving accounts was of executed trade union leaders in Lota, who, after expressing their concerns for the families they were leaving behind, sang workers' songs to a guitar accompaniment. During the reburial, in what must rank as one of the most odious acts of the Aylwin regime, Vasili Carrillo, a political prisoner, was denied permission to pay a tribute to his father, Isidoro; but this didn't prevent the electoral politicians from joining the procession. See *Fortin Mapocho,* July 16, 1990, p. 28.

6

The Political Economy
of the Aylwin Government

Our economic program rests on three essential foundations: guaranteeing economic stability by fighting tirelessly against inflation along with maintaining basic macroeconomic equilibrium; achieving, within the framework of an open market strategy, a greater degree of, and better, integration of the Chilean economy in the world economy; accentuating the process of investment in people, through intense, durable, and systematic action on the part of the state, to open up opportunities for middle class and poorer Chileans.*

—Alejandro Foxley[1]

The Export Model:
Continuity, Consensus, Consolidation

Patricio Aylwin's electoral victory in December 1989 energized the long-cherished hopes of Chileans that the end of the Pinochet dictatorship would also bring about an end to the widespread suffering and poverty inflicted upon them by more than a decade and a half of neoliberal economic policies. Tapping the power of this deeply rooted sentiment, the Concertación de Partidos por la Democracia, the incoming civilians' political coalition, chose a campaign slogan, worded to confidently presage: La Alegría Ya Viene (Happiness is coming!). The carefully crafted government program of the incoming coalition insinuated significant socioeconomic improvement: the savage capitalism of the Chicago Boys would be replaced by a kinder, gentler development strategy unimaginatively christened as "growth with equity."[2]

After Aylwin's March 1990 inauguration, expectations remained high that previously expressed concerns about social justice would translate

---

All quotations originally in Spanish have been translated by Fernando Ignacio Leiva.

into policies redressing the severe socioeconomic injustice and anguish resulting from Pinochet's rule. Given the magnitude of these expectations, shortly after assuming his post as finance minister, Alejandro Foxley felt obliged to beseech the public, "Let us be judged after four years have passed, not after six months."[3]

During the second half of 1991, it became apparent that Foxley's request for a "grace period" lasting the full duration of the Aylwin administration was going unheeded: Chuquicamata and El Teniente copper workers went on strike; national health and teachers' unions organized "illegal" work stoppages; the coal miners of Curanilahue held regional demonstrations protesting rising layoffs and governmental passivity in the face of the imminent collapse of the regional economy; Mapuche Indian organizations, with a vigor and autonomy that surprised the Concertación coalition, initiated combative mobilizations to defend their land and cultural rights. The "honeymoon" period between the newly elected civilian government and the expectant masses seemed to draw to a close.

In this chapter, we will examine the general orientation[4] of the Aylwin government by reviewing its discourse and practices during its first two years at the helm of the state apparatus. Specifically, we will explore how the Aylwin government's view of *who* should run the economy and *how* it should be run has influenced its macroeconomic performance and its ability to satisfy popular aspirations. The purpose of such an exercise is to throw light on some central questions about the fate of the neoliberal model during the post-Pinochet period:

- What modifications, if any, has the growth with equity strategy introduced into the economic model structured by Pinochet?
- How has the Aylwin government's emphasis on consensus building and concerted action altered the preexisting configuration of class power and the "degrees of freedom" previously enjoyed by transnational capital and local corporate conglomerates?
- What mechanisms for social control and "governability" are being deployed to suit the present development strategy and new political conditions?
- Do these two years of elected government suggest that social equity and export-oriented capitalist accumulation are indeed compatible?

The opening section below reviews the Concertación government's general economic orientation as reflected in the growth with equity development strategy it has adopted. The second section examines the underlying assumptions of such a strategy, the major policy initiatives carried out during these two years, and the results of policy implementation.

Economic Orientation

The Three Pillars of Aylwin's Development Strategy

In his first report to Congress on the state of public finances,[5] Foxley identified the three pillars supporting the civilian government's development strategy: (1) an "unbreakable commitment" to macroeconomic stability, (2) a "fuller and improved commercial and financial integration with the world economy," and (3) the enhancement of social services "within the constraints of a balanced fiscal expenditure program." Foxley's succinct exposition of the main components of the Concertación politico-economic project is revealing in three important respects. First, if the development ideology of a particular class alliance can be inferred, among other factors, from its views on the role of foreign capital and on the proper role of the state in the economy vis-à-vis the private sector, as well as from the general objectives the alliance manifests in the relationship between investment and consumption,[6] then Foxley's definition provides sufficient material for a preliminary identification of the "magnetic conceptual poles" that orient the direction of the Aylwin government's politico-economic intervention. Second, Foxley's description reveals, in a nutshell, the self-imposed economic boundaries that constrain the government's political initiative. Recall that during his inaugural speech, President Aylwin set forth the five grand objectives of his government as follows: "(1) achieve national reconciliation, (2) consolidate and perfect the democratic system, (3) promote social justice, (4) support the economic growth, development, and modernization of the country, and (5) reinsert Chile in the international community."[7] The resources and energies allocated to the achievement of these goals has been conditioned by the general guidelines directing economic strategy. Third, each of the pillars formulated by Foxley contains elements inherently in contradiction: macroeconomic equilibria versus the satisfaction of popular demands; internationalization and export competitiveness versus improved wages and labor rights; alleviation of the symptoms of massive poverty versus uprooting its structural causes. The capacity to maintain the knife-edge balance among these antagonistic goals has decisively influenced the ability of the government to effectively implement its policies, accomplish its predefined goals, and maintain electoral support.[8] How these tensions embedded in the formulated development strategy have played themselves out during these two years provides a valuable entry point for investigating the political economy of the Aylwin regime.

The Guiding Principles: Boeninger's Mark

As has been argued previously, the intellectual origins of the growth with equity strategy are to be found in the shifts made by Christian Democratic and Socialist intellectuals during the years 1983–1989. More precisely, formulation of the fundamental principles for the Aylwin government's macroeconomic policies began in 1984, when Edgardo Boeninger synthesized a consensus among neoliberal ideologues, Christian Democrats, and renovated Socialists in his theory of change under democracy. It is not surprising, therefore, that when, in 1990, a group of CIEPLAN analysts[9] set themselves the task of explaining the foundations of the Aylwin government economic policy, they repeated almost word for word, the principles outlined by Boeninger six years earlier. The link between the theory of change under democracy and Aylwin's economic strategy is indisputable.[10]

According to CIEPLAN analysts, the basic guidelines defining the strategic direction of the Aylwin government are as follows:

1. To construct a stable legal and institutional framework for the development of economic activities.
2. To maintain a market economy open to international flows.
3. To give priority to the struggle against poverty.
4. To defend macroeconomic balance, stability, and a "gradualist approach" to social progress.

These four strategic directives define the "rules of order" to be followed by the Aylwin government in the ranking of politico-economic objectives. Hence, the orientations above prescribe that, in spite of massive social needs and accumulated injustices, the government should undertake no measures that could be interpreted as an "intolerable threat" by the capitalist class or the armed forces. Consequently, the governing coalition's prime directive—its overriding mandate to defend private property—excludes any redistributive efforts that might affect property rights or jeopardize export competitiveness. Likewise, the internationalization of the economy and the humoring of international investors have priority over the satisfaction of the socioeconomic needs of the impoverished. The campaign against poverty must be tightly circumscribed and subordinate to the requirements of macroeconomic balance, fiscal austerity, and the hegemony of the market.

Two Years of "Growth with Equity"

To assess the deployment of Aylwin's development strategy, we proceed to examine each one of the three pillars upon which it rests: macroeconomic equilibrium, increased internationalization, and reinforced social programs. In each case we review (1) the original assumptions, (2) the measures and policies adopted during the 1990–1991 period, and (3) the main economic and political results. Though necessarily general, this overview captures the main political criteria, the problems, and the outcomes of two years of economic management by the successors of the Chicago Boys.

The First Pillar: Defense of Macroeconomic Equilibrium

A central component of the economic discourse and practice of the Concertación coalition during these first two years has been the zealous safeguarding of macroeconomic equilibrium. Although the coalition appears to respond to "plain economic common sense" devoid of ideological or class considerations, closer scrutiny reveals that such a commitment conceals the application of a particular brand of policies that maintain grave distributive disequilibrium generated under the military regime. Reflecting his belief that macroeconomic equilibrium plays a role as a disciplining mechanism for popular demands, Foxley has pointed out, "If an economy can pass the test of fiscal equilibrium, then *social activists learn to respect the government's authority and the private sector becomes willing to invest*" [emphasis added].[11]

Policies to Preserve Macroequilibrium

To safeguard basic macroeconomic balance, Aylwin's economic team was forced to apply two major policy packages during the 1990–1991 period. The first was a 1990 stabilization and adjustment program aimed at controlling inflationary pressures and reducing imports in order to reestablish the balance in the foreign trade account. In June 1991, only three months after claiming the successful completion of the 1990 adjustment policies, the Aylwin administration was compelled to implement a second set of measures. This time, the objective was to control both the surplus of foreign exchange in the economy and the resulting decline of the exchange rate. A brief analysis of these two efforts reveals the ephemeral nature of macroeconomic balance in a small and open economy such as Chile's. Likewise, the two measures evidence the extent to which Aylwin administration policies implemented to maintain equilibrium are biased in favor of export-competitiveness based on cheap labor and on unregulated access to Chile's natural resources. In addition, the measures show how the defense of economic macroequilibrium is based on the preservation of major macrosocial disequilibrium engineered by the neoliberal policies and repression of the previous regime.

TABLE 6.1   Real Gross Domestic Product by Expenditure Type (annual growth rate)

	1987	1988	1989	1990	1991
Gross domestic product	5.7	7.4	10.1	2.1	6.0
Private consumption	4.8	9.6	8.4	0.7	5.4
Government consumption	−2.1	4.7	0.9	1.6	3.6
Gross capital formation[a]	16.2	10.7	20.8	6.9	−1.0
Exports	8.8	6.1	15.7	7.6	12.9
Imports	17.0	12.1	25.3	0.6	8.5

[a]Refers to gross fixed capital formation
SOURCE: Banco Central, *Boletin Mensual* no. 771 (May 1992), p. 1,333.

Adjustment in 1990. In 1988, facing an upcoming electoral contest and enjoying the US$1 billion bonanza of additional fiscal revenues due to higher than expected international copper prices, the military regime increased government expenditures and reduced corporate and income taxes. As a result, during the last two years of Pinochet's rule, aggregate demand increased by 23 percent while GDP only grew at a slower 18 percent rate.[12] The outpacing of GDP by aggregate demand was quickly reflected in a rapid increase in imports and growing inflationary pressures. Nonfood consumer imports doubled from US$690 million in 1988 to US$1,234 million in 1989; the Consumer Price Index (CPI) shot up from 12.7 percent in 1988 to 21.4 percent in 1989. After Pinochet's electoral defeat in the plebiscite, his finance minister, Hernán Büchi, began to apply a mildly contractive policy, which Foxley and Ominami intensified once the new government assumed office.

Through the combination of restrictive monetary and fiscal policies, and in tight coordination with the autonomous Central Bank, the Aylwin administration began enforcing a strict adjustment program. On the monetary side, the Central Bank took measures to raise market interest rates, whereas on the fiscal side disbursements for different budgetary items were purposefully delayed. As can be seen from Table 6.1, private consumption fell from an annual real rate of growth of 8.4 percent in 1989 to only 0.7 percent in 1990, while the expansion of imports plummeted from 25.3 percent in 1989 to a mere 0.6 percent in 1990.

These corrective policies succeeded in "cooling off" the economy; the quarterly rate of GDP growth fell drastically from 5.5 percent during the first quarter of 1990, to rates of 0.8 and 0.2 percent during the second and third quarters of that year. The Aylwin government was able to decelerate economic activity from an annual rate of 10 percent (measured in terms of GDP) in 1989 to 2.1 percent in 1990. Inflationary pressures, however, remained, due to the effects of a government-decreed increase in minimum wages and high petroleum prices. Measured by the CPI, yearly inflation during 1990 was 27.4 percent, a figure well above the 21.4 percent rate for the previous year. However, the tendency toward rising inflation after the second half of 1989 appeared to have been broken by the fourth quarter of 1990.[13]

The June 1991 Package. By the second quarter of 1991, the rate of inflation had once again shot up to 6.2 percent, reaching an accumulated rate of 27.3 percent for the previous twelve-month period. This time, however, macroeconomic imbalances did not originate in expansionary policies but rather in the open economy strategy of development itself. Due to the successful expansion of exports, as well as to the influx of short-term speculative capital, the Chilean economy—in sharp contrast with other economies of the region—began to face the destabilizing consequences of a foreign exchange glut! Accumulated international reserves derived from balance-of-payment transactions reached US$2.37 billion at the end of 1990, a significant increase over the US$437.4 million of 1989. This increase was due to the influx of US$2.65 billion in external funds, mainly in the form of foreign direct investment and short-term speculative capital taking advantage of the differences between declining U.S. interest rates and the relatively real higher rates prevailing in Chilean financial markets.

By June 1991, accumulated reserves held by the Chilean Central Bank totaled US$5.65 billion.[14] Thus, after moving out of the external finance constraints of the early 1980s, the Chilean economy had made the transition to the no less problematic situation of being swamped by foreign exchange surplus (see Table 6.2).

Such a surplus generated powerful negative macroeconomic effects. On the one hand, the excess of dollars tended to lower the real exchange rate, thus damaging the competitiveness of Chilean exports. On the other hand, the Central Bank was forced to prop up the declining exchange rate by soaking up excess dollars through the sale of its securities. Such a policy tended to increase monetary emission, which augmented inflationary pressures and undermined macroeconomic balance.

Drowning in Dollars

Aylwin's second major macroeconomic policy package sought to overcome the pressure exerted by the inflow of dollars on export competitiveness. As the deluge of dollars continued, the exchange rate fell, which made it difficult to follow a restrictive monetary policy.

The policy package finally jointly proposed by the government and the Central Bank consisted of the following measures:

- An across-the-board lowering of import tariffs from 15 to 11 percent.
- A 2 percent reduction in the value of the dollar and a reapplication of the original exchange rule, which accounted for international inflation in its crawling peg policy.

TABLE 6.2   International Reserves and Real Exchange Rate

Month	Net Reserves[a] (US$ billion)	Real Exchange Rate[b] (base 1986=100)
1990		
April	13.20	111.63
May	3.54	111.08
June	3.79	108.37
July	4.15	107.17
August	4.37	108.14
September	4.29	106.56
October	4.99	105.43
November	5.40	108.90
December	5.35	109.01
1991		
January	5.53	108.67
February	5.73	110.00
March	5.84	107.45
April	5.68	103.62
May	5.79	99.54
June	5.65	98.11
July	5.56	98.57
August	5.76	99.67
September	5.81	100.98
October	5.93	98.01
November	6.29	99.03
December	6.64	100.29

SOURCES: [a]Banco Central, *Boletin Mensual* no. 767 (January 1992), p. 146.
[b]Banco Central, *Informe Económico y Financiero*, February 15, 1992, p. 29.

- A stamp and seal tax applicable to short-term foreign credits.
- An increase in gasoline taxes of 40 percent in 1992, and of 35 percent after 1993.
- A 20 percent obligatory reserve deposit on short-term foreign credits.
- The granting of permission to private banks to engage in external trade financing activities among countries other than Chile.

By the end of 1991, this new array of policies seemed to have achieved its objective. Year end inflation for 1991 had fallen to 18.7 percent, slightly above the target annual rate of 18 percent; gross reserves grew only US$37.6 million during the last quarter of 1991, as opposed to US$71.2 million for the same period in 1990, indicative of an initial success in curbing the incoming tide of foreign exchange.

However, the apparent success of these policies did not prevent independent observers from noticing the blatant dissonance between the 1990 measures and those implemented in 1991. Whereas in 1990 the means to reestablish macroeconomic balance had been drastic reduction of imports, the policy intervention of 1991 sought to restore macroeconomic stability using opposite means, namely by sharply increasing imports.

To deal with the flood of dollars, Aylwin's economic team chose to "burn off" excess foreign exchange rather than attempt to find a productive destination for the US$6 billion in accumulated reserves. The June 1991 policies promoted increased consumption of imported durable and luxury goods and overseas travel by upper middle class sectors (travel to the United States by Chileans increased by 21 percent in 1991); these measures did little to improve job opportunities for unemployed young people, whose official unemployment rate remained at over 13 percent. In fact, in 1991 the annual rate of gross domestic expenditures in gross fixed capital formation declined 1 percent in real terms. Thus, in spite of its short-term success,[15] the June 1991 package posed critical questions about the medium- and long-term effects, as well as the strategic implications, of maintaining macroeconomic stability in a small and open economy such as Chile's.[16]

Cracks in the First Pillar

A review of the efforts to maintain macroeconomic balance—the first pillar of Concertación's development strategy—reveals that during Aylwin's first two years, it was maintained at the expense of raising productive investment and forgoing a policy of industrial and technological development, even when the resources for such an effort were abundantly available.

Additionally, these two years suggest a contradiction between maintaining macroeconomic balance and increasing the internationalization of the economy. During 1991, as in previous years, Chile's relatively small economy was extremely vulnerable to the disequilibrating effects induced by the inflow of short-term speculative capital or by changes in international prices and interest rates. The policies implemented to correct such imbalances (burning off "excess" foreign exchange through increased imports) in turn led to further vulnerability and increased social inequality. The beneficiaries of the chosen policies were the bloc in power and the consumers of imported luxury goods. The path chosen to attain macroeconomic balance further reduced the range of alternative policy options, that is, productive investment, state incentives for research and development, deepening the internal market, and so on. Yet, ironically, the cause of this imbalance, the unrestricted internationalization of the Chilean economy, constitutes the second pillar and real core of the Christian Democratic-Socialist coalition's development strategy.

The Second Pillar: Further Transnationalization

A Strategic Objective

Accelerating the integration of Chile's productive and commercial structures into the global capitalist economy, in the eyes of the Aylwin administration, provides the chief lever for securing the much-sought objectives of dynamic economic growth, increased social harmony, and lasting political stability. Therefore, what Foxley describes as "greater and better integration into the world economy" constitutes the real driving force behind Concertación's economic development and political strategy. For this reason, "modernization through internationalization" rather than "growth with equity" would be a more accurate description of the Concertación coalition's strategic goal.

Internationalization of productive and commercial structures in concordance with the terms dictated by international capital is envisioned as the key "modernizing" force for overall societal development. According to Christian Democratic and renovated Socialist theorists, the internationalization of the Chilean economy offers the advantage of fusing the realization of three critical goals—economic growth, broadening social consensus, and reducing social polarization—without the inconvenience of having to modify preexisting private property rights. Such a view reveals an important conceptual shift from the previous programmatic stance.

In the 1950s and 1960s, while in their structuralist mode, Christian Democratic and Socialist theorists made the state the purported depository of social rationality. Today, in the wake of the neoliberal offensive, and after their conversion to the wonders of capitalist restructuring, Christian Democratic and Socialist theorists have reached the conviction that the only bearers of societal rationality are the forces of the international market and the globalization of capital. To an important degree, the internationalization of the Chilean economy, successfully initiated by Pinochet, has become "the motor force of history" for them and a welcomed "civilizing" force. Thus, they proclaim:

> There does not exist a rational objective [the task of modernization] that can elicit greater public adherence than this. ... All of us want to consume in a civilized manner, therefore we cannot produce or export in a primitive manner. We all want information and entertainment of an international level. ... Chile must deepen and improve its dynamic orientation toward the international economy.[17]

Modernization through internationalization is defended through a technocratic-dogmatic discourse asserting that the globalization of economic, commercial, and financial structures is both desirable and inevitable.

Keeping pace with technological change and avoiding being left behind by the "information age" and the trends of the twenty-first century requires full participation in the globalization of markets and international capital flows. Concertación theorists argue that, independently of our will, globalization is the one and only truly "democratic" force in the world today: People want videocassette recorders, McDonalds restaurants, and brand name imported sneakers. The conception of economic and social development that is currently being uninhibitedly embraced by Christian Democratic and Socialist intellectuals and political leaders can at best be described as a mongrelized version of the Euro- and U.S.-centric modernization theory of the 1950s, updated with neoliberal-spawned awe for the capitalist international market and the seductive powers of consumerism. They explain their intellectual shift in an almost heroic manner, saying it

> reflects the evolution of conception undergone by the more progressive groups in Chile after a decade and a half of military government, and [has been] influenced by profound changes in the world economy. These conceptions are the result of a drawn out process of reflection and analysis, *which has sought to preserve the positive elements of the structural reforms carried out by the Pinochet regime*, incorporating them within the framework of the progressive tradition, embodied in the Chilean democratic system [emphasis added].[18]

That ideas change in the face of a changing world is not surprising. The surprise lies in the extent to which Christian Democratic and Socialist intellectuals have allowed the direction of change to lead to reformation of their world vision, in order to conform to the dictates and conditions imposed by transnational capital.

Why Greater Internationalization?

The devotion of the Chilean economy to increased internationalization must be explained, beyond ideological factors, by Christian Democratic and Socialist recognition that the undisputed engine for capitalist expansion during the 1984 to 1989 period was the explosive growth of exports. Based on this trend, Foxley and Ominami have set themselves a goal: to ensure that exports rise to 35 percent of GDP from the current 30 percent, a performance that, in their view, would be "comparable to nations with a clear exporting tradition, such as Denmark and Sweden."[19] To achieve that objective, however, "emphasis must be placed on predictable policies that guarantee a competitive and stable real exchange rate, and on policies that are framed in an environment fostering international trade."[20] The nucleus of export promotion policy under Aylwin is to continue export incentives granted under Pinochet and to maintain a stable macroeconomic environment, low and even export duties, and a high and competitive exchange rate.[21]

Aylwin's economic team postulates that a high rate of export growth would lead to rapid expansion of employment levels and rises in wages and fiscal revenues. Sustained export growth would also be the key for ensuring governability, since the prospects of socioeconomic improvement in the near future "would promote acceptance of redistributive gradualism."[22] Nevertheless, Aylwin's economic team was aware that to maximize the alleged benefits of export growth, future expansion should increasingly come from nontraditional goods. If, under Pinochet, export expansion had been based almost exclusively in resource-intensive products (mining, fruit, fishing, lumber), Aylwin would promote the gradual transition to a second export phase, which, though still heavily based on primary products, would incorporate a greater number of value-added exported goods. In Foxley's view, greater internationalization of the Chilean economy would also be the driving force behind the transition from export competitiveness based on cheap labor and the depredation of natural resources to competition based on increases in productivity. Hence, the key for the economic, as well as political, success of the Concertación regime lies in ensuring a deeper and better transnationalization of the Chilean economy.

Toward "Improved" Internationalization

According to CIEPLAN analysts, the strategy of internationalizing the Chilean economy has four subcomponents: (1) ensuring access to international markets, (2) increasing foreign direct investment, (3) developing a loan program with multilateral lending agencies (World Bank, IDB, International Finance Corporation [IFC], and so on), and (4) reaching agreement with private commercial banks on the renegotiation of the external debt. In light of the promises to preserve Pinochet's economic model, the transition in Chile did not alter the interest or confidence of foreign investors. Before Aylwin's first anniversary in office, many of these objectives had been achieved: the external debt had been renegotiated and Chile had returned to the voluntary credit market, and significant loans had been obtained from multilateral lending institutions, such as the World Bank and the IDB. According to the *Comité de Inversiones Extranjeras* (Committee for Foreign Investment), between January 1, 1988, and October 1989, authorized foreign direct investment had reached US$4.35 billion, of which US$2.4 billion had materialized. Whereas in 1989 materialized FDI[23] had reached US$898 million, it climbed to US$1.13 billion in 1990, reaching US$1.15 billion in 1991. In spite of these increases, foreign direct invest-

TABLE 6.3   Foreign Direct Investment, 1990–1991 (in millions of US$)

	1990		1991	
	US$	Percent	US$	Percent
Authorized FDI				
Total value	1446	100.0	3394	100.0
Mining	–	–	2304	67.9
Services	–	–	510	15.1
Manufacturing	–	–	334	9.8
Forestry	–	–	140	4.1
Other	–	–	106	3.1
Total authorized	1446	100.0	3394	100.0
Materialized FDI				
Total value	1132	100.0	1150	100.0
Mining	–	–	554	48.2
Services	–	–	193	16.8
Manufacturing	–	–	157	13.6
Other	–	–	246	21.4
Total materialized	1132	100.0	1150	100.0

SOURCE: Comité de Inversiones Extranjeras, *El Mercurio,* December 18, 1991.

ment in Chile has remained heavily centered in the mining sector. During the period from 1974 to 1981, mining received 84.7 percent of authorized FDI; its share fell to 57 percent between 1982 and 1989. In 1991, mining represented 67.9 percent of authorized FDI (see Table 6.3).

Reasons for Investors' Confidence

In addition to predictable policies, "a greater and better internationalization of the Chilean economy" required that the state provide adequate signals regarding its commitment and willingness to remove all obstacles—either economic or political—that could stand in the path of internationalization. The first two years of the Aylwin government reveal that it has given ample guarantees and credible signals in this respect. During the years 1990–1991, the already lenient rules on the operation of foreign capital were further relaxed, productive and speculative capital flows increased; the democratic image of the first civilian government in almost seventeen years was used effectively to gain greater access to European and Asian markets and to introduce Chile into the U.S. generalized system of preferences. Furthermore, World Bank and IDB requirements that juridical changes be made to further privatize public enterprises and services (train freight, public works, ports, and the state-owned copper corporation, Corporación del Cobre [CODELCO]) were scrupulously followed. The freight section, the most profitable area of operations of *Ferrocarriles del Estado* (state railways) was privatized in exchange for a

World Bank loan. Constitutional law was modified so that CODELCO could develop joint ventures with private capital; the health system was further decentralized and semiprivatized to the satisfaction of international investors. Import duties were lowered from 15 to 11 percent, and both Foxley and Ominami actively spoke out during Washington trips in favor of "fast track" approval for the Bush initiative and the signing of a free trade agreement with the United States.

The Third Pillar: Novel Social Programs

Governability Through "Integration to Development"

The social policy designed by Concertación technocrats consistently subordinates redistributive concerns to the preservation of macroeconomic balance and the increased internationalization of the Chilean economy. Rather than engage in a radical redistribution of income and wealth, Aylwin social policy seeks to dissipate social demands and control social conflicts. Both the concern over governability, which has eclipsed concern over redistribution, and the gaping abyss between discourse and reality can be explained as outcomes of two interrelated factors: (1) the ideological framework behind the growth with equity development strategy, and (2) the structural requirements of export-oriented accumulation.

Growth and Investor Confidence as Key Objectives

Concertación economists are firmly convinced "that growth rates of at least 5 percent of GDP are necessary to bring about an improvement in the economic situation of the population."[24] According to their initial estimates, such a pace of economic growth requires that the rate of investment climb and remain at a level equivalent to at least 20 percent of GDP. The main lever perceived as capable of achieving the 20 percent target rate is local and transnational private capital, given that, after the 1973 military coup, the state significantly reduced its role in determining the level of total investment. Safeguarding investor confidence, particularly that of transnational investors, is seen as the key variable for achieving the desired goals; within this logic, macroeconomic stability, increased liberalization, stable relative prices, and rising investor confidence determine the critical path for improving the lot of the more than 5 million Chileans living below the poverty line.

In the tautological logic of Concertación theorists, the successful closing of the circle—high investment rate by private capital → high economic growth → social harmony—requires a previously existing climate of social peace. Under the present conditions of elite convergence and defeat of the Left, the Aylwin government knows fully that social mobilization and rising popular demands have little chance of destabilizing the government or setting off military reaction. Popular unrest, however, could muster the capacity to upset the favorable investment climate generated by the previous sixteen and one-half years of military repression. In order to create the conditions necessary for investment rates of 20 percent of GDP, "it is imperative that social and economic conflicts be kept at "bearable" levels. This presupposes that unsatisfied social demands must be channeled and that at least a partial solution must be given to them."[25]

Autonomy of Distribution from Accumulation

The Aylwin government's commitment to sustain economic growth based on exports and its promises to improve the distribution of income within a framework of strict macroeconomic equilibrium are both based on the assumption that no inherent contradiction exists between these objectives. In other words, Concertación economists trust that it is possible to harmonize increases in international competitiveness with greater internal social equity. This view implicitly presumes that the government can apply a strategy of growth independently of the redistributive strategy, with each strategy having its own logic, but being mutually reinforcing.[26] The basis and scope of Concertación social policy rests on this assumption: It is necessary to administer and channel social conflict until the trickle-down effect kicks in.

The Role of the State

The state assumes a crucial new role within this context: It must promote a system of political and social negotiations capable of reformulating social demands within the strict parameters dictated by the "objective restrictions of the system."[27] Constant political intervention is required by state functionaries at the institutional level (in Congress, on the Board of the Central Bank, and so on), in the political parties, and in the social organizations themselves. In such venues, government functionaries and representatives of the political class must act as tireless propagandists for social collaboration, social pacts, and consensus-building initiatives. They must also actively broker agreements among relevant social actors, as well as act in unison to isolate and neutralize potential challenges to the *democracia de acuerdos*, or brokered democracy.

The second role entrusted to the state is that of alleviating the situation of the poor, implementing programs offering subsidies and self-help projects that ensure governability. Although this second task was also carried out under Pinochet, under Aylwin the disciplining of labor and controlling of the impoverished has so far relied more on co-optation and the extension of clientelistic relations than on coercion and repression. Thus,

Concertación social policy *combines continuity of social assistance programs* initiated by the military dictatorship *with a greater reliance on new mechanisms of social co-optation* made possible by the elected character of the government.

The shift from repression to co-optation required, however, modifications of existing state institutions and creation of appropriate organs to implement this new policy. In July 1990, the Aylwin administration created the Ministry of Planning and Cooperation (MIDEPLAN), which was to be responsible for "evaluating and harmonizing the action of the ministries in the social areas (labor, health, education, and housing) around the Program of Integration to Development."[28] MIDEPLAN was to coordinate the work of two specialized bodies, the Agencia de Cooperación Internacional (ACI) and the Fondo de Solidaridad e Inversión Social (FOSIS). ACI would be responsible for obtaining funding from international private and governmental agencies for the Concertación social programs. FOSIS would be in charge of funding and assisting locally based self-help projects presented by municipal governments, NGOs, and, in theory, local grass-roots organizations. In addition to MIDEPLAN, the Aylwin administration created two other agencies, the Instituto Nacional de la Juventud (INJ) and the Servicio Nacional de la Mujer (SERNAM), both aimed at "integrating" their targeted sector into the development process. With respect to labor-capital relations, the government actively promoted the signing of a social pact between the most important trade union organizations and the Confederación de la Producción y el Comercio (CPC), the powerful class organization of Chile's owners.

Disciplining Labor Through Co-optation

The critical variable in Concertación's politico-economic plan is its capacity to co-opt labor. In exchange for small increases in consumption and marginal improvements in the legal conditions affecting the functioning of unions, the Aylwin government expects the leadership of the Chilean trade union movement to accept capital's unobstructed access to the exploitation of labor and abide by key components of labor flexibility enshrined in Pinochet's 1981 labor code. In the words of Concertación theorists, the initial task of the government with respect to the labor movement is "to make workers feel, on the one hand, as though they are participants in the system and its potential beneficiaries, while, on the other hand, ensuring that they do not demand immediate wage improvements since this would endanger the international competitiveness of Chilean production." To make things perfectly clear, they stress that "this competitiveness would also be threatened if we were to return to the rigid labor legislation that regulated labor relations before 1973."[29]

The instruments to be used to achieve the objective were the ideology of social consensus and the two basic agreements signed by the trade union leadership of the Central Unitaria de Trabajadores (CUT) and leaders of CPC. The first of these agreements, the Marco de Referencia para el Diálogo, was signed on January 31, 1990; the second, and more important, document, the Acuerdo Marco Tripartito, was signed on April 27, 1990.[30] Through these two documents, Chilean capitalists imposed their vision of social and economic development on the leadership of CUT, obtaining their promise to restrict wage and political demands to the tight parameters assured by the continuity of the neoliberal model.

The signing of the Marco de Referencia represented a significant strategic advance for the capitalist class. By endorsing that document, the CUT leadership, headed by Christian Democrat Manuel Bustos and Socialist Alejandro Martínez, (1) accepted a definition of economic development that equated it with economic growth, conquest of international markets, and increased investment, (2) guaranteed the respect for private property and the right to work, (3) recognized private enterprise as the most important agent of economic development, and (4) expressed confidence in the market as an efficient mechanism for the allocation of resources. The Acuerdo Marco outlined a shared socioeconomic plan between owners and workers, in which they agreed to cast their lot with the success of the open economy and the export-oriented strategy. The Acuerdo Marco established a mechanism for regular consultation whereby "technical commissions" representing CPC and CUT would meet regularly to engage in "dialogue" on points of interest.

In exchange for its support of the economic model, the trade union movement obtained an increase in the minimum wage (granted by the government, not the capitalists) and miniscule gains facilitating the legalization of trade union activity.

However, through the Acuerdo Marco, the existing Christian Democratic and Socialist leadership has attempted to definitively close the book on Chile's class labor movement, which, during the last century, defended an anticapitalist historical project for Chile. These two agreements have provided the means for the Concertación government and the capitalist class to gain the collaboration of an important part of the trade union leadership in disciplining Chilean workers. In sharp contrast with the best leadership tradition in Chile's pre-coup working class history, the current leadership of the trade union movement has willingly become "labor lieutenants" of the capitalist class, actively contributing toward confining worker demands within export model parameters.

The new role prescribed for Chilean workers and the labor movement is aimed at strengthening the competitiveness of Chilean exports. Toward this effort, workers must contain wage demands, requesting wage increases only when there are increments in productivity. Workers should also contribute by replacing the traditional confrontational stance vis-à-vis capital with cooperative relations within an enterprise. The new conception of labor-capital relations stresses that cooperation on the shop floor is crucial for technological innovation, economic growth, and improvements in the working-class standard of living.

The Acuerdo Marco, therefore, represents the abandonment of the historical platform of the Chilean working class, as contained in the 1953 founding principles of CUT. In its place, the current CUT leadership has endorsed the "modernization through internationalization" approach and the trickle-down theory as the means for improving the socioeconomic lot of Chilean workers. It has accepted that wage increases be calculated on the basis of future inflation and increases in productivity. Rather than representing their constituency and ensuring the organization of the unorganized, the current leadership's main concern is to deliver what it promised to the bosses at the negotiating table; it must demonstrate its ability to discipline the rank and file and isolate those leaders who will not go along with the renovated and more "modern" trade unionism promoting class collaboration.

One of the Concertación's strategic goals is to construct a new political class (*clase dirigente*) steeped in the new principles of elite democracy and committed to the internationalization of productive and commercial structures. The signing of the Acuerdo Marco represents a significant change in the orientation of the organized trade union movement and a qualitative advance toward Concertación's objective of "committing key leaders of political parties, and of business and trade union organizations, to the stability of these fundamental rules of the game, which apply to both the political and the socioeconomic levels."[31] The new rules of the game require a trade union movement willing to restrict its demands and political activity to the boundaries allowed by the export model. Just as Chile's negotiated democracy requires an elitist political style from politicians and government officials, the collaborative labor-capital agreements require an elitist style on the part of trade union leadership, which must resist pressures to effectively democratize CUT.

Political Parties and Labor's Autonomy

How could such a major shift in the orientation of the Chilean trade union movement take place?[32] According to Aylwin's minister of labor,[33] the answer lies in the fact that "nearly 70 percent of the top rank leaders of the country's most important trade union organizations are at the same time very active militants of the political parties that make up the government coalition." The shift also has to do with the level of control exercised by political parties over the leadership of the trade union movement. Thus, Minister of Labor Cortázar confidently states, "the risk of spontaneous rejection of agreements at the top is decreased by a sense of collective identity that is bonding trade union leaders with the government, namely, through the strong system of parties. This point is reflected in an exemplary manner by the advisers to the trade union organizations, all of whom are invariably linked to the political system." As the leadership of CUT increasingly becomes an Aylwin government instrument, utilized to placate and control labor unrest, there is mounting pressure from below to reject the current leadership of the trade union movement, and a growing number of trade union leaders is calling for the democratization of CUT and the development of an autonomous labor movement.[34]

Through the ideology of consensus and the Acuerdo Marco, the Concertación coalition and the Aylwin administration have struck a major victory in the legitimation of the capitalist restructuring carried out by Pinochet. They have institutionalized the fall in the value of labor power and have consolidated the neoliberal legislation ensuring that capital has the flexible labor force it requires to compete internationally. Thanks to the acquiescence of the present CUT leadership, capital's hegemony over labor, denied to it under the military dictatorship, has made important advances under Aylwin.

Poverty Programs That "Invest in People"

Better Targeting, Not Redistribution

Continuity of neoliberal policies also manifests itself in the Aylwin government's preservation of the basic methodological approach used by the Pinochet regime to design its social programs. In this regard, Concertación analysts assert that, "the advances of the military government, with respect to the diagnosis of problems and the targeting of social expenditures, must be recognized."[35] Thus, the vast machinery overseeing social control and "efficient" social spending—the targeted allocation of social expenditures and the classification of the poor into different strata according to socioeconomic profile—is not only celebrated but improved upon.[36] Nevertheless, the Aylwin government considered it necessary "to further develop the targeting of specific groups for expenditures rather than isolated individuals, thereby raising efficiency in the supply of social services."[37]

By incorporating this new emphasis into previous "advances," the Aylwin government has preserved and expanded the past technocratic orientation of using social policy as a means of ensuring social control. Whereas under Pinochet social policy and social expenditures were an integral part of overall national security doctrine and counterinsurgency strategy, under Aylwin these elements are used to sustain governability through the institutional channeling of conflicts and the strengthening of clientelistic relationships between the state and social groups.

Differences from Pinochet's Programs

Concertación technocrats insist that in spite of these continuities, their conception of social policy differs from the military regime's in at least three important respects: (1) the identification of the root causes of social problems, (2) the role assigned to social groups in defining policy, and (3) the manner in which social programs are to be funded.[38] A review of these three alleged differences reveals, however, that in no way do they challenge the export-oriented model of capital accumulation or modify the basic neoliberal orientation of economic policy.

Roots of Poverty. According to Concertación social policy experts (Dagmar Raczynski, Sergio Molina, Alvaro García), the dictatorship identified the origin of social problems in the *lack of access to goods.* In their view, Pinochet's social policy sought to provide the impoverished with those consumer goods that they lacked. The Concertación coalition's diagnosis envisions poverty "as *the product of economic, political, and cultural marginality*" [emphasis added].[39] As Alvaro García, Socialist vice-minister of MIDEPLAN, further clarifies, "I believe that introducing the poor to the market is the only solution possible. If poverty and underdevelopment have existed in Latin America, *it has been exclusively or fundamentally due to the marginalization that these social groups have had from the market* [emphasis added]."[40]

Such a conceptualization, rather than being a novel approach, represents a throwback to mid-1960s marginality theory, modified by grafting onto it the neoliberal concept of the "subsidiary role of the state." Whereas in the past the state was conceived as the agent that had to incorporate the marginalized into the development process, the updated conception places the market at the center of this integrative process.

The Role of "Beneficiaries." A second avowed difference is that the Pinochet regime saw the poor as objects and as passive recipients of assistance; the Concertación coalition sees the poor "as subjects of their own development, and in that sense, the role of the state is to complement and reinforce the effort that they [the poor] themselves carry out."[41] The apparent "progressive" character of this definition is seriously brought into question when one considers that the "participation of the poor" in the self-provision of services constitutes one of the dominant characteristics of the current effort by multilateral lending institutions and "enlightened" neoliberalism to privatize social programs and raise the efficiency of these programs without increasing fiscal expenditures. Thus, the World Bank's 1990 *World Development Report* suggests that "to be really effective from a cost point of view, interventions should not only be well directed to the chosen target groups, but should also be carefully formulated to satisfy the specific needs of the poor. ... In general, in those programs that have been successful, the beneficiaries, the poor, have participated both in the design phase and in implementation."[42]

Source of Financing. The third difference between Pinochet and Aylwin's social policy allegedly resides in the different sources of financing for social programs. According to Concertación technocrats, the Pinochet dictatorship sought to redirect a constant level of social expenditure by "giving fewer benefits to middle-income groups, more benefits to the poor."[43] Concertación promised that once it came into the government, it would apply a progressive taxing scheme so that social expenditures would be paid for by Chile's higher income groups. This professed difference vanished into thin air when, shortly after occupying his cabinet post, Minister of Economics Ominami announced that to finance increased social expenditures, instead of taxing corporations and the rich, he would be raising the IVA (a value-added tax) from 16 to 18 percent, an increase to be most seriously felt mainly by working- and middle-class Chileans.

The Real Innovation in Social Policy

From a critical perspective, the truly innovative nature of post-Pinochet social policy lies elsewhere—in the Aylwin administration's capacity to appropriate and channel the social energy of subsistence organizations, such as soup kitchens, consumer co-ops, grass-roots women's organizations, and health groups, all of which mushroomed under Pinochet. The distinguishing trait of Concertación's social policy from 1990 to 1991 rests in its capacity *to identify and tap the energy of popular grass-roots organizations, particularly the energies deployed by shantytown women in pursuit of ensuring the social reproduction of the urban poor.* The government's ability to subordinate these organizations is inextricably linked to the work of progressive social scientists and NGOs, which, under Pinochet, maintained a close and contradictory relationship with the grass-roots organizations.[44] Their research and contacts provided them with the necessary information to design and implement a well-coordinated strategy of co-optation.

Discovering the Role of Shantytown Women

In the mid-1980s, for example, Dagmar Raczynski, a noted sociologist and member of CIEPLAN, concluded after extensive study that the *pobladora*, the shantytown woman, was the key actor in residential and local areas, acting as a central provider of social services, visiting the municipality in search of assistance, caring for children, being active in parent-teacher meetings, occupying the forefront in the supply and demand of community-based social services. In sharp contrast to the Chilean Marxist Left's neglect of this social sector—induced by the strong productionist bias still prevalent—Concertación social policymakers were able to understand the key role played by pobladoras in the overall functioning of society. Based on such understanding, Raczynski and her collaborators proposed the following:

> a first priority is that diverse initiatives be formulated by the local government (municipality), by the community itself, and by private institutions, which open up spaces for the social participation of women, particularly women who are mothers, where they can find an answer to their needs, receive training and simultaneously empower the energies that they pour toward social services. *We point out the necessity that women incorporate themselves into the provision and participate in the delivery of "communitarian services,"* supporting such tasks as the delivery of health, education, child care, care for the elderly and the sick, and cultural and recreational activities [emphasis added].[45]

Thus, Raczynski and Concertación analysts proposed that the Aylwin administration *institutionalize the nonremunerated productive labor of women at the household and community level*, and that this be done in the name of affirming the social role of women. This line of reasoning led the Aylwin administration to establish FOSIS and SERNAM and to massively force upon organized shantytown women training courses on microenterprises and microentrepreneurs.

The apparent feminist content of these policies evaporates when one places these policies in the context of the functioning of a model of accumulation, oriented toward export, which maintains its competitiveness on the basis of the superexploitation of labor and the transfer of the costs of reproduction from the state and private enterprises onto the shoulders of working-class people and their families and, particularly, women.[46] That the institutionalization of nonremunerated community-based domestic labor be couched within the discourse on participation and legitimizing the social role of women reveals the absence among Concertación female social scientists of a combined class and gender perspective along the lines developed by Marxist feminists elsewhere.[47]

Women and Microentrepreneur Training Programs

The Aylwin administration, unable or unwilling to combine a class and gender approach, has so far implemented social policies of "investing in

TABLE 6.4   Budget for the Fondo de Inversión Social (FOSIS) (in millions of current Chilean pesos: US$1=Ch$350)

	1990	1991
Youth training	–	214.0
Peasant irrigation	238.8	–
Microenterprise support	307.9	–
Consumption	100.6	–
Social projects	856.6	1085.8
Rural programs	–	1165.8
Youth national institute	–	593.4
Other	–	346.3
Total	1503.9	3405.3

SOURCE: Compiled on the basis of Secretaría de Comunicación Social, *La Gente* (June 1991), p. 19.

people" rather than lifting the women's burden or significantly improving the situation of the poor, and these policies have begun to generate noticeable perverse effects. For community organizations to participate in the delivery of social services, they must first acquire legal status, which enables them to sign contracts with municipal authorities. Such institutionalization (legalization) of grass-roots organizations has tended to break the community-, gender-, and class-based solidarities of the past, replacing them with values of individual entrepreneurship and individual success. The result has been the disappearance of many community-based organizations. Second, the training programs on microenterprises and microentrepreneurship egg the urban poor on to take initiatives that have little economic viability. Rather, they provide the basis for an intertemporal political exchange in which present-day sacrifices and continuities are accepted by the poor, who are given expectations of future benefits to be received "after completing the training course as microentrepreneurs." As can be seen from Table 6.4, just over 20 percent of FOSIS funds in 1990 were designated to support microenterprise training and development programs.

Pandering to a Failed Policy

An in-depth review of income-generating projects promoted by Pinochet's Servicio Nacional de Empleo (SENAEM), by the United Nations Development Fund for Women (UNIFEM), and by the Catholic Church in poor neighborhoods, evidenced an extremely high failure rate for microenterprise programs for the poor. The few economically successful experiences were those in which (1) the productive units were born out of personal initiative and not induced by NGOs or government, (2) market and profit criteria were clearly dominant, (3) individual work was duly valued, and (4) the participant-owners were highly skilled workers with years of experience that gave them the necessary knowledge on sources of raw materials, the importance of quality control, and marketing outlets for their production. The study concluded that "the induced creation of small productive units ... is neither an efficient nor viable policy for generating stable employment or adequate income. The efforts that have to be exerted are enormous, the period of maturation unknown and unforeseeable, and the drop-out rate of participants and the mortality rate of enterprises is high."[48]

Yet, in spite of this damning evaluation of previous experiences carried out in Chile to promote microenterprises, the Aylwin administration *has made microenterprise training and funding a key component of its social policy toward the poor!* If past experience and the market itself had shown the nonviability of microenterprises for the poor, and these conclusions had been reached by Concertación analysts themselves, then why has the Aylwin administration deployed so much political, human, and material effort into reconverting social organizations into microenterprises?

One possible answer is that, although failures in economic terms, such efforts are effective mechanisms for politically controlling the poor and for breaking the historical base of collective action for Chile's dispossessed. These programs are geared toward developing the "psychosocial traits" required to convert an organized pobladora into an entrepreneur able to successfully compete in the market. The traits of successful microenterprises have been shown to be willingness to enforce the division of labor, to accept an efficient line of authority and leadership, and willing subordination to the logic of market criteria.[49] The diffusion and acceptance of such values and behaviors constitute the necessary components for the consolidation of bourgeois hegemony over the organized urban poor, in a sector where shantytown women have played a crucial organizing role in the past.

A final perverse effect of the Concertación "investment in people" programs has been the transformation of the delivery of social services into a profitable activity. The availability of state funds for training programs has generated the creation of new NGOs, many of them owned by state functionaries and by Concertación militants. Privy to insider information, political contacts, and influence, these NGOs are the ones that win the lucrative public contracts for training, organization, and delivery of services to poor communities. The ensemble of state funds, municipal functionaries, professionals working for NGOs tied to governing political parties, and favored local leaders has created the institutional and financial configuration for corruption, co-optation, and clientelism.

Aylwin's social policy can be criticized for launching a process in which the poor are told to become actors without having access to the economic resources and the political power to take effective control over their own

TABLE 6.5   Greater Santiago: Distribution of Personal Income by Deciles

Deciles	1969	1979	1988	1989	1991
1	1.3	1.4	1.2	1.2	1.2
2	2.4	2.4	2.2	2.3	2.5
3	3.3	3.2	3.0	3.1	3.3
4	4.3	4.1	4.0	4.0	4.3
5	5.4	5.0	4.9	5.1	5.3
6	6.7	6.5	6.2	6.3	6.5
7	8.6	8.4	8.2	8.0	8.1
8	11.6	11.8	11.7	11.0	10.9
9	17.4	18.1	18.8	17.4	16.6
10	39.0	39.1	39.8	41.6	41.3

SOURCE: Programa de Economía del Trabajo, *Series de Indicadores Económico-Sociales: Series Anuales 1960–1991* (Santiago: PET, 1992), Table 8, p. 73.

destiny. Aylwin's "progressive" social policy emphasizing decentralization and participation is not an instrument for a profound democratization of Chilean society; it responds more to a vision that seeks to legitimize the privatization of social services and the transfer of the costs of production of labor onto the shoulders of the poor themselves.[50] The discourse on "investment in people," on "affirming the social role of women," and on promoting "local development," though attractive components of the Aylwin administration's social policies, seek to diffuse and contain conflicts within the limits of manageable local space, shielding the societywide structures of power and knowledge, as well as the economic model, from popular challenge and control.

Results of the Social Policy

Through limited increases in social spending (US$250 million in 1990), the Aylwin government seems to have momentarily tempered the socially polarizing thrust of capitalist accumulation. Nevertheless, the dominant tendency remains the regressive redistributive push of the current pattern of economic growth. This persistent inequality is reflected in how the distribution of personal income has evolved during the 1988–1991 period. During this three-year period, Chilean GDP grew at an average annual rate of approximately 6.1 percent, while exports expanded at an average of 12 percent a year. Yet the data available for Greater Santiago presented in Table 6.5 show how the poorest 10 percent of households saw no change in their participation in the distribution of income precisely during a period of explosive economic growth.

Whereas between 1989 and 1990, the participation of the poorest 20 percent of households in total income increased from 4.6 to 4.9 percent, in

TABLE 6.6   Total Income Distribution According to Quintiles

Quintile	Oct.–Dec. 1978	Oct.–Dec. 1988	Sept.–Nov. 1989	Sept.–Nov. 1990
1 (poorest 20%)	4.55	4.23	4.6	4.9
2	9.54	7.54	7.9	8.4
3	14.11	10.86	11.3	11.5
4	19.91	16.93	16.6	17.2
5 (richest 20%)	51.89	60.44	59.6	58.0
Total	100.00	100.00	100.0	100.0

SOURCE: Instituto Nacional de Estadísticas, Encuestas Suplementarias de Ingresos. Quoted by Hugo Fazio, "Resúmen Económico" (June) (Santiago: Instituto de Ciencias Alejandro Lipschutz, 1991), p. 27, mimeo.

TABLE 6.7   Average Monthly Household Income, 1989–1991 (converted from pesos, October 1991:US$1=Ch$359.06)

Quintile	1989	1990	1991
1 (poorest 20%)	95.88	102.89	107.73
2	167.36	174.42	181.43
3	235.14	239.27	243.15
4	345.53	359.94	357.94
5 (richest 20%)	1242.00	1208.89	1073.50
Average	417.18	416.68	392.75

SOURCE: Instituto Nacional de Estadísticas, Encuesta Suplementaria de Ingresos. Quoted by *La Nación*, March 27, 1992, p. 16.

1990 the richest 20 percent of households obtained 58 percent of total income, slightly down from the 59.6 percent of 1989, but significantly above the 51.8 percent that these households obtained in 1978 (see Table 6.6). The latest available figures for 1991, presented in Table 6.7, show that—measured in real terms—the average monthly household income of the poorest fifth of households went up from US$102.89 in 1990 to US$107.73 in 1991; the same data show that the average monthly income for all households *fell* from US$416.68 in 1990 to US$392.75 in 1991.

Although these figures show slight improvement in income distribution, the immense disparities that have accumulated over the past two decades are not being solved by the timid poverty-alleviation programs so far implemented by the Aylwin government. On the contrary, the gradualist approach accepts the drastic concentration of wealth and massive impoverishment brought about by the restructuring of Chilean capitalism under Pinochet.

Whether the present expansive phase will consolidate the tendency for the expansion of absolute poverty to be replaced by increases in relative poverty[51] still remains to be carefully assessed.

TABLE 6.8   Whole Country National Unemployment Rate in Two Surveys (percent)

	INE	U. of Chile
1980	10.4	12.1
1981	10.8	11.7
1982	19.6	21.1
1983	16.8	22.2
1984	15.4	18.8
1985	13.0	16.3
1986	10.8	13.9
1987	9.3	12.7
1988	8.3	11.8
1989	6.3	10.0
1990	6.0	10.0
1991	6.5	9.0[a]

[a]Figures for March 1991.
SOURCES: CIEPLAN, *Set de Estadísticas Económicas* no. 87 (Santiago: CIEPLAN, 1991), mimeo, and Banco Central, *Informe Económica y Financiero* (February 1992).

More Jobs, But at What Wages?

Study of changes taking place in the labor market is important and requires further scrutiny. Estimates for 1991 provided by INE put the national unemployment rate at 6.5 percent of the labor force, a rise over the 6.3 percent rate in 1989 and 6.0 rate in 1990. These figures look impressive, given the high levels of unemployment of previous decades. However, as shown in Table 6.8, INE figures do not coincide with those provided by the University of Chile: The total country unemployment rate for 1991 should be 9.0 percent, not the INE figure of 6.5 percent. Although they use different sample sizes, both of these institutions use the same methodology, considering respondents to be employed if they say they had worked for money for more than one hour during the previous week. Both surveys indicate a downward trend in the unemployment rate.

INE figures for Greater Santiago have to be scaled up by at least 70 percent if one follows the PET methodology, considering a respondent to be employed if the respondent claims to be. Following this second methodology, PET estimates that in June 1988, the unemployment rate for Greater Santiago was 18.0 percent; in June 1989, it was 16.6 percent; and in June 1991, it was 14.3 percent, as opposed to INE's figure of 8.1 percent.[52]

Beyond the methodological question, these disparate figures suggest that, over the last two years, increases in GDP and employment have relied heavily on labor-intensive and so-called informal activities. The impressive official employment figures would thus conceal crucial information about the quality of the jobs being created.

The general wage index (for all workers, including remunerations paid to professionals and corporate executives) presented in Table 6.9 shows

TABLE 6.9   General and Construction Sector Real Wage Index (base 1970=100)

	General	Construction
1970	100.0	100.0
1972	126.6	–
1978	76.0	93.1
1979	82.2	98.6
1980	89.3	107.2
1981	97.3	113.1
1982	97.6	108.1
1983	86.9	80.7
1984	87.1	69.8
1985	83.2	58.5
1986	84.9	54.2
1987	84.7	53.1
1988	90.3	57.0
1989	92.0	61.4
1990	93.7	65.1
1991	96.9	66.4[a]

[a]Data for August 1991.

SOURCES: CIEPLAN, *Set de Estadísticas Económicas* no. 87, tables 11 and 13 (Santiago: CIEPLAN, 1991), mimeo, and Programa de Economía y Trabajo, *1991–1992 Economía y Trabajo en Chile Informe Anual* (Santiago: PET, 1992), Table 13, p. 246.

that as of October 1991, real wages had still not recovered to their 1970 levels. If one considers the wage index for the construction sector presented in Table 6.9, the situation is much bleaker; here, wages remained roughly 35 percent below their 1970 levels. In spite of modest improvements in income distribution, official employment rates, and the general wage rate, the Aylwin administration has not appreciably altered the drastic fall in the value of labor power under Pinochet.

Temporary Social Co-optation, Not Durable Social Equity

Popular perception reflects the limited modification in the socioeconomic situation for the estimated 40 percent of the population living below the poverty line and reveals growing dissatisfaction with the government's gradualist approach. A July 1991 poll[53] carried out by SUR Profesionales in the popular sectors of Conchalí, Pudahuel, Cerro Navia, La Cisterna, La Granja, and San Ramón, aiming to "discover and evaluate from the perspective of the poor the government and state's social policy," reflected the popular perception that meager changes had occurred in personal socioeconomic situations. Poll results indicated that whereas "66.1 percent of those polled thought that their personal and family situation would improve with the arrival of a new government," only 9.5 percent declared that what the Aylwin government had done for the poor "was as good as we expected." Indicative of the gap between official figures and people's perceptions, 67.6 percent of those polled responded that the country's economic growth "favors the rich," while only 8.5 percent said that it "favors the poor." Other indicators of prevailing discontent showed in the 45.4 percent of respondents who agreed with the statement that "the present government cares more about private entrepreneurs and has forgotten about the poor," while 42.7 percent agreed with the statement that "the government is not giving concrete solution to the problems of the poorer sectors of society."

The Concertación coalition, though not able to display significant progress in paying the "social debt" to the poor, has nonetheless scored important successes with its social policy. In political terms, the Concertación's social policy has had initial success in co-opting urban shantytown grassroots organizations, channeling their energies into municipal assistance programs, participation in microentrepreneur training programs, and the preparation of self-help projects to be submitted to the state for funding approval. Concertación social policy has also had limited success in the co-optation of a significant sector of the trade union leadership, obtaining active endorsement from it to develop a system of collaborative relations with capital.

Can the present situation of co-optation be maintained and expanded in the future? Will the discontent currently being expressed by a still relatively small sector extend itself geographically and socially, surpassing the mechanisms for social control put in place by the Aylwin administration? The answers to these questions are inextricably linked to the future evolution of Chile's popular movement and to its capacity to nurture and re-create, under the present conditions, the popular democratic spirit and traditions of past struggles.

Conclusion: Whither "Growth with Equity"?

The choice of a particular development strategy is strongly influenced by the *ideology* and the *material interests* of a country's governing groups.[54] In this chapter, we have analyzed how Concertación's recurrent rhetoric supporting social integration and its declared concern for social justice masks a clear bias in favor of local and transnational capital. This is not happenstance; it is an inherent element of the negotiated transition and of the endorsement of the export-oriented economic model made by Concertación policymakers before the December 1988 plebiscite.

In November 1988, Alejandro Foxley, one of the architects of the Concertación's strategy, offered the Chilean ruling classes the following transaction: If the private sector promised to "modernize itself, create jobs, seek more equitable conditions for the labor force," he pledged that Concertación politicians and the future civilian government would work, side by side with the private sector, to legitimize the existing economic order in the hearts and minds of Chilean people.[55] The analysis presented in this chapter indicates that Aylwin's economic team has religiously kept its part of the bargain.

Under the facade of the supposedly more benevolent "growth with equity" development approach, the Aylwin government has implemented macroeconomic policies and a development strategy that are but a seamless continuation of the neoliberal model under Pinochet. Moreover, through the discourse of "national reconciliation" and "social equity," the Christian Democratic-Socialist coalition has contributed toward broadening the sociopolitical base of support for the economic model originally implanted by Pinochet.

If the Pinochet and the Aylwin regimes are compared in terms of four key politico-economic relationships—the connections between local and international capital; between labor and capital; between the role of the state and private property rights; and between capital accumulation and distribution—one finds that each of these relations has been conserved without significant modification. Protected by rhetoric about social pacts and consensus building, the Aylwin government has attempted to facilitate the unfettered reproduction of these basic class relationships rather than modify them.

In this light, any conclusions reached through historical assessment of the Aylwin government's role will depend on the length of the historical period against which it is appraised. If the starting point is the triple crisis (economic, ideological, and political) of the system of domination that began to afflict Chilean society after the mid-1960s, then the striking historical characteristic of the Christian Democratic-Socialist government is that it expedited the legitimation of the violent restructuring of Chilean capitalism executed under Pinochet, rather than that it engineered the "return to democracy."

The overview of the Aylwin regime's political economy presented in this chapter attests to the seriously flawed nature of the fundamental assumption sustaining the Concertación development strategy, namely, that export-oriented capitalist accumulation and social equity are compatible objectives, naturally resulting from the unrestrained operation of market forces and the preservation of macroeconomic equilibrium.

Even high-level Concertación and governmental officials have been forced to recognize the flawed nature of this assumption. A confidential document, originally prepared to evaluate the first eighteen months of government and to chart the government's political course for the next two years, indicates a hardening of the option in favor of export growth at the expense of social programs. The classified document, leaked to the press, warns top government and coalition officials:

It is necessary to be clear that, in the short run and even to some extent in the middle run, there is no full compatibility between raising the levels of investment to achieve economic growth, on the one hand, and the accomplishment of spectacular successes with policies to eradicate poverty, on the other. Economic growth is a necessary condition for the permanent eradication of poverty; and a higher rate of growth requires the channeling of important resources toward investment; in other words, *it requires that we avoid the temptation of achieving tangible and immediate social improvements that would result if these resources now channeled toward investment were rerouted toward consumption* [emphasis added].[56]

The leaked document offers clear indications that the fundamental assumption about the alleged autonomy of the logic of accumulation from that of distribution—the linchpin of the growth with equity strategy—was also being sacrificed at the altar of political realism. Thus, the document advises:

It becomes indispensable to create a nationwide awareness of this reality because there exists the tendency to believe that present day constraints that impede a greater degree of satisfaction of multiple social demands are caused by the transition, that is, by the power that "authoritarian enclaves" confer to the opposition. *This is a dangerous illusion that would generate enormous populist pressure on the next government* [emphasis added].[57]

In other words, the real constraints faced by Aylwin's economic team are of a self-imposed doctrinal nature (commitment to transnational investor confidence) rather than of an institutional or political character (authoritarian enclaves). Acknowledging that social demands are not going to be adequately satisfied during the period from 1992 to 1994, the document asserts that the Concertación government must prepare to effectively resist "populist" pressures.

Faced with the prospects of increases in the intensity and number of social conflicts during the remaining two years of the Aylwin government, the cited document calls for the formation within the government of "a structure of coordination to design strategies for the preemption and resolution of conflicts." This strategy, the document suggests, contemplates the incorporation of three essential elements: (1) "the inadmissability of actions that create pressure, such as illegal work stoppages and strikes, (2) the postulate that when confronted with such measures the government will resort to all the mechanisms stipulated by the existing legal order, and (3) the defense of the legitimacy of police force operations in the face of street demonstrations and other sorts of actions that do not conform to currently existing legal dispositions."[58]

In the relatively short period of twenty-four months, the elected-civilian Aylwin government seems to be prepared to drop all pretenses that social demands are going to be adequately satisfied. To defend macroeconomic balance and the further internationalization of the Chilean economy, the Aylwin government is willing to garrison itself in Pinochet's 1980 constitution and resort to police repression. Thus, the contradictory character of the Aylwin regime and its growth with equity development strategy resides in the fact that, playing on the long-suppressed hopes of Chileans in the name of "democracy," the government is committed to diffusing and enforcing the values, attitudes, and political practices compatible with export-oriented capitalist accumulation.

If one based calculations on the still-significant support for the Aylwin government and considered the relative ease with which the Christian Democratic-Socialist coalition has constructed the "blessed normalcy" characteristic of undisputed capitalist hegemony, one could mistakenly conclude that the contradictions of the export-oriented model of capital accumulation might remain without being acted out by popular social forces. The Aylwin government seems to be taking no such chances, however.

Notes

1. See Alejandro Foxley, *Exposición Sobre el Estado de la Hacienda Pública: Presentación del Ministro de Hacienda* (October 23, 1990) (Santiago: Ministerio Secretaría General de Gobierno, Secretaría de Comunicación y Cultura, 1990), p. 16.

2. To get a flavor of these promised changes, see the section, "Bases Programáticas Económico-Sociales," of the *Programa de Gobierno de la Concertación de Partidos por la Democracia,* subsection 4, p. 19, on "social justice" states: "The nation must decisively confront the challenge of fighting poverty. For that purpose it is necessary to recognize that it is *the central problem being faced today by the nation,* and that it is necessary to generate the collective will to allow for resources to be mobilized in the necessary amounts to confront the problem and to apply sustained measures to progressively advance towards the eradication of extreme poverty" [emphasis added].

3. See the Foxley interview by Eliana Gaete in *Revista APSI* no. 368 (November 19–December 2, 1990), p. 58.

4. This chapter eschews empirically identifying the "class nature" of the alliance represented by the Aylwin regime. A full analysis of the development model being implemented by the Aylwin regime requires establishing the class nature of the coalition of social classes, class fractions, and social groups that give it its main orientation and share in the objective benefits. Barbara Stallings investigates ways to identify the class nature of an alliance in her book, *Class Conflict and Economic Development in Chile, 1958–1973* (Stanford: Stanford University Press, 1978). Rely-

ing on Poulantzas, she points out that alliances are formed in various ways: by a hegemonic class fraction that gives the alliance its main orientation; by a power bloc composed of the rest of the dominant classes; by allied classes, which share in the objective benefits; and by supporting classes, whose backing is garnished through ideological illusions. From an empirical point of view, the identification of the class nature of an alliance offers, according to Stallings, four possibilities: (1) analysis of the voting base (which helps identify allied and supporting classes, (2) establishment of who benefits the most from the policies carried out by an alliance once in power, (3) examination of the formal channels for exerting power or influence, and (4) examination of the informal channels in which influence is exercised. However, undertaking such a task here is clearly beyond the scope of this chapter.

5. See Foxley, op. cit., p. 4.

6. See Stallings, op. cit., p. 63.

7. Secretaría de Comunicación y Cultura, *Folleto Informativo* no. 2 (Santiago: Ministerio Secretaría General de Gobierno, 1991), p. 2.

8. These contradictory aims, rather than being liable to weaken the internal coherence of the development strategy, are envisaged by Aylwin's economic team as a source of enhanced political maneuverability and ascendancy. Foxley indicates that "the awareness that one has a quota of limited power has generated a new form of doing politics that attempts to establish agreements with those that think differently, overcoming the old antagonistic and confrontational styles of the past." See *El Mercurio*, September 15, 1991, pp. A–1 and A–13.

9. See Joaquín Vial, Andrea Butelmann, and C. Celedón, "Fundamentos de las Políticas Macroeconómicas del Gobierno Democrático Chileno (1990–93)," *Colección Estudios CIEPLAN* no. 30 (December) (Santiago: CIEPLAN, 1990).

10. Recall from Chap. 4 that Boeninger's five points included: (1) the need for substantive agreement on fundamentals, (2) explicit recognition of private property, (3) gradualism in socioeconomic change, (4) economic growth as the priority, with distributive efforts subordinated to growth, and (5) increasing social equity to lead to political legitimacy and long-run stability. Although the connection between these fundamentals and Aylwin's economic strategy can be seen as a commendable example of political capacity and coherence, the point here is to examine the societal impact of these guidelines as they reflect a consensus among different fractions of the capitalist class and its political representatives.

11. *El Mercurio*, September 15, 1991, p. A–13.

12. See Banco Central, *Boletin Mensual* (June 1991).

13. PET, *Indicadores Económico-Sociales* no. 96 (November) (Santiago: PET, 1991), p. 2.

14. See Banco Central, *Indicadores Económico Financieros* (May 1992).

15. The persistent problem of macroeconomic instability due to the open nature of the economy and the erosion of the effects of the June 1991 measures led Aylwin economic authorities to adopt a de facto reevaluation of the peso in January 1992.

16. These concerns were raised, albeit timidly, by economists sympathetic to the Concertación coalition but not directly involved in the government. See, for example, *Indicadores Económico-Sociales* no. 91 (June) (Santiago: PET, 1991).

17. See Eugenio Lahera, "Modernización: Tarea Nacional Permanente," *El Mercurio*, December 13, 1991, p. A–2. This is an op-ed piece that exemplifies the

modernization discourse so popular among Christian Democratic and Socialist intellectuals. Lahera is a consultant to ECLAC and he is close to the Concertación government.

18. See Vial, Butelmann, and Celedón, op. cit., p. 64.

19. See Foxley, op. cit., p. 7.

20. Ibid.

21. See Vial, Butelmann, and Celedón, op. cit.

22. See Stephany Griffith-Jones, "Introduction," *Colección Estudios CIEPLAN* no. 31 (March) (Santiago: CIEPLAN, 1991), p. 6.

23. Figures for the 1988–1990 period come from Gustavo Marin, "Chile Hacia el Siglo XXI: Crisis del Capitalismo y Recomposición de las Clases Sociales," *Documentos de Trabajo* no. 43 (October) (Santiago: PRIES-CONO SUR, 1991). Data for 1991 come from *El Mercurio*, December 18, 1991, and include information available at the year's closing session of the Comité de Inversiones Extranjeras. A detailed analysis of foreign direct investment during the 1980s is forthcoming: Patricio Rozas, "La Inversión Extranjera en Chile," *PRIES-CONO SUR*.

24. Vial, Butelmann, and Celedón, op. cit., p. 57.

25. Ibid., p. 58.

26. See Griffith-Jones, op. cit.

27. See Oscar Muñoz, "Estado, Desarrollo, y Equidad: Algunas Preguntas Pendientes," *Colección Estudios CIEPLAN* no. 31 (March) (Santiago: CIEPLAN, 1991).

28. See *La Gente* no. 1 (January 1991), p. 15. *La Gente* is published by the Secretaría de Comunicación y Cultura.

29. See Vial, Butelmann, and Celedón (1990), op. cit., p. 79.

30. For a fuller account of the contents of the Acuerdo Marco, see Rodolfo Fortunatti, "Concertación Social, una Oportunidad Histórica," *Economía y Trabajo en Chile. Informe Anual 1990–1991* (Santiago: PET, 1991), and Jorge Ayala, "El Acuerdo Marco: Gobierno, Empresarios y Trabajadores," *Análisis y Perspectivas* no. 2 (May) (Santiago: Centro de Investigaciones Economicas y Sociales, 1990).

31. See René Cortázar, "El Proceso de Cambio y la Concertación Social," *Transición a la Democracia: Marco Político y Económico*, comp. Oscar Muñoz (Santiago: CIEPLAN, 1990), p. 71.

32. See Fernando Leiva, "La Concertación Social y el Acuerdo Marco: ¿Hacia el Disciplinamiento del Movimiento Sindical Chileno?" *Materiales de Economía* no. 1 (April) (Santiago: Grupo de Economistas del Movimiento por la Autonomía Sindical [MAS], 1991), pp. 4–9.

33. See Cortázar, op. cit., pp. 86–87.

34. See the document, MAS, ed., "Por Una Propuesta y un Proyecto Propio de los Trabajadores," discussed at the First Encounter of Trade Union Leaders, August 29, 1991, Santiago.

35. See Vial, Butelmann, and Celedón, op. cit., p. 68.

36. For an analysis of the advantages and disadvantages of the "Ficha CAS," the socioeconomic profile used at the municipal level to target social subsidies, see Dagmar Raczynski, "La Ficha CAS y la Focalización de los Programas Sociales" (Paper presented at the Seminario Estadísticas Socioeconómicas y la Realidad Nacional, sponsored by FLACSO, the Instituto Nacional de Estadística, and the

United Nations Research Institute for Social Development [UNRISD], Santiago, July 17–18, 1991).

37. Vial, Butelmann, and Celedón, op. cit., p. 68.

38. See Alvaro García, "Programa de Gobierno de la Concertación de Partidos por la Democracia: Aspectos Socio-Económicos," *Encuentro Nacional de ONG con Partidos Políticos* (September), Martín Gárate and Juan Vergara, eds. (Santiago: 1989), p. 39.

39. Ibid.

40. Ibid., p. 47.

41. Ibid., p. 39.

42. See Banco Mundial, 1990: Informe Sobre el Desarrollo Mundial 1990: La Pobreza (Washington, D.C.: World Bank, 1990), p. 4. One should note that, when speaking about "participation of the poor," both the World Bank and the Aylwin administration are referring to the poor who are willing to have their "participation" mediated by NGOs, and not to the poor who are organized on a regional and national level and who mobilize politically around their needs.

43. See Alvaro García, "Las Orientaciones de la Política Social," *Colección Estudios CIEPLAN* no. 31 (March) (Santiago: CIEPLAN, 1991), pp. 131–140.

44. The majority of key positions and governmental posts have been filled with men and women formerly affiliated with the NGOs. For useful, but generally uncritical analysis, see Brian Loveman, "Las ONG y la Transición a la Democracia en Chile," in *Desarrollo de Base (Grassroots Development)* 15, 2 (Washington, D.C.: Inter-American Foundation, 1991). A more critical, though limited, assessment is presented in Fernando Ignacio Leiva, "'They Give Us Wings But Clip Our Wingtips': Grassroots Organizations and Popular Education around Economic Issues" (Paper presented to the Latin American Studies Association (LASA) Congress, Miami, December 3–4, 1989).

45. See Dagmar Raczynski, "Apoyo a Pequeñas Unidades Productivas en Sectores Pobres: Lecciones de Políticas," *Notas Técnicas CIEPLAN* no. 133 (September) (Santiago: CIEPLAN, 1989), p. 87.

46. The tendency of capital to transfer the costs of reproduction to working class families, and particularly to women, has been pointed out in our previous work. See Henry Veltmeyer, "Surplus Labor and Class Formation on the Latin American Periphery," in Ronald Chilcote and Dale Johnson, eds., *Theories of Development* (London and Newbury Park: Sage, 1983); Fernando Ignacio Leiva and James Petras, "Chile's Poor in the Struggle for Democracy," *Latin American Perspectives* 13 (Fall 1986); and also Taller PIRET-Grupo de Investigación Sobre los Trabajadores Desplazados (GISTRADE), *Los Trabajadores Desplazados de Chile* (Santiago: Taller PIRET, 1987).

47. We are referring to the body of work developed by noted social analysts such as Lourdes Benería, Norma Chinchilla, Carmen Diana Deere, Magdalena León, the late Suzana Prates, Martha Roldán, Helen Safa, Cynthia Truelove, and many others.

48. See Raczynski, 1989, op. cit., p. 78.

49. Ibid.

50. For a critical review of the discourse on decentralization, see José Luis Coraggio, "Las Dos Corrientes de Descentralización en América Latina," in

Cuadernos del CLAEH/Revista Uruguaya de Ciencias Sociales no. 56 (May) (Montevideo, Uruguay: Centro Latinoamericano de Economía Humana [CLAEH], 1991), pp. 63–78. Also by the same author see, "Poder Local y Poder Popular," *Cuadernos del CLAEH/Revista Uruguaya de Ciencias Sociales* no. 45/46 (August) (Montevideo: CLAEH, 1988), pp. 101–120.

51. See Alvaro Díaz, *El Capitalismo Chileno en los 90: Crecimiento Económico y Desigualdad Social* (Santiago: Ediciones PAS, 1991).

52. See "Segunda Encuesta de Empleo," *Documento de Trabajo* no. 68 (Santiago: PET, 1989); and Berta Teitelboim, "Tercera Encuesta de Empleo en el Gran Santiago: Empleo Informal, Desempleo y Pobreza," *Documento de Trabajo* no. 89 (March) (Santiago: PET, 1992).

53. See Francisco Martorell, "El Gobierno y los Pobres: La Deuda Impaga," *Revista Análisis* no. 400 (September 30–October 13, 1991), p. 10. Another nationwide poll by CEP shows a drastic fall in support for the Aylwin government. Whereas in June 1990 support for Aylwin reached 73.6 percent and only 8.8 percent expressed opposition, by July 1991 those approving Aylwin's tenure had fallen to 49.8 percent. The percentage rejecting it had almost doubled, climbing to 15.3 percent. A more recent indicator of rising discontent was the 6.6 percent of the vote gained by the Communist party and the Movimiento de Izquierda Democrático Allendista (MIDA) in the June 1992 municipal elections.

54. See Keith Griffin, *Alternative Strategies for Economic Development* (London: Macmillan, 1989), p. 227.

55. Foxley's offer, made in a November 1988 speech to ENADE, was as follows: "Let each one of us do his part. What we democrats today are offering is to work side by side with the private sector, neither against the private sector, nor in a parallel track to the private sector. We are willing to contribute, in the modest measure of our capabilities, to change the climate and the general approach with which the economic model is discussed in public debates." See Alejandro Foxley, "Bases Para el Desarrollo de la Economía Chilena: Una Visión Alternativa," *Colección Estudios CIEPLAN* no. 26 (June) (Santiago: CIEPLAN, 1989), p. 185.

56. *La Segunda*, October 14, 1991, p. 11.

57. Ibid.

58. Ibid., p. 12.

7

Social Movements and Electoral Politics

The Rise and Fall of Social Movements

The apparent paradox of declining democratic grass-roots organizations in the transition from a military dictatorship to an electoral regime has not yet been adequately analyzed. At the superficial level, there are the self-serving arguments of regime intellectuals who claim that the electoral regime is now the custodian of the interests, values, and democratic aspirations of the movements, that the latter's historical "functions" have been exhausted (their function was to defeat the dictatorship), and that the contemporary period requires new, and higher, or more mature, forms of political representation, namely, the electoral-party regime managed by intellectuals, lawyers, and other members of the political class.[1] In a milder version of this discourse, the movements are assigned the subordinate or supplementary role of collaborating with the electoral regime in implementing the latter's policies. Hence, although the movement rhetoric is retained, it is largely seen as being voiced by a chorus led by electoral conductors. The ideologues of the electoral-party regime inadvertently concede the main issue in dispute: that the popularly organized democratic social movements that once had the capacity to create an aware and participatory citizenry have been marginalized in the name of a "higher" form of democracy. The crucial issue in this conception of democracy is the clearly elitist framework in which the political process is described: Mass movements are perceived as threats to the political class, which is seen as the only group capable of upholding democracy.

There is little historical, empirical, or theoretical justification for this elitist position. In the first instance, it was large-scale mobilizations by the social movements that secured the basic structural changes in the late 1960s and 1970s—and that gave effective voice and power to the poor in their struggle to extend democratic decisionmaking to the workplace, neighborhood, and other venues.[2] More recently, it was the mass social movements in the neighborhoods that forced Pinochet and Washington to seek electoral negotiations with the political class as an alternative to mass confrontation.[3] High levels of citizen political activism, debate, and organization—the civic culture essential to any conception of democracy—were the product of social movement activity; and it ebbed with the extension and intervention of the electoral party machinery and the dominance of the professional intellectual class. Movement democracy is government for the people, of the people, and by the people. In the electoral elite conception, it is government of the people, by the professionals, for the stability of the existing order. The fate of the social movement thus has wider implications for the larger political system, for the nature of political representation, and for the future development of democratic politics. An analysis of the current state of movements and their recent trajectory is a necessary precondition for understanding their future prospects, and for that matter the prospects for a political transformation in which the popular classes exercise political power.

Stages in Social Movement–Regime Relations

The relationship between the electoral party apparatus and the social movements has gone through several stages: (1) during the Pinochet period: relative autonomy of movements to parties, (2) in the transition toward electoral politics: increasing subordination of movements to parties, (3) in the immediate aftermath of the electoral period: party supremacy and demobilization of movements, and (4) in the postelectoral period: divergent paths either toward state incorporation or toward reactivation and autonomy of movements.

The social movements manifest their greatest strength, autonomy, and independence during the late Pinochet period, first, before the electoral parties seize the initiative in negotiating the transition with Pinochet; and, second, in the period following the consolidation of the electoral regime, at the end of the electoral transition. In between, that is, in advance of the elections and in their immediate aftermath, the political scene was dominated by party professionals, technocrats, and their entourage of academic advisers and former members of NGOs, who demobilized the movements, atomizing their members and inculcating in them an attitude of expectation and prudence toward forthcoming regime programs.

The initial reaction of movement supporters was to withdraw from active participation, to join in government-sponsored programs and organizations, and to petition legislative and executive officials to meet basic needs embedded in electoral campaign programs. Essentially, the first year of the Aylwin government (1990) can be described as one of movement expectation—the notion that neighborhood and workplace reforms would be forthcoming through the regime's own initiatives in consultation with the grass-roots organizations. Those expectations were not met either during the first or the second year. In 1991, during the second year, a clear and perceptible change among movement supporters had taken place in Chile—the mood had swung from guarded expectation to general dissatisfaction and, in some cases, to limited protest, a prelude most likely to lead to more extended protest and struggle during the year to follow.

As the electoral period unfolds, there is a bifurcation in the social movements between those sectors that lend themselves to the new clientelistic regime, narrowing their political goals and social aspirations and limiting their political activity, and those that challenge the new electoralist regime by occupying the new spaces for participation and demand-making, contesting the hegemony of the new political elites.

The relative influence of each of the two "perspectives," the "electoralist-clientelist" and the "autonomous movementist," varies in direct relation to its historical proximity to the electoral realignment (the defeat of Pinochet). In the period closely following the elections, while popular expectations were still high and fear of authoritarian reversal was still pervasive, the electoral-clientelistic forces were clearly in ascendance. As time passed without consequential change in socioeconomic conditions, and perhaps with regression in some areas (unemployment, declining state social spending, and economic stagnation), the "halo effect" around the regime dissipated. Socioeconomic issues of everyday and local concern took on increasing precedence, local representatives of the state regime lost "credibility," and the autonomous movement adherents were in a position to regain their influence.

The tension between the electoral-party regime and the social movements described by this sequential pattern is not inevitable: The regime could combine a program of vigorous social reform and subtle organizational co-optation to effectively undermine movement reactivation. But there are good reasons to doubt the effectiveness of that strategy. First, the regime is committed to promoting the neoliberal economic model, based on supply-side economics, tight controls on inflation, and gaining investor confidence.[4] This basically "trickle-down" approach is hardly likely to make much of an impact on the poor. Second, the formidable organizational apparatus that the regime has at its disposal—the intellectual cadres and their "training institutes"—does not represent the electoral base or grass-roots party members in the neighborhoods. Even in the initial postelectoral period, there were indications that local Socialist activists were joining electoral slates with Communist and MIR supporters against the Christian Democrats in local community elections.[5] Local party activists are not always "unconditionally" pro-electoralists, particularly if pressures mount in the community. Third, there is a substantial nucleus of grass-roots community leaders and activists who have not been demobilized or co-opted and who can serve as "reference points" in countering ineffective government programs. The existence of the "class- and movement-conscious" group is crucial to any movement revival. Its capacity to act is, however, influenced to some degree by the evolution of the crises in the Communist and related leftist parties and depends on the emergence of a new national political movement that subordinates electoral to movement politics. The very restrictiveness of the electoral political system in the post-Pinochet period is a result of the political defeat of the social movements in 1986. And it is this contradiction between the emergence of electoral politics in the narrow confines of the authoritarian state and neoliberal economic model that provides the social movements with their greatest opportunity and challenge: to broaden and deepen democratic politics, without succumbing to regime blandishments.

Reactivation of Social Movements in the Second Year

The most striking aspect of the new political structure in Chile is the highly concentrated power in the hands of certain key ministers (ministries of finances and economy) in the regime and their unconditional defense and promotion of the existing concentration of economic power in the hands of export-oriented economic conglomerates. This centralized ministerial power among self-styled "technocrats" is exacerbated by arrogant and unilateral formulation of decisions that adversely affect major sectors of the populace.[6] Many movement activists and leaders are as much appalled by and hostile to the style of dictating policy as they are repelled by the substance of the private investor bias of the policies.

The term, "technocrats," is used with ironic intent—because at the same time the ministers and their advisers are using technocratic jargon ("efficiency," "productivity," "competitiveness"), they are deeply involved in fashioning a thoroughly *class-biased* program that continues to weaken the organizational capacities of labor while it furthers existing socioeconomic inequalities. Technocratic rhetoric thinly glosses over the politics of employer-oriented capitalism. "Efficiency" in heightening output from labor for capital is matched by total ineptness in securing the efficient outflow of essential social services and providing basic goods to farm workers and squatters. The rather simplistic and naive applying of the notion of "efficiency" to investor goals—and ignoring the misallocation of budgetary resources to the military instead of to the working poor—is one glaring example of the self-serving nature of these "technocrats." The politics of the ministers is much closer to Adorno's *authoritarian* than to Veblen's technocratic engineers:[7] Their servility to the economically powerful is matched by their arrogance to the poor.

It is this combination of authoritarian political style and investor-oriented economic policy that has reactivated popular opposition and eroded expectations among the populace.

The most obvious indicator of popular disenchantment with the neoliberal regime is found in public opinion trends.[8] Between June 1990 and July 1991 the approval rating of the Aylwin government declined from 73.6 percent to 49.8 percent, a drop of almost one-third. In terms of political self-definition, there has been a massive turning away from the traditional parties: The percentage not identifying with any party increased from 22 percent in June 1990 to 34 percent in July 1991, an increase of over 50 percent. Given the elitist style of politics imposed by the technocrats, it is not surprising that almost 87 percent of the respondents claim not to participate in politics—clearly a case in which the current regime has failed to engage the active participation of the mass of citizens. The decline in participation is further reinforced by the alienation of most citizens from interest in politics: 71 percent expressed little or no interest in politics. In regard to the "progress" of the country, 50 percent felt the country was stagnant or in a state of decadence—hardly an optimistic assessment of the "economic miracle" much touted in the business press. In this regard, the economic czar of neoliberal policy, Minister of Finance Foxley, experienced a very substantial decline in approval, from 65 percent to 54 percent, between April and June 1991.

Five primary concerns that the populace thought the government should direct greater effort toward solving included crime, health care, employment, poverty, and salaries. It is safe to assume that the socioeconomic problems engendered and sustained by the neoliberal economic model contribute greatly toward causing these concerns and the accompanying alienation and decline in government support. Political alienation extends to perceptions of the "political class." Across the board, "established leaders" linked to the transitional process have experienced a decline in popular confidence: The most striking decline is among Catholic bishops (from 35 to 26 percent), business leaders (from 14 to 8 percent), and government ministers (from 29 to 25 percent). Clearly, the probusiness bias of the regime is not shared by the vast majority of the public.

Into the second year of the Aylwin regime, disillusion and apathy toward government policy and the leadership surrounding it seems to be the general tendency among the public—tendencies that are even more pronounced among lower income groups, as our interviews with target groups suggest. Clearly, the regime's policies favoring export-oriented investors and its elite technocratic style of government are in discord with the egalitarian and democratic traditions of the general public. The expectations generated by the electoral campaign have dissipated and the second year finds an increasing loss of confidence in proestablishment leaders. The efforts toward the rearticulation of new autonomous activity—both in the trade union strikes and in new forms of struggle in the shantytowns—are the first public manifestations of this disenchantment.

In order to focus on the advanced forms of public protest and the re-emergence of social movement activity, we interviewed and participated in public discussions with local and national leaders, activists, advisers, and researchers of three types: shantytown organizers, farm worker leaders, and trade unionists and advisers. In addition, we interviewed researchers working closely with the activist groups. Among the shantytown dwellers, we focused on two types of leaders, interviewing, on the one hand, local leaders of health groups, the "common kitchens," and "popular economy" organizations, and, on the other, leaders of the neighborhood councils (*junta de vecinos*). The choice was made in part to include both supporters of the current government in the neighborhood councils and local leaders who were independent of the party-state apparatus. Among the farm worker leaders, we interviewed both progovernment and antigovernment leaders. In the area of labor, we chose to focus on a strategic union, that of the copper workers, because of its importance to the economy and its long tradition of organization, and because it appeared to embody and express more clearly the underlying malaise of workers to the regime's labor policy.

Shantytown Dwellers, Farm Workers, and Labor: Growing Disenchantment

We met with a group of about sixty local community leaders from most of the largest shantytowns in Santiago to evaluate the positive and negative features of the transition.[9] The net result, which presented a balanced and objective evaluation, was negative. The discussion first focused on identifying the positive changes. Most participants noted the greater openness of local officials to discussing problems, the decline in fear of state harassment, and the government's promotion of neighborhood councils. But there were differences in degree regarding even these positive changes: There were mixed reactions to the issue of police repression. Some shantytown dwellers emphasized its decline, whereas others insisted that in their neighborhoods police raids and harassment of young people continued, citing incidents as recent as the previous week. There was common agreement that state "disappearances" had ceased and the "right to life" had been secured. There was some debate among the pobladores over the government's request that the neighborhood councils police neighborhoods and denounce youth who take drugs or engage in "terrorist" activity—and this raised a question on whether government support of "local participation" was merely a subterfuge for mobilizing communities to support the state.

Regarding the changes that took place during the transition and that negatively affected shantytown organizations, local leaders cited "dialogue without positive resolution of basic problems." The principle issues included housing, employment, and health care—none of which had even begun to be faced, according to most participants. In this regard an "open letter" from the pobladores of San Ramón,[10] issued in a municipal *cabildo* (town meeting), cited a survey in which 92 percent of the residents lived in poverty or in "extreme poverty" and 70 percent of families were not able to feed themselves at the minimum nutritional level. The open letter pointed out that "We pobladores are fed up with the bad experiences we've had with candidates who make promises to the pobladores during election periods and who know little or nothing of the life or survival of the people." The open letter went on to attack the Christian Democratic deputy representing the district for blaming the pobladores for their own misery. The letter also denounced government officials who speak of "projects" and insufficient budgets as they "continue the same economic model of the dictatorship."

There was an increasing sense among the pobladores' leaders that inconsequential "open door" policies and "dialogues" were ploys to give the appearance of concern as they continue the same policies as the previous regime.

The second major negative comment revolved around the "decline in popular organization and participation in their own organizations." Despite the government's rhetoric, the pobladores' leaders cited the efforts by the regime to co-opt local leaders in state-sponsored organizations and the disillusion with broken promises leading to withdrawal as principal causes for lower levels of involvement. The local leaders cited the absence of media space and communications networks—their monopolization by the state and corporate interests and the outlawing of locally controlled radio stations—as an additional factor undermining local organization. The local leaders described a three-phase process to disarticulate autonomous local organizations: (1) initial contact for dialogue, (2) presentation of proposals that divide the organization (over issues regarding the degree of autonomy of organization versus integration with the state in order to obtain scarce resources), and (3) subsequent dissolution of the organization, under the pretext that problems would be resolved "now that there is a democratic government."

Besides criticism of the government, changes in the behavior of the church were also viewed negatively. In the postelectoral period, numerous criticisms were made of church leaders restricting popular access to space in parish halls, opposing autonomous organizations, and turning away from popular base communities engaged in social struggles to engage in the practices of traditional paternalistic charity. NGOs, which had previously worked with the people, were increasingly described as appendages of the state, serving as linkage groups tying local groups to a state policy of restricted demand-making.

Faced with largely negative experiences during the transition, the local leaders turned to discussion of future choices. The first priority was the need to strengthen local organizations, to reactivate the apathetic who had grown disillusioned with government policy and organization. Here there was sharp debate over whether the neighborhood councils could be transformed into autonomous organizations to serve local interests or whether they "don't serve—they serve the government." Some of the local leaders had been elected to councils and hoped to raise issues to confront the regime, as they simultaneously continued their activity in the social organizations.

Most poblador leaders agreed that new organizations and new approaches needed to be developed in the post-Pinochet context. They emphasized recovering the positive experiences of the past and forgetting party divisions by building independent organizations. These proposals largely reflect the negative perception local leaders held concerning the electoral parties, which had come in and cannibalized local organizations for immediate electoral ends, setting local people off in rivalries unrelated to their local needs.

The pobladores confronted the problem of the "isolation of social groups" by focusing on specific social issues and dividing the responsibility for them among soup kitchen organizers, health workers, and so forth. They proposed town meetings and other multisectoral structures that can unify diverse social organizations in common struggles. In a final impassioned statement reflecting both the bitterness directed toward state technocrats and the resolve of the activist shantytown women, one militant woman leader stated: "We gave our struggles of seventeen years to those who denounce us for destabilizing democracy. ... Our role for the future should be to denounce them, reorganize with different organizations, organize ourselves, not from above (like the NGOs), educate the people politically—politics is necessary in solving problems. Without knowledge you become an instrument of government. Sectoral groups need to be superceded. We must go to the roots of sectoral problems."

It was very clear that a dramatic and perceptible shift had taken place among pobladores in the course of the second year of the Aylwin government. The disorganization and disorientation of militant leaders was being replaced with a sense of new purpose and direction in organization. The former isolation of groups and critical exchanges among them were lessening: common ground was emerging among activists, leaders, and the increasingly disenchanted residents of the poblaciones. The first organized steps taken were the convening of town meetings, where specific problems concerning paved roads, garbage pickups, and delivery of basic health care were addressed. These meetings drew, once again, hundreds of residents to confront the do-nothing politicians they had elected. Although there were common critical positions, there were differences over the organizational forms popular organizations should use to mount their struggles—some opted for existing organizations; others promoted the democratized neighborhood councils; and still others advocated developing new organizational forms, like the cabildos.

The critical point of the discussion, however, was the strong tendency to question and remain independent of the electoral parties and the state, even as the social movements were themselves becoming a new base for political action and electoral politics at the level of local organizations—electing and supporting locally recognized leaders. There was also recognition of the new terrain to be traversed, in which yesterday's allies (church officials, NGOs) may turn out to be today's adversaries, and yesterday's apathetic neighbors may turn out to be active supporters in town meetings. The *vertical* alliances between established institutions and the poor, which originated under the dictatorship, are being replaced by *horizontal* alliances among the previously segmented groups in the poblaciones. The process of creating the new movements from previous organizations and newly elected ones is, however, fraught with difficulties, yet it is opening new opportunities for growth. Two case studies nicely illustrate this process: those of a soup kitchen (*olla común*) and a neighborhood council (*junta de vecinos*) in Lo Hermida.

The Common Kitchen in Lo Hermida

The decline of autonomous social organizations—despite the continuing basic needs they serve—was best illustrated in our research by the conditions surrounding a common kitchen in Lo Hermida. The fundamental problem was the erosion of support by outside agencies (such as the church and NGOs), accompanied by the turn toward collaboration and direct funding by regime-controlled "solidarity" organizations.

According to one of the women organizers of the common kitchen, "Of four projects [operating prior to the elected regime], only one project remains and the food supply covers only eight days instead of thirty. ... After sixteen years of work with the church, we were ousted from their facilities with one week's notice. The archbishop issued the order. ... We now have to increase our efforts to obtain food, funds, and space to serve the needy families of this sector."

The rationale that church officials and members of the NGOs have offered to the local organizers for abandoning the common kitchen was reiterated by one missionary: "Because democracy has arrived there is no need to continue the programs. ... You don't need us." The fact of the matter is, however, that no new government programs have emerged to feed the indigent families dependent on the common kitchens. The *ideology* of the church hierarchy and the overseas governments backing the NGOs dictates that they channel resources directly to the new electoral regime at the expense of the democratically controlled local organizations. Along with this ideological shift toward the Christian Democratic regime, the church has also reoriented its work to provide what the women leaders of the common kitchen described as "fraternal help, a return to charity: food baskets and prayer meetings within a paternalistic framework."[11]

The church and the NGOs have gone full cycle. By supporting the local communities and creating ties during the popular insurgency against the dictatorship, they were able to gain influence and create dependent relations; thus they can subsequently use their leverage to orient the local organizations toward becoming an appendage of the new regime.

Aided by proregime sociologists studying the poor, the regime agency, FOSIS, obligated the common kitchen to make direct agreements with the agency to obtain any resources. Previous channels moved resources from overseas government agencies to NGOs to the social organizations; such goods are now detoured via the regime. Along with the new effort to dominate civil society, the regime has now drawn distinctions among the poor, imposing an order of priority in relief assistance. There are only two categories: those in "extreme poverty" (those without work, those who, as one woman described it, "have nothing of nothing") and those in "poverty" (without stable work). These invidious distinctions devised by the professionals (many are former leftists and former human rights advocates from the research institutes and the church) are the basis of insidious "means tests" to determine who qualifies for the meager resources dispensed for survival.

To receive funding for their common kitchen or similar projects, local movement activists must submit their proposals to FOSIS. The politics of the process is best described by one of the women leaders in the common kitchen: "To obtain funding you need to get support from above. Many former NGO professionals now run FOSIS and much depends on who is in charge of decisions in FOSIS. It is best to know someone in the Intendencia [Santiago city government]—particularly if you share their politics. If you were active in their party, it would help get your project funded. Otherwise it is a long, drawn-out bureaucratic process."

The example of the Lo Hermida soup kitchen illustrates the tendency of the electoral regime to develop a particularistic, clientelistic approach toward the shantytowns. Contrary to the rhetoric of its ideologues, as the regime further deregulates and lessens the state's role in the economy, it increases the role of the state in and over civil society. Built into the politicization of the regime's poverty program is an antagonistic attitude toward autonomous social movements that are not part of its electoral apparatus. The scarce resources allocated toward poverty amelioration are used to segment the poor and to undermine local initiatives.

From the opposite viewpoint, the meager resources, bureaucratic delays, and political tests have had the effect of further alienating local community leaders and provoking apathy among the regime's electoral supporters, who feel that their expectations have been frustrated.

The Neighborhood Council in Lo Hermida

In the aftermath of the presidential elections, the regime quickly passed a law (December 1989) democratizing the neighborhood councils. Under Pinochet, the dictator appointed the local mayor, who in turn appointed the local president of the neighborhood council. Backed by state repression on the one hand, but having to cope with large-scale unemployment on the other hand, the mayor presided over a council of elected delegates from the local neighborhoods. The anti-Pinochet opposition in the shantytowns combined militant opposition outside the councils with struggles voiced by the elected delegates. Thus the newly elected leadership of the councils was a product of organized forces from both inside and outside the previous structures. The newly democratized neighborhood council leadership that we interviewed was located in Lo Hermida, and its newly elected president is a supporter of the Socialist party and the PPD (Party for Democracy).[12] According to the president, monthly dues for membership in the junta are 50 pesos a month (roughly 13 U.S. cents). According to his figures, 3,500 of the 6,000 residents registered to vote, 1,300 paid their dues, and 950 voted. There were 19 candidates (12 women and 7 men) and 6 were elected, including one woman. The progovernment coalition (mostly Christian Democrats and Socialists) elected 4 council members; the pro-Pinochet Right, 2.

Government propaganda has focused its program for grass-roots organization in part on the development of the neighborhood councils. Along with the regime's municipal reform proposals and its efforts to organize elections for local government, the neighborhood councils are seen as part of the "democratization" process. As the initial elections demonstrate, the major parties of the government and the Right have directly intervened in the local elections. Many social movement leaders commented that the parties had displaced independent local leaders—in many cases local activist women.

In evaluating positive developments under the new neighborhood councils, the progovernment council president cited mostly local initiatives. He mentioned the proliferation of a variety of youth, sports, and ecology groups organized under the umbrella of the councils. He pointed to "projects," including small-scale efforts to create green zones, as well as proposals to extend paved roads in the neighborhood. In the latter case, however, the regime demanded that the shanty dwellers pay 15,000 pesos to have the paving work done—almost one-half month's pay for most. It is no wonder that the urbanization program is hardly progressing.

Concerning health care, the council president cited a "doctor who comes voluntarily on Saturdays for three hours and attends 120 people a month"—out of 15,000 residents—to assist the understaffed local clinic. The gap between the local communities' expectations and the regime's performance was described by the president in terms of the declining involvement of local residents in council activities: "There has been a decline in participation since the fall of the dictatorship. Why the decline in interest? People had expectations in the government and feel deceived. The transition process is slow. Communication is super-bad between the national government and the councils. Only having 'friends' in national government opens doors."

Contrary to what regime ideologist Tironi claims, declining popular participation is not due to lack of interest in politics but rather to people feeling they have been deceived and have wasted their time in organizations that have few resources to solve their problems. The communication gap between the regime and their electoral base in the shantytown is not evident at the other end of the social spectrum—where chief executive officers of local and international corporations and banks have frequent exchanges, lunches, and meetings with top government officials. Communication between the armed forces commanders and the ministers is frequent and the regime is quite attentive to their concerns. On the other hand, according to the council president, the major exchange between the regime and the communities takes place through the regime practice of "holding forums, to inform the public, not to listen or permit the 400 people in attendance to present their demands."

At the national level, the council president cited the increase in the minimum wage to nearly US$100 a month as its major achievement, but he went on to mention that "the transition is different, but not so different. ... I don't always defend the government."

The main problem for the council president was "explaining the shift in the political economic policies" of his party (the Socialists) from Allende's social reform agenda to the current probusiness neoliberal policies. Although he made an effort to promote the new party line, it was clear that he saw it as a temporary tactical move. "We are reviewing past experiences, the changes in Eastern Europe. We want to avoid brusque changes. I understand the need to postpone changes if they provoke the Right. ...

Things would be boycotted. Neoliberalism is a tactic, not a strategy to avoid provoking the Right. It is not clear what definitions the parties of the Left will take. I hope the new changes do not prejudice the interests of the people. The Socialist party and the PPD will have to define their future."

It is clear that the local leaders in the councils are not tied unconditionally to the regime or to the national leadership of their parties. They have dual loyalties: to the national party and to the interests of the local communities. If the time frame for implementing unrealized programs is increased, the tensions between the local militants and professionals at the national level are likely to increase. The recognizable decline in participation in a single year has already provoked a small crisis in the council leadership. The absence of resources is likely to deepen that crisis and increase the possibility of conflicts and confrontations between the councils and the local and national government, as well as within the governing parties, particularly those of the Socialists and the PPD.

It is unlikely that the councils will end up dominating neighborhood politics. For one thing, the council leadership is unrepresentative of the women who generally lead the block committees. In the district of Lo Hermida, of the 45 block committees we analyzed, 25 were led by women (55 percent), whereas the council itself contained only 1 woman (16 percent). Of the 3,200 recorded members of the council, only 320 were paid up (mostly, according to the president, because of special needs, i.e., obtaining residency papers) and less than 50 show up at regular meetings. From the vantage point of popular participation, local decentralized decisionmaking, and concrete delivery of services, the regime's policy toward "local democracy through the councils" is largely a failure. The initial loyalty and support is ebbing even among local militants of the governing party, who, for now, rationalize neoliberal policies as tactical. When they discover that the "tactic" is in reality a long-term strategic conception—it is doubtful that the regime will be able to hold on to its followers, short of putting them on the state or municipal payroll.

Trade Unions and the Regime

Interviews with labor consultants and researchers, as well as leaders of farm workers, advisers, and mining workers, reveal a pattern of increasing discontent. Experiences of rebuffs and perceptions of neglect and outright hostility to basic labor demands, including legal rights, salary demands, and job security issues have provoked the ire of labor. The reactions of labor have varied. Sectors of the leadership for farm workers continued to speak the language of critical support to the government[13] (with the accent on "critical"), whereas labor officials in the mining sector spoke of confrontation and described the first wave of militant strikes and conflicts with the regime. We proceed below to examine the socioeconomic context and contradictory relationship between agro-export farm workers and mine workers and the electoral regime.

One researcher who has spent years studying the conditions of the rural labor force described the much-praised agro-export economy as a "modern sector that lives in extreme poverty."[14] After investigating the electoral regime's attitude toward the 600,000 seasonal farm workers, this same researcher noted that its programs have had little impact on improving their lives. Another study, conducted by Sylvia Venegas, on seasonal workers found that over 70 percent were either living in poverty or indigent.[15] What little technical assistance is provided by the National Institute of Agricultural Research is directed at what are described as "mercantile peasants"—those producing a surplus for the market; subsistence farming and the role of women in agricultural development are completely ignored. In fact, INDAP, the Institute for the Development of Agriculture, deliberately excluded discussion of the role of women and technological transfers in agrodevelopment, much to the chagrin of the wife of a leading World Bank official, as she had indicated an interest in the role of women in development during a recent visit to Chile.

The government has not modified the Pinochet model in the least to accommodate farm worker interests. According to researchers, only incremental changes within the model that do not result in budget increases are considered. And only technical assistance proposals within the rigid confines of the agro-export strategy are even discussed. According to congressional investigations by Deputy Juan Pablo Letelier, one of the congresspeople to take an interest in farm workers, agricultural workers earned less in 1990 than in 1989. Entrepreneurs paid less to workers under the electoral regime than under Pinochet, wages declined from 1,500 pesos (US$4.30) a day to 1,300 (US$3.70) to 1,400 pesos.[16] Agricultural researchers describe the trade union in the countryside as having made "no gains" under the electoral regime. Firings of trade unionists continue. Fear of employers is pervasive among farm workers. There is no support in the executive branch for granting farm workers the legal right to strike during harvest or of permitting unions to organize at the municipal level. What activists thought were legitimate demands just a year ago—and some of them, such as the right to strike, were even incorporated in the electoral campaigns—are now considered "exotic." The Foxley-led economic team has turned the political agenda to the right. The fear of employers inculcated during the Pinochet dictatorship has not been relieved by the electoral regime's single-minded support of the grower. Traumatized by past terror, ignored by the current regime, the farm worker lacks a positive image of the trade unions. The agro-export model—and

Foxley's "macroeconomic" policies favoring agrobusiness—creates uncertainty among farm workers, which is a key factor blocking effective organization.

Hopes and Realities for the Temporeros

The labor force in the Chilean countryside numbers close to 700,000, of which the great majority are seasonal wageworkers (temporeros) employed in the agrobusiness export sector.[17] The Pinochet regime oversaw the massive transformation of small and cooperative farmers, tenant farmers, and sharecroppers into seasonal wageworkers. The stimulus was an agrarian policy that abrogated the land reform law, promoted exports, and increased interest rates, thus increasing the value of land and encouraging landowners to lower labor costs. Permanent tenants were replaced by seasonal wage laborers. Previously there had been one seasonal worker for every four permanent workers; now there are 50 seasonals for each permanent worker.[18] There are currently approximately 600,000 seasonal farm workers, of whom only 60,000 are organized.[19] In the pre-Pinochet period, organized rural workers exceeded 200,000, the majority of whom (130,000) were affiliated with the Communist-Socialist "Ranquil" union.[20] Today the Communist-led SURCO union has only 10,240 members, and most of those are concentrated in the north (Norte Chico) distributed among communes, small farmers engaged in cooperatives, and dispossessed peasants. Seasonal workers organized by SURCO number only 3,720, composing 37 percent of its membership and less than 1 percent of the seasonal labor force.[21] The strongest single union is the Christian Democratic Union, with almost 50 percent of the local union affiliates, the remainder being distributed among the Socialists, Communists, and MAPU.[22] The decisive factor in accounting for the precipitous decline in rural organization was state policy, which had been a permissive policy from the mid-1960s to 1973, but became a highly effective state terrorist policy throughout the Pinochet period. Seventy-eight local and national leaders and union activists were executed or "disappeared" by the Pinochet regime, thousands of other peasant union members were arrested, tortured, and "registered"—that is, blacklisted from future employment. State terror induced mass fear, which, according to all union organizers, is still present among peasants.[23]

During the Pinochet period, the agrobusiness class ruled the countryside in an absolutist fashion: State terror reduced agrarian wage laborers to the neoclassical ideal of being a mere "factor of production." Security of land tenure and labor rights for peasants were replaced by "labor flexibility" (meaning concentration of the power to hire and fire in the hands of agrobusinessmen) as the ideal of agricultural policymakers.[24]

The account of the condition of farm workers by technical researchers is in line with descriptions given by farm worker leaders. Juan Ahumada, head of SURCO, one of the leading unions, describes government policy as deliberately causing "atomization of farm workers and their subordination to production committees controlled by employers, thus undermining trade union organization."[25]

The progovernment president of the National Peasant Commission, Rigoberto Turra, attempted to provide a "balanced account" of government performance regarding farm workers. On the positive side, he cited the fact that "peasants can be heard, the public offices are open, the regime talks about greater participation."[26]

On the negative side, he cited "insufficient advances on labor laws, salaries, and collective bargaining." Regarding legislation on firings, the new law does not offer the least protection: Employers need only to cite "the necessity of the farm operations" to fire workers—thus continuing their arbitrary and absolute power to fire any employee. Notions about the "necessity of the firm" have not been used to promote technical changes, according to Turra, but "have been motivated by the desire to rid firms of union organizers." Massive firings of unionists have elicited no protest from the government, according to all union leaders present at our interview. Turra pointed out that the government's position on the minimum proportion of workers needed to form rival and divisive unions is actually worse than the employers'. The unions proposed a 15 percent minimum of workers in any firm as the basis for a union; the employers proposed 10 percent; and the government, 5 percent. The government policy was clearly directed at spawning union rivalries, even at the expense of its erstwhile supporters among the farm workers.

The farm workers further complained that absolutely no consideration was given to reenacting the law allowing unionization of farm workers by the municipality—Law 16625 passed during the previous Christian Democratic government in 1967. Instead, the regime proposes a type of company union (*sindicato eventual y transitorio*) that denies farm workers the right to strike or engage in collective bargaining—thus violating the International Labor Organization's principles on collective bargaining. In case of strikes, the new labor legislation allows employers to continue hiring strikebreakers or "replacements" if workers reject a contract in which the employers agree to increase wages in accordance with the level of inflation.

As one progovernment union leader remarked in an understatement, "There are not going to be profound changes under this government."[27] This comment was made after the union leaders noted that even their modest proposals to regulate water rights in order to provide greater access for small producers was rejected, along with greater access to credit for small farmers. On the salary issues, the union leaders confirmed what independent observers had already noticed: Wages had declined in 1990. Contract workers received 973 pesos (approximately US$3) a day, whereas noncontract workers received 1,059 pesos a day, according to a survey of 110 farm workers.[28] The difference between the two groups reflected the fact that noncontract workers (approximately three-fourths of those in the survey) are not covered by any social legislation.

While the president of the CNC claimed union organization was growing—from 60,000 to 80,000 over the past year—the difference was largely accounted for by a nebulous category described as "pre-unions."[29] These figures were disputed by the leader of SURCO, who argued that "mobilization is very low and in the summer of 1990–1991 there was no movement, less activity, and strikes were sporadic; the struggle is latent." Where workers go on strike, as in Los Andes, "the employers truck in 100 workers to replace the strikers with impunity." All union leaders agreed that the employers are more repressive under the electoral regime than they were in the final period of Pinochet's dictatorship. Their explanation is that the employers "want to put the government in a bad light." A more plausible explanation is the unconditional support given to the employers by the Aylwin-Foxley regime.

Faced with the dilemma of having to continue to support their party leaders in the regime or becoming totally irrelevant, the union officials proposed a "new perspective," arguing that "class conflict is latent and we need to enter a new stage toward mobilization. It is clear the regime lacks will. ... We need to work with other organizations and parties...to press our demands."[30]

The futility of lobbying government ministers is becoming apparent even to the progovernment Socialist leaders of the CNC: "We are in the doors of the Minister, but if we talk for three years more and there are no solutions ... ? The government, not the Right, cuts off the labor law in the Senate. The government doesn't listen." The arrogance and low regard with which the Foxley technocrats regard the farm worker leaders, specifically, and labor unions, in general, was evident in a poignant remark made by the president of the CNC: "The government spoke of participation during the first year. For us, participation meant discussion with the authorities around a table. In practice, the government formulates programs and sends the labor law to Congress and notifies the unions two days before. There is neither participation nor consultation."[31] Even the narrow conception of "participation" defined by these trade union officials (negotiations around a table) is rejected by the technocratic economic elite. Subservient to agrobusiness, but arrogant to union leaders—this is another description of the authoritarian development style cultivated by intellectuals-turned-state-managers.

In a moment of anger and reflection, one of the agricultural union leaders concluded: "The unity of farm workers in agriculture is distant ... there is a lack of will. The reason unity does not advance is because of the parties. To unify the farm workers we must be independent of the parties."[32] One might add, particularly of the government parties.

The paralysis of the farm unions linked to the regime and the arrogant and arbitrary rejection of their minimal demands by regime technocrats is slowly generating opposition, even among party loyalists. It is interesting to note that one of the more moderate union leaders referred to the militant ongoing strike of the copper workers' union as "an example of a practical measure" that the farm workers' union should consider. To the extent that urban-based movements (public sector unions, industrial unions in the factories and mines) began to break with the proregime mystique and challenge its economic policy, these actions are likely to create a favorable milieu in which agrarian unions can overcome the fear of the past and the bureaucratic and legal obstacles of the present.

Both rural unionists and independent observers agree that the current regime's rigid adherence to the neoliberal export model offers no relief to the farm workers: The choice is either independent class action or continued impotence and organizational stagnation.

Subordination or Autonomy?

The prospect for organizing the mass of farm workers, however, is not as bleak as it appears if substantial organizational and strategic changes can take place in the union movement. First, the bulk of the sporadic strikes that took place in the mid-1980s, particularly in 1986–1987, were led by women, almost all newly incorporated into the labor force.[33] Yet, in a meeting with the top leadership of all the rural unions, there was not a single woman present, nor was the role or the demands of women ever voluntarily brought up, despite the fact that the vast majority of packing house workers are women.[34] Secondly, there are indications that the "lack of consciousness" much commented upon by the older top leadership does not capture the evolving process in the countryside: There is a growing sense among many workers of their common exploitative position; there is a growing understanding of distinctly conflictual relations, which is a prelude to collective organization.[35] To capitalize on this potential basis for expanding class awareness, the labor unions can build a program of activities that meets cultural needs in the context of political organizing.[36] In this regard, autonomous unions intent on building class-conscious organizations come into conflict with efforts by the church hierarchy and its professional collaborators to subsume labor and capital in common organizations that obscure exploitative relations in the name of providing social services and social harmony.[37] In the new electoral context, the union leadership's "passing the political line" down from the top, and its dependence on "lobbying" the legislature for legal and political support have shown few results.[38] Without a strong movement from below, without the potential threat of mass strikes and the subsequent loss of income, neither the president nor Congress has any reason to respond to the unions. In other words, the union leadership has a mistaken reading of Chilean social history, as well as of the present situation. Workers' rights have been the product of mass struggle; legal changes have codified, not created, those rights. The process of elite negotiations with the employers, encouraged by the Socialist and Christian Democratic government parties, has yielded very little. As the head of the National Confederation of Peasants described it: "For seventeen years the entrepreneurs were used to having all power and receiving unlimited state aid. To meet with the unions was a joke. With Aylwin the dialogue advanced only 20 percent, that's all. The agro-industrial entrepreneurs have no culture of dialogue; they only know how to dominate, backed by the banks, the armed forces, and the courts. Since the government is fragile, our demands are moderate."[39] Yet, even the limited demands of the progovernment unions have been rejected by the electoral regime. And the much-vaunted "legalism" of the Chilean people, often commented upon by the governing coalition and the union leaders, is a very class-selected and myopic view of the origins of the current legal order. The present restrictive laws were imposed through violence by the military coup and the illegitimate regime of terror. The laws legislated by the democratically elected regimes were overturned—the laws that permitted municipal unions the right to strike during harvest and that prohibited unjust political firings.[40] To the extent that the peasant unions follow the lead of the electoral regime and continue to consider the arbitrary laws imposed by violence as "legitimate," they have created a major obstacle to the organization of farm workers. The union's public discrepancy with the government on the new labor legislation is a first step toward defining an independent union position: The unwillingness of the government to impose specific constraints on firings is too strong a concession to the employers for even the most ardent union advocates of the regime.[41] The union officials are conscious not only of their tenuous hold over the membership but also of their capacity to lose influence if they continue subordinating their members' demands to the regime's alliance with the investor class.

Although union leaders have a minimum program of legal rights on the table, some of them have indicated a willingness to reduce their demands to a single one: legal recognition of compulsory dues payments (*cotización obligatoria*) from all workers in a unionized enterprise. Even here, the government objects, arguing that only unionized workers should be obliged to pay dues. The emphasis given to organizational financing through top-down agreements once again reflects the legal-bureaucratic style of politics. Instead of gaining the allegiance of the workers and their willing payment of dues in return for effective union representation of their interests and struggles, union officials argue that financial independence will allow them to proceed to build the organization and expand membership. Thus far, the strategy has not worked and it is unlikely to in the near future: Compulsory dues will be the product of a mobilized, union-conscious leadership, not the result of a fragmented union movement representing less than 10 percent of the labor force. The union officials proclaim their formal autonomy, and, in the aftermath of the failure of the electoral regime to meet their minimum demands in the proposed new labor law, they have taken a critical position. The problem of the relationship between the electoral regime and parties and the rural trade unions remains. The commitments of the Socialist and Christian Democratic party regime to expand and consolidate the existing neoliberal model is particularly antithetical to the programmatic needs of the farm workers for several reasons. Politically, the agro-export sector has particularly strong ties to the right-wing parties and the armed forces, with both of whom the regime is cultivating working relations. The regime's economic team, Finance Minister Foxley and Economics Minister Ominami, has given priority in the economic sphere to promoting investor confidence and increasing exports of "nontraditional" products, i.e., fruits and timber. Socially, the regime is intent on promoting programs of social assistance (through the Solidarity Fund) to the rural poor within the existing framework, thus building a peasant electoral clientele independent of the unions. In political, economic, and social matters, the electoral regime and the peasant unions are on divergent courses. This does not preclude the regime's making partial wage concessions, or increasing social services, or keeping the door open for "dialogue" with the union leadership. It does mean, however, that the legal labor framework of the previous regime will remain practically intact to promote the agroindustrial elite's "competitiveness." Ultimately, the union leadership will have to choose whether to persist in its loyalty to the electoral regime while playing a marginal role among farm workers or whether to pursue an independent course of organization, mobilization, and class conflict that will probably involve opposition to the regime.

Copper Miners: Privileged Labor or Militant Vanguard?

Nothing captures the spirit of the times as aptly as the copper workers' strike at El Teniente mine and their confrontation with the Concertación regime and its principal Christian Democratic and Socialist ministers and bureaucrats. On one side, the strike was led by a group of young rebel underground miners striking to raise incomes disproportionately for the lowest-paid miners, and, on the other side stood Socialist former trade union lawyers and advisers, now working for the government, denouncing them as "privileged laborers," striking "against Chilean society."[42]

The copper workers' strikes at Chuquicamata and El Teniente mines represent a watershed in the relationship between the electoral regime and the popular social movements: they are the first open confrontation between labor and regime in a strategic sector of the export economy. The strikes provide insight into the nature of the government's response to popular opposition to its close working relations with the military and its technocratic style of rule. Just as significant is the emergence within the trade unions of a new generation of combative trade union activists who are not only independent of the major parties (even though some are affiliated with them) but are determined to make their demands heard above and beyond the existing trade union and party leadership.

Without entering into the complexities and all of the nuances of the strike (which began in July 1991), it is important to call attention to several significant events.

1. Ninety-seven percent of the workers voted to strike, even though 14 of the 15 leaders "did not expect a strike vote."
2. The workers represented by Union Eight—the underground miners—presented a single collective contract favoring the lowest-paid workers, whereas the maintenance and above-ground workers favored across-the-board increases.
3. Union Eight workers walked off the job, whereas the leaders of the 15 unions signed a pact to postpone the strike. The following day all workers went on strike—making the strike "illegal" according to the Pinochet labor code enforced by the electoral regime.
4. The following day, 5,000 workers stormed the union hall, literally putting all 15 leaders "up against the wall." According to one labor adviser present, a labor attorney "saved the lives of the leaders by calling for a re-vote on the strike: 89 percent voted in favor and the strike continued."

As a result of this confrontation, according to one labor adviser, "the leaders cannot come into agreement with the bosses without consulting the bases ... and they will not be elected next time despite long-standing personal and clientelistic ties."[43] The government of technocrats launched into a spurious demagogic propaganda campaign accusing the miners of being privileged and seeking more pay at the expense of fewer hospitals for the poor. The workers effectively undercut this rhetorical outburst by pointing out that the Concertación government continues the Pinochet dictatorship's policy of handing over to the military 10 percent of gross copper sales—US$230 million annually. Eliminating this handout to the military would, the miners argued, make a major contribution to hospitals and housing, so pathetically lacking in the current Concertación budget.

Within the governing coalition, the presumed Socialists were most aggressive in rejecting the miners' demands, particularly those of one Iván Valenzuela, a "Socialist" economist who was formerly an adviser to the trade unions and a member of an NGO. One of the ploys used by Concertación was to accuse the strikers and their leaders of being "Communist-inspired," despite the fact that most of the workers had voted for the Concertación coalition in the previous congressional elections.

In both copper strikes, the workers' reactions to the Concertación regime was significant. According to one union adviser in the forthcoming elections the mayoral and council candidates will have to come before the trade unions to be queried on their position on the strike. It is likely that workers will present their own candidates for council in some cases. Among miners in Chuquicamata, young workers—in the cohort between 25 and 35 years of age—have formed a nucleus under the leadership of Hernán Santelices that has established a radio station and a labor weekly, and plans to form a workers' party based on the trade unions, similar, but not identical, to its counterpart in Brazil.[44] This nucleus of young militant workers emerged during the struggle against the dictatorship and is not easily bought off with simple wage increases. They have raised basic issues of worker co-participation in the industry and are pushing for a say in decisions on training and promotion. Their slogan is Yesterday for Democracy, Today for Dignity.

The government is fearful that the copper workers' strikes will serve as an example, particularly after their success in defying the regime and obtaining better contracts. The whole neoliberal strategy, rigidly adhered to by the Aylwin-Foxley regime, is based on low wages and high profits to sustain the inflow of foreign capital and to stimulate domestic investment from the major conglomerates. References to the militant tactics, autonomous action, and economic successes of the copper miners have been heard among the leaders of the farm, health, and food workers.

The age cohort of young militants and new leaders among the copper workers is found in other trade unions and in the neighborhood organizations. Santelices has put forth a promising proposal to organize a "national encounter" of trade unionists and intellectuals to elaborate a counterprogram based on basic needs in response to the current regime's investor-oriented strategy. The goal would be to present the program to the next Congress of CUT, moving it toward a more independent position and away from its current policy of collaboration and subordination to the government.

Conclusion

It is ironic, but not inopportune, that the better paid but highly organized copper workers in the strategic export sector have taken the lead in challenging the neoliberal regime and providing a possible leadership role for the more impoverished sectors of the Chilean population. A snowballing effect could once again activate the social movements and undercut the ascendant authoritarian-elitist style of politics that has emerged in the postelectoral period. It is possible, and probably likely, that the sporadic strikes by labor in the second year of the electoral regime are a dress rehearsal for a much more generalized and conflictual period in the third year. Certainly the current regime's rigid adhesion to its budget priorities and investment and fiscal incentives puts it on a collision course with reactivated social movements. Much of the discontent is emerging precisely among those local activists and militants who originally supported the Concertación government and who are now becoming deeply disenchanted with the arrogant style and investor bias of the government.

The dogmatic statement that electoral politics equals democracy is open to serious question in light of the experiences of grass-roots organizations. If democracy means the growth of autonomous social movements, citizen interest and involvement in politics, representation of local interests in national politics, and the flow of influence from the bottom to the top, then the Chilean experience suggests that the emergence and consolidation of the electoral political organizations has not promoted democracy. Our study, based on interviews and observations, concludes that electoral politics in Chile means the subordination of social movements to hierarchical party structures and the selective incorporation of activists into the party and state; the displacement of active citizens by state functionaries and the resultant withdrawal and passivity of former participants; the transmission of elite discourse to local affiliates and the transcendence of investor priorities over local social needs; the marginalization of ongoing social mobilization, the atomization of former participants, and the ascendancy of professional politicians and authoritarian technocrats.

The electoral process operates around elitist structures that disarticulate the foundation of democratic politics. Although the electoral process provides one of the basic ingredients of democratic politics—free choice of representatives—the organizations, activities, and information that underlie the electoral process are subject to elite manipulation and control. Moreover, in the aftermath of the elections, the dominance of nonrepresentative structures undermines any effective influence over policy decisions. In this context, the electoral system functions as a facade for an authoritarian structure of politics and for elitist political organizations. Likewise, the context allows us to understand the Chilean transition as a transition from a closed, repressive, centralized military regime to a more open authoritarian, elitist, elected-civilian regime. The state framework (military, judicial, and civil bureaucracy and class structures) remains almost identical. Change within this context involves a "circulation of elites"—within the broad confines of an expansion of civil liberties, personal freedom, and public safety. The initial impression of sweeping political changes takes place at the level of the procedures for elections. But at the level of the process for making decisions, the key referents of decision-making remain highly restrictive—as much so as in the past, if we look at some mundane indicators, such as budget or macroeconomic policy. The very process of decisionmaking—with its technocratic style—is an imitation of the previous regime's, with little or no participation of, or consultation with, the newly enfranchised popular classes or organizations. The ritual gestures toward greater openness and dialogue are largely symbolic—devoid of consequential policy changes, as almost all representatives of the social organizations have noted. And the combination of substantive influence for the investor classes and symbolic gestures to the poor marks the elitist character of the political transition.

Notes

1. Typical articles of this genre written by the renovated Socialist intellectuals-turned-functionaries are: Eugenio Tironi, "Crisis, Desintegración y Modernización"; Manuel Antonio Garretón, "Partidos Políticos, Transición y Consolidación Democrática"; and José Joaquín Brunner, "La Intelligentsia: Escenarios Institucionales y Universos Ideológicos." All are to be found in a special issue of *Proposiciones* entitled, "Chile, Sociedad y Transición," no. 18 (January) (Santiago: Ediciones SUR, 1990).

2. Juan Espinoza and Andrew Zimbalist, *Economic Democracy in Chile* (New York: Oxford University Press, 1986); James Petras and Morris Morley, "Socialist Movements and the Political Class in Latin America," in Petras and Morley, *U.S. Hegemony Under Siege* (London: Verso, 1990), pp. 157–189. The renovated Socialists have been engaged in systematic distortion and denigration of the popular power movements during the Allende period, labeling grass-roots efforts to implement social changes and new organs of power as "extremist excesses" and projecting their current accommodation with bankers, generals, and corporations as the model behavior for the populace.

3. See James Petras and Fernando Leiva, "Chile: The Authoritarian Transition to Electoral Politics: A Critique," *Latin American Perspectives*, 15, 3 (Summer 1988), pp. 97–114.

4. See President Aylwin, "Capital Foráneo Debe Contar con Normas Estables," *El Mercurio*, July 19, 1991, pp. A–1 and A–12; "Aumento de 81.5% en Relacion a 1989: Inversiones Extranjeras por U.S. $874 Millones Aprobados al 11 de Julio," *El Mercurio*, July 13, 1990, p. B–1.

5. "PS, PC y MIR Ganan en las Juntas Vecinales," *El Mercurio*, July 17, 1990, p. C–3.

6. For a description and favorable presentation of the new technocrats, see Patricio Silva, "Technocrats and Politics in Chile: From the Chicago Boys to the CIEPLAN Monks," *Journal of Latin American Studies* 23 (May 1991), pp. 385–410.

7. See Theodore Adorno, *The Authoritarian Personality* (New York: Harper, 1950) and Thorsten Veblen, *Engineers and the Price System* (New York: A. M. Kelley, 1965).

8. The following public opinion data is drawn from a survey by CEP-Adimark between June 28 and July 20, 1991. The findings were reported in *La Segunda*, August 2, 1991, pp. 10–19.

9. Approximately sixty community leaders from most of the important shantytowns were represented. The meeting took place August 7, 1991, in the meeting hall of the Confederation of Construction Workers. The meeting was organized by Promoción e Intercambio de Recursos Educacionales y Tecnológicos (PIRET), a Santiago-based center of popular education. The interviews cited are from this meeting.

10. "Carta Abierta a los Pobladores de San Ramón con Motivo del Cabildo Comunal," Grupo de Salud Poblacional "Llareta" (Llareta Community Health Group), La Bandera Township, July 28, 1991.

11. Interviews at Zona Oriente Lo Hermida, August 5, 1991, with a group of four organizers in the common kitchen movement.

12. Interview with the president of Junta de Vecinos Lo Hermida; other interviews with council leaders took place in Capilla Sara Gajardo in Pudahuel.

13. The interviews with the farm worker union leaders took place in the headquarters of CNC, August 5, 1991. The president, Rigoberto Turra, and the executive board member, Juan Ahumada, were the main interviewees. Juan Ahumada and Oscar Valladares were also interviewed the previous year in July 1990.

14. Interview with María Elena Cruz, researcher at GIA, August 5, 1991.

15. Ibid.

16. Ibid.

17. The exact figures greatly depend on the time of year, and on whether one includes transport and related processing activities. The estimates run from approximately 500,000 workers (interviews with María Elena Cruz, GIA) to 600,000 (staff of GEA) to 700,000 (Juan Ahumada, Confederación "El Surco").

18. José Bengoa, Jaime Crispi, María Elena Cruz, Cecilia Leiva, *Capitalismo y Campesinado en el Agro de Chile* (Santiago: GIA, 1980); María Elena Cruz and Cecilia Leiva, *La Fruticultura en Chile. Un Area Privilegiada de Expansión de Capital Agrario* no. 3, vols. 1 and 2 (Santiago: GIA, 1982); Rigoberto Rivera and María Elena Cruz, *Pobladores Rurales* (Santiago: GIA, 1984); and María Elena Cruz, *De Inquilinos a Temporeros de la Hacienda al Poblado Rural* no. 21 (Santiago: GIA, 1986).

19. The concept of temporary workers is under scrutiny since there are great variations between rural- and urban-situated farm workers and between workers

in the north, south, and central parts of the region. Employment of "temporaries" varies from five months to ten months a year. See the survey by Sylvia Venegas, "Los Tipos de Trabajadores Frutícolas y su Situación Ocupacional," Santiago, GEA, July 1990. Mimeographed.

20. Interview with Oscar Valladares, treasurer of Movimiento Unitario Campesino y Etnias de Chile, July 13, 1990.

21. Interview with Juan Ahumada, executive board member of CNC, July 18, 1990.

22. Ibid.

23. Interview with eight members of the Executive Committee of the National Peasant Commission, July 19, 1990.

24. Ibid.

25. Interview with Juan Ahumada, president of Confederación Nacional Campesina "El Surco" and executive board member of CNC, August 5, 1991.

26. Interview with Rigoberto Turra, president of both CNC and the Socialist Nehuén Confederation, August 5, 1991.

27. Interview with the farmworker union leaders took place in the headquarters of CNC, August 5, 1991. The president, Rigoberto Turra, and executive board member Juan Ahumada were the main interviewees. For a brief critical appraisal in the official publication of the CNC, see "Transición Democrática, Buen Comienzo, Pero ..." *Tierra*, nos. 68–69, October 15–December 15, 1990, pp. 12–14.

28. *Encuesta de Remuneraciones de Temporeros* (Santiago: Comisión Nacional de Campesina, 1991), mimeo.

29. According to the official publication of the CNC, only 2,000 new trade union members were signed up in 1990. See *Tierra*, nos. 68–69, October 15–December 15, 1990, pp. 39–40.

30. Interview with CNC executive board members, August 5, 1991.

31. Ibid.

32. Ibid.

33. Interview with Juan Ahumada, July 18, 1990.

34. Interview with CNC executive board members, July 19, 1990. Interview with María Elena Cruz, then a GIA researcher, July 18, 1990. For the role of women see Sylvia Venegas, op. cit., p. 9. In her survey, Venegas found that women are more likely than men to seek organized solutions to job-related problems, and the higher the concentration of women, the greater the differential. Among packing-house workers, only 16 percent of the men looked toward collective action as compared to 25 percent of the women.

35. Interview with Juan Ahumada, July 18, 1990.

36. During our July 18, 1990, interview, El Surco leader Juan Ahumada described a range of cultural and social activities as integral elements of any successful unionization effort: "Sports, recreation, and culture are the best way to appeal to young seasonal workers. We have to move from festivals to union assemblies; in this fashion attendance increases from 10 to 500."

37. One such proposal for labor capital collaboration is found in Gonzalo Falabella, *La Casa del Temporero en Santa María. Proyección de una Experiencia en Transición* (Santiago: SUR, 1990), mimeo.

38. Faced with a government-proposed reform of the labor code that met some of their basic demands, the leadership outlined a strategy directed toward (1) mobilizing and educating parliamentary groups, (2) arranging a series of meetings with the progovernment party alliance and Concertación, and (3) mobilizing and organizing the rank and file to pressure the president and the congress to modify the president's proposal. Interview with executive committee members of CNC, July 19, 1990.

39. Interview with CNC executive committee members, July 19, 1990.

40. On April 27, 1967, President Frei signed Law 16625, the peasant unionization law, supported by the Christian Democrats, the Socialists, and the Communists. The current regime of Christian Democrats and Socialists has expressed no interest in revising legislation from the 1960s.

41. Over 2,000 arbitrary firings of farm workers, most of whom were trade union members, occurred during the harvest of 1990 without any government response to the petitions of the CNC. See *Tierra-Carta* no. 3, June 1990.

42. Interview with one of the chief trade union advisers of the National Confederation of Copper Workers, August 9, 1991.

43. Ibid.

44. A highly informative interview of Hernán Santelices is found in "La Rebelión de los Viejos," in *Página Abierta*, August 5–18, 1991, pp. 2–3.

8

Limits to Aylwin's "Growth with Equity"

Success and Contradictions of the Model

International development and financial institutions have conferred lavish praises on the Aylwin government's handling of the economy during the two-year "transition to democracy." Indeed, viewed from the angle of traditional macroeconomic indicators, the Aylwin government's management of the economy during the period 1990–1991 can claim significant achievements: GDP grew at the rate of 2.1 percent in 1990 and 6.0 percent in 1991 while inflation decelerated from an annual rate of 27.3 to 18.7 percent during these two years. Exports continued expanding, reaching US$8.9 billion in 1991, and, as can be gathered from Table 8.1, international reserves attained record levels. Social programs marginally helped improve the distribution of income, and though results so far have been limited, the rhetoric surrounding the new programs, which "integrate the poor to development," remains impressive. According to official figures, unemployment declined to 6.5 percent at the end of 1991, while, as shown in Table 8.2, real wages grew, though at rates below increases in productivity. Rates of profits showed a rising tendency as Chile entered its second year under civilian rule. According to the Santiago Stock Exchange, the 1991 rate of profits before taxes for 109 of the largest enterprises surpassed the previous rates of 31.8 percent in 1989 and 27.6 percent in 1990. During 1991, this upward tendency was maintained: Earnings rose from 28.2 percent during the first quarter of 1991 to 29.5 percent during the second, reaching 33.6 percent in the third.[1]

Indicators such as these have fueled a climate of triumph among Concertación economists, one that is reminiscent of the frenzied self-righteous enthusiasm of the Chicago Boys prior to the 1981 crash. Concertación policymakers confidently assert that, if present trends are maintained, in twenty years Chile will double its per capita GDP and workers will be able to quadruple real income during their lifetimes.[2]

However, these impressive indicators cannot be fundamentally attributed to the technical proficiency of Aylwin's economic team or solely to

167

TABLE 8.1   Selected Macroeconomic Indicators (in annual percentage rates and USR millions)

	1987	1988	1989	1990	1991	1992
Gross domestic product (%)	5.7	7.4	10.1	2.1	6.0	10.4
Inflation (%)	21.5	12.7	21.4	27.3	18.7	12.7
Real exchange rate	104.2	108.3	101.8	99.2	95.5	88.5
Unemployment (%)	9.3	8.3	6.3	6.0	6.5	4.9
Real wages (%)	−0.2	6.5	1.9	1.8	4.9	4.5
Current account	−808.0	−167.0	−767.0	−824.0	101.0	−583.2
Exports	5223.7	7051.8	8080.0	8309.9	8929.4	9986.1
Imports	3994.3	4833.2	6501.9	7036.8	7353.5	9236.9
Balance of trade	1229.4	2218.9	1578.9	1273.1	1576.0	749.2
Capital account	899.0	277.0	841.0	988.0	−422.0	398.0
Capital	944.0	1009.0	1278.0	3356.0	816.0	2896.0
Foreign investment	923.0	1011.0	1583.0	1014.0	453.0	604.0
Other	21.0	−2.0	−305.0	2342.0	363.0	2292.0
Reserves	−45.0	−732.0	−437.0	−2368.0	−1238.0	−2498.0

SOURCE: Compiled on the basis of data obtained from Banco Central, *Boletín Mensual* no. 767 (January 1991) and no. 784 (June 1993).

TABLE 8.2   Participation of Wages in the Gross Domestic Product, 1987–1992 (annual percentage rate of change)

	GDP	Employment	Average Productivity[a]	Real Wages	Share of Wages in GDP[b]
1987	5.7	3.5	2.2	−0.2	−2.4
1988	7.4	4.9	2.5	6.5	4.0
1989	10.0	5.2	4.8	1.9	−2.9
1990	2.1	2.0	0.1	1.8	1.7
1991	6.0	0.7	5.3	4.9	−0.4
1992	10.4	4.1	6.3	4.5	−1.6
1987–1992 Average	6.9	3.4	3.5	3.2	−0.3
1990–1992 Average	6.4	2.6	3.8	3.6	−0.2

[a]Productivity equals rate of change in GDP minus rate of change in employment.

[b]Wage Share of GDP equals rate of change in real wages minus rate of change in average productivity.

SOURCE: Rafael Agacino, "El modelo no garantiza la equidad," *Los Tiempos,* May 9, 1993, p. 26. Reprinted with permission.

the favorable economic climate created by the newly elected civilian regime. Rather, these indicators express and are connected to two related phenomena. First, since 1985 Chilean capitalism has been experiencing a process of sustained recuperation and expansion, to the point that by 1991 most macroeconomic variables have regained and even surpassed their 1981 levels. Second, the Concertación coalition and government committed itself to maintaining the export-oriented model, applying policies similar to its openly neoliberal predecessors. The expectations of Chilean and transnational investors were therefore not affected by the transition and the change of government. On the contrary, the large conglomerates that dominate the Chilean economy sense that they have entered a new historical period. They envision the Aylwin regime actively pursuing the consolidation of the structural transformations and the legitimation of the violent realignment of class power carried out under Pinochet.

Contradictions

Nevertheless, favorable macroeconomic indicators also obscure powerful unresolved contradictions brewing beneath the apparently calm surface of economic success. In the case of a small, open economy such as Chile's, the contradictions of the export-oriented model of accumulation have been evaluated as (1) promoting the superexploitation of labor, (2) increasing dependency and economic vulnerability to international shocks, (3) fostering the concentration of power and wealth, and thereby increasing social polarization, (4) intensifying the transnationalization of the capitalist class and its concomitant opposition to effective redistributionist policies, and (5) intensifying the plunder of natural resources and the degradation of ecological systems.[3] After 1989, each one of these contradictions has continued maturing and intensifying under the tenure of the Aylwin administration.

Four "Gordian Knots" of Aylwin's Strategy

Far from resolving these contradictions, the modernization through internationalization development strategy enthusiastically applied by Foxley and Ominami seems to have raised them to new levels. Hence, these contradictions began to forcefully manifest themselves during the first two years of the Aylwin government in the form of four persistent afflictions of the "growth with equity" development strategy:

1. The contradictory relationship between export competitiveness and a significant improvement in real wages.
2. The tension between exchange rate and monetary policy, fueled by the very success of the open economy strategy.
3. The conflict between the continuation of subsidies to formerly bankrupt private banks and the political need to increase social spending.
4. The lack of appropriate institutional conditions to allow advancement to an idealized "second phase" of the export model.

TABLE 8.3   Evolution of Real Exchange Rate and Revised Real Wage Index, 1980–1987

	Real Exchange Rate Index[a]	*Total Revised Real Wage Index*[b]
1980	106.8	95.0
1981	93.2	105.0
1982	103.9	110.3
1983	124.1	91.1
1984	129.8	86.5
1985	159.8	80.0
1986	175.9	81.5
1987	182.0	81.2

[a]Base 1980–1981=100.

[b]Base 1980–1981=100. The revised real wage index has been constructed by Meller on the basis of data provided by a private on-going survey of 4,000 enterprises.

SOURCE: Compiled on the basis of Patricio Meller, "Revisión del Proceso de Ajuste Chileno de la Década del 80," *Colección Estudios CIEPLAN* no. 30 (Santiago: CIEPLAN, 1990), Table 2.6, p. 29. Reprinted with permission.

Each of these four nodal problems needs to be taken into account when assessing the economic performance of the Aylwin government and the future perspectives for the growth with equity development strategy.

Export Competitiveness and Real Wages

The export boom experienced during the second half of the 1980s was based to a great extent upon the successful enforcement of an adjustment package that made the devaluation of the peso the central policy instrument.[4] According to the Central Bank figures presented in Table 8.3, the real exchange rate underwent an increase of over 80 percent between 1981 and 1987: Its index climbed from 93.2 to 182.0 during the period. To achieve an increase in the competitiveness of the Chilean economy of such magnitude (and ensure that such gain was not eroded by inflationary pressures) a 20 percent drop in real wages was required. Analyzing the nature of Chile's adjustment process and the basis of the increased competitiveness of Chilean exports in world markets during the second half of the 1980s, Patricio Meller, a CIEPLAN economist, noted "the greatest portion of the real devaluation has been obtained through a significant reduction in the unitary cost of productive factors, a reduction that has hinged more on reducing the return to productive factors (specifically the price of labor), rather than on increases in productivity. Up until 1987, keeping real wages depressed constituted the key factor in validating a real devaluation."[5]

This inverse relationship between variations in the exchange rate and the level of real wages during the period 1980–1987 is clearly illustrated by the data presented in Table 8.3. These figures reveal that the secret of the purported success of the Chilean economic model is to be found, *not in the set of socially neutral and technically more appropriate neoliberal policies, but in capital's ability to destroy labor's capacity to defend the value of its labor power.* The competitiveness of Chilean exports and the dynamism of the model vitally depended on keeping labor disciplined. This fact is well understood by exporters, neoliberals, and Concertación technocrats: If wages rise too quickly, exporters could not readily convert these increased costs into a higher price for their exports. Given its highly competitive nature, the world market fixes an unyielding ceiling on price hikes.[6]

If wages increase, exporters will demand a higher exchange rate (a depreciated peso) so that when they convert export earnings to domestic currency, they will command a greater number of pesos per product sold and, therefore, be in a better position to cover rising production costs.

If the level of real wages should increase too rapidly, or the peso appreciate significantly, profit margins and the competitiveness of Chile's resource-intensive exports (minerals, fruit, lumber, and fishing) could be seriously damaged. Yet, after 1987, and with escalating intensity after 1988, one of these two variables experienced significant shifts in a direction that threatened the dynamism of Chile's export model. Real wages during the years 1989–1991 increased at an average annual rate of 3.6 percent. But, as indicated in Table 8.2, this increase was well below the 3.9 percent average annual rate at which productivity increased for the same three-year period. Thus, of the two critical variables determining the competitiveness of Chilean exports—wages and exchange rate—increases in real wages during the Aylwin regime have so far been of a nonthreatening character. However, the same could not be said for the steady decline in the exchange rate index, reflecting the strong appreciation of the peso during 1990 and 1991 (see Table 8.4). The factors behind the appreciation of the peso during these two years illustrate the ephemeral character of macroeconomic balance and the vulnerability of the open economy development strategy.

Open Economy and Macroeconomic Balance

A fundamental shortcoming of the Chilean model seems to be that its very success undermines the competitiveness of exports and weakens the capacity of government authorities to maintain macroeconomic balance. As exports expand, as they have since 1985, the number of available dollars in the hands of exporters increases. As this swelling number of dollars is bought by the Central Bank at a depreciating dollar value, monetary emission increases.

Since 1988, this tendency has been further intensified by the differential between Chilean and U.S. real interest rates. Because Chilean interest

TABLE 8.4   Real Exchange Rates and Real Wages, 1986–1992

	Nominal Exchange Rate[a] (Ch$/US$)	Real Exchange Rate Index[b]	Total Real Wage Index[c]
1986	192.90	100.00	–
1987	219.41	104.15	94.40
1988	245.01	108.27	100.58
1989	266.95	101.76	102.59
1990	304.90	99.23	104.40
1991	349.22	95.47	109.52
1992	362.58	85.81	114.46

[a]Average nominal observed exchange rate.
[b]Calculated by multiplying the nominal rate by relevant international inflation and dividing by the domestic prices index. Does not include Chile's Latin American trading partners.
[c]Average yearly real wage index; base: December 1982=100.
SOURCE: 1986 to 1991 data from Banco Central, *Informe Económico y Financiero*, June 30, 1992, pp. 27–29; 1992 data from Banco Central, *Informe Económico y Financiero*, August 15, 1993, pp. 27–29.

rates from 1990 to 1991 were higher than international rates, there was a potent incentive for the influx of short-term speculative capital into the economy.[7] The combined effect of export expansion and the liberalization of financial markets and capital flows led to the flooding of the Chilean economy with excess dollars. With particular intensity during 1990 and 1991, structural factors kept reproducing a chronic and growing inconsistency between exchange rate and monetary policy.

As a result of the marked appreciation of the peso, the real exchange rate index (nominal exchange rate multiplied by international inflation over domestic inflation), which in 1989 stood at 101.76, steadily declined to 85.81 by 1992. Faced with a depreciating dollar, the Association of Exporters of Manufactures (ASEXMA) expressed concern that the growth rate of non-copper exports had been steadily diminishing since 1987. Non-copper exports, which had grown 22 percent in 1986, grew at only 21.6 percent in 1988, at 11.6 percent in 1989, and at only 11.2 percent in 1990. ASEXMA traces this deterioration of the competitiveness of the Chilean export sector to the progressive decline of the exchange rate.

According to ASEXMA figures, in real terms the dollar had depreciated 18 percent in 1990 and 6.5 percent during the first 11 months of 1991, with respect to the Unidad de Fomento (UF), a measurement of constant buying power. A shoe exporter, who in December 1988 would sell his product at US$18 or its equivalent to cover his costs, by November 1991 was being forced to sell the same product at US$20 in Germany, US$21.7 in Japan, US$21.8 in England, and US$21 in the United States, in order to break even. Thus, exporters of manufactured products complained, "Due to the lower exchange rate (appreciation of the peso), we are forced to readjust our prices in dollars above the level of international inflation, which has resulted in lost opportunities for many of our members."[8]

Who Benefits? Who Bears the Costs?

Faced with a declining real exchange rate, the Central Bank committed itself to stem this downward push by acquiring excess dollars. During the eighteen-months in which the price of the dollar was stuck to the floor of the price band, the Central Bank bought US$4.5 billion, or the equivalent of 50 percent of total export earnings for 1991.[9]

These measures by the Central Bank to prop up the price of the dollar relative to the peso led to a rise in the monetization of the economy. During 1991, for example, money held by the public (M1A) grew at a rate of 38 percent, whereas money demand grew at only 28.6 percent, resulting in an excess of liquidity of 7.3 percent.[10] To counteract this effect, Banco Central authorities attempted to withdraw money from circulation (sterilization) by selling securities in the internal market. However, this was not a cost-free operation. To attract buyers and sell its debt, the Central Bank had to pay interest rates above the value of what it was obtaining by depositing the bought dollars at international interest rates. The cost of these operations for the Central Bank was about US$100 million, an amount equivalent to approximately 0.5 percent of GDP.[11]

The context outlined above starkly portrays the extent to which a high degree of integration with the world economy has seriously eroded Chile's autonomy in determining monetary as well as exchange rate policy. Attaining macroeconomic balance, a key policy objective, has been progressively undermined by the very success of the open economy development strategy. Apparently, fiscal policy would be the only variable remaining under control of the economic authority. Nonetheless, in the case of Chile, fiscal policy and the level of spending are conditioned by international interest rates and the constitutional norms defining the level of defense spending at 1989 levels in real terms. One must also add to these limitations the existence of a Central Bank deficit induced by the post-1983 US$6 billion rescue of bankrupt private financial institutions. Thus, if and when inflationary pressures arise, and considering Concertación's lack of the political will to confront the armed forces or the financial groups, it is highly probable that future adjustments will be made by decreasing social spending.

"Subordinate Debt": Lingering Costs of a Bail-out

Contrary to the claims of its propagandists, the imposition of neoliberalism in Chile resulted *in the expansion of state intervention in the economy,* rather than in the state's retreat from economic affairs.[12] A strengthened state role was necessary not only to repress and discipline labor and violently restructure property rights; it was also a prerequisite for transferring the burden and costs of salvaging the insolvent private banking system onto the shoulders of society.

The private financial system rescue caused the public sector to suffer losses estimated at between US$6 to US$9 billion. Such a loss led to a debt of the public sector with the Central Bank, which, as of December 31, 1989, had reached US$6.97 billion, or 31 percent of all Central Bank assets.

Massive state subsidies to private banks under Pinochet live on under Aylwin in the form of the "subordinated debt."[13] In 1991, the subordinated debt of ten private banks to the Central Bank totaled approximately US$3.4 billion. Of the US$3.4 billion owed, 20 percent of those in debt pay no interest, while the other 80 percent pay a conveniently low 5 percent rate. Additionally, no deadline has been specified for the indebted banks' debt payment. The Banco de Chile, responsible for US$1.25 billion or 36.53 percent of the total owed to the Central Bank, would take thirty-three years to pay what it owes, if it were to enjoy a profit rate of 30 percent a year during that period! The Banco de Santiago, owing US$1.16 billion or 34.1 percent of the total, would take seventy-two years to pay, if it faced the extraordinary situation of 30 percent annual rate of return during that time span. Yet, because of lenient conditions, both banks have engaged in a strong modernizing drive, installing automatic bank teller machines all over the country, knowing full well that their debt is unpayable and that the Aylwin government will have to decide how to make up the losses.

It is symptomatic of finance capital's continued hegemony that the Aylwin administration maintains this blatantly unjust mechanism for transferring surplus from the national economy to private banks. Two different figures give an approximate idea of the magnitude of this process: The tax reform of 1990 boosted governmental funds available for increased social spending by US$250 million; during the same year, the favorable terms of interest enjoyed by the indebted private banks represented the transfer of US$370 million.[14] In other words, *during 1990 there was a net transfer of US$120 million, which went not to the poor but to the private financial sector.* Additionally, the financial cost of this policy to the Central Bank represents a revenue loss equivalent to US$180 million a year, and projections are that this amount grows annually at a 5 percent rate. This quasi-fiscal deficit represents the monthly transfer of approximately US$2.3 million to the private financial sector.

Once again, the situation outlined so far shows that beneath the surface of macroeconomic equilibrium and positive economic indicators there festers a serious problem of inequality and potential financial instability. While praise for Foxley's "responsible" macroeconomic management by

Aylwin's economic team continues to gush forth from the privileged, so too a mechanism continues to operate that transfers surplus from the whole of the economy to the private financial sector. Whereas adequate increases in social expenditures for health and education are denied by using the need for macroeconomic balance and the "impersonal" rules of the market as excuses, Aylwin's economic team willingly bends those rules to service the needs of Chile's financial elite.

A "Second Phase" of the Export Model

Foxley's Dream, Workers' Nightmare?

In the environment of increasing globalization and restructuring of the world economy, experience shows that there are two basic routes toward attaining and maintaining international standards of competitiveness: (1) depressing real wages and living standards and concentrating on standard products and production methods, or (2) increasing productivity through technological advances and improved education and training.[15] In the case of Chile, international competitiveness and the expansion of exports was accomplished by using the first of these routes: the increased superexploitation of labor (accompanied by intense depredation of natural resources). As previously indicated, after 1985 the export promotion policy of high and stable exchange rates was sustained by a drastic reduction in living standards and a considerable reduction of real wages.

The passage toward exports with a greater value-added content is seen as crucial for maintaining the long-term competitiveness and market share of Chilean exports. Aylwin's economic team is therefore convinced that the transition from natural resource–based to manufactured exports holds the key for promoting lasting economic dynamism and augmenting societal harmony. The idealized vision of Chile's capitalist class as Schumpeterian entrepreneurs willing to take risks leads both Foxley and Ominami to have faith in the ability of the market mechanism and the appropriate corporate response to bring about the passage to this "second phase" of the export model. In their eyes, increased internationalization will goad capitalists to base the future competitiveness of their exports on increased investments in technological innovation.

To bring about a change in Chile's export profile, Foxley and Ominami's choice policies have been to provide greater incentives for international capital and to enthusiastically embrace the Free Trade Agreement between Chile and the United States.

A cursory analysis of the composition of exports would seem to indicate that their dream of a second phase of the export model was becoming a reality: Industrial exports climbed from 33 percent of total exports in

TABLE 8.5   Exports Classified According to Major Sectors (in millions of US$)

		Agriculture and Sea		Manufacturing			Total
	Mining[b]	Total	Fresh Fruit	Total	Fishmeal	Cellulose	Exports (FOB)
1986	2096.1	683.0	478.9	1412.1	315.1	192.6	4191.2
1987	2603.3	796.3	531.0	1824.1	362.5	264.9	5223.7
1988	3848.3	930.4	584.1	2273.1	458.9	310.2	7051.8
1989	4472.8	994.5	543.5	2612.7	507.8	321.1	8080.0
1990[a]	4590.2	978.6	703.8	2741.2	379.6	314.9	8310.0
1991[a]	4393.0	1220.8	948.6	3315.6	464.6	305.4	8929.4

[a]Data for 1990 and 1991 are provisional.
[b]Mining includes copper.
SOURCE: Banco Central, *Informe Económico y Financiero* (February 1992), Table 26, p. 32.

1990 to 37 percent in 1991. In dollar terms, Table 8.5 shows that industrial exports went up from US$2.74 billion in 1990 to US$3.32 billion in 1991.

However, these apparently impressive figures require closer scrutiny. Of the US$574 million increase in industrial exports between 1990 and 1991, 56 percent of that expansion corresponded to natural resource–based products with low levels of industrial transformation. Of the US$500 million increase, US$83.5 million corresponded to fishmeal, US$56.5 million to wood chips, sawn wood, and wood panels, US$81.6 million to fish, and US$65.3 million to fuel derivatives.[16]

Making a virtue out of necessity, Aylwin's economic team currently hopes that the combined effects of an appreciating peso and lower import tariffs will stimulate exporters to launch a process of technological innovation. Nevertheless, a number of different studies has convincingly argued that the preconditions for the transition from competitiveness based on superexploitation to competition based on increases in productivity are rooted in factors related to institutional and class structure rather than in appropriate market signals. Among some of the necessary preconditions prevailing in East Asia but absent in Latin America, these studies mention: (1) the existence of an endogenous technological core, (2) a strong domestic entrepreneurial class, (3) a developmentalist state, and (4) a relative level of independence from external financing constraints. Compared to the experience of East Asia, the institutional and social conditions necessary for effective industrial policies are missing. What is lacking in Chile is what one author calls the conditions for the "effectiveness of intervention."[17]

Effective state intervention to bring about economic transformation requires that the state is able both to formulate and to implement coherent economic strategies. A prerequisite for formulating a consistent strategy is a degree of autonomy of the state from the dominant class or class fractions, which enables the state to pursue goals that do not reflect the interests of these groups and may even go against their short-term interests.[18]

Lacking the institutional preconditions for the articulation of state-induced industrial policy, the Foxley-Ominami team, in its attempt to increase manufactured exports, has no other option but to resort to facilitating the access of international capital to cheap Chilean labor. Even before taking his cabinet post, Foxley pandered to the idea that "Chile is a potentially important platform for exports to Pacific Ocean markets. We will open our doors to businessmen from other countries who wish to set themselves up here and export to Pacific markets."[19]

Instead of increases in productivity through technological innovation, we are likely to see the growth of manufactured exports relying on the increasing informalization of labor-capital relations and establishment of *maquiladora*-type operations. Taking advantage of the labor code created by Pinochet and sanctioned by Aylwin and egged on by intensified competition from Latin American countries completing the processes of capitalist restructuring, Chilean exporters will most likely resort to strategies that replace their stable wage force with contract workers, temporary labor, and outsourcing through the use of homework or subcontracting. As in other countries, exporting firms will tend to reduce the reliance on full-time wageworkers earning fixed wages and fringe benefits. The experience of other Third World countries has been that competitiveness is maintained through measures that discipline and "flexibilize" the labor force and that broaden the use of subcontracting, temporary workers, homework, and other measures tending to informalize labor-capital relations.[20] The Aylwin administration's active support for the expansion of informal enterprises and their linkage into the export strategy anticipates that informalization of labor-capital relations, not technical innovation, will be the fulcrum for increasing manufactured exports in the coming years.

Incapable of articulating a national industrial policy or a national policy of technological development, the Aylwin government presents a strategy to increase manufactured exports that depend on new forms of superexploitation of labor. Instead of greater social harmony and sustained economic growth, we are likely to observe in coming years the emergence of the acute social, economic, ecological, and political problems that accompany the development of export platforms and maquiladora production. If, in fact, such a pattern is repeated, Foxley's dream of increasing manufactured exports could well transform itself into a living nightmare for Chilean workers.[21]

Toward an Alternative Model of Development

For both economic and political reasons, the replacement of the current export-oriented model is a prerequisite for the full democratization of Chilean society. In the current intellectual and political context of increasing economic globalization, crumbling of the statist-Socialist model, and political defeat of popular democratic forces in Chile, the search for an alternative model of development becomes a demanding task. The basic guidelines for such an alternative are to be found in the Chilean people's experience of democratic struggles over these last twenty-five years—events which still have not been adequately evaluated by the Left. It is from that experience that important lessons can be drawn, to enrich and make viable an alternative development model to replace the current "modernization through internationalization" strategy.

Chile's recent history clearly demonstrates that alternatives to the neoliberal authoritarian state model must begin with a restructuring of the state apparatus—for political as well as socioeconomic reasons. The current state—the military, judiciary, and higher permanent civil officials—is committed to preserving the prevalent organization of wealth, power, and prosperity. In order to change the balance between the state and civil society, and redistribute income, land, and state subsidies from capital to labor, the state must be transformed: A popularly elected regime would face endless blockages, or even a coup, if it attempted to implement democratic social changes or to elaborate an alternative economic model. Reductions in the military budget, including the transfer of the US$300 million copper tax to civilian uses, would certainly generate more productive and socially useful projects benefiting the salaried majority. The reform of the judiciary—early retirement of the Pinochet-appointed Supreme Court judges—would bring the judicial system into line with the democratic process.

Second, the relationship between the state and civil society and the economy would need to be transformed before an alternative socioeconomic model could be implemented. The current ascendancy of technocrats, which limits effective representation to large-scale investors—foreign and domestic—while inhibiting the organization of civil society, would have to change. Trade unions, neighborhood groups, farm workers' associations, as well as consumers, women, and ecologists would be directly represented in defining "macroeconomic policy." The rule by technocrats and former leftist politicians controlling clientelistic organizations would be replaced by a strengthening of autonomous forms of self-representation, that is, councils elected at the workplace and neighborhoods—similar to the industrial and municipal councils that developed during the Allende government. Civil society would be freed of state tutelage while the economy would be regulated through diverse mechanisms in which these self-management councils would play an important role. These changes in institutional parameters are necessary preconditions for the successful application of the policy of the new self-managed social economy (similar to a democratic socialist system).

The design of economic policy must fit with the social values and priorities of civil society—quality of life, not GNP, should define development goals. In the first instance, economic policy should be directed toward recovering the enterprises privatized by the Pinochet regime, often sold at absurdly low prices—usually to cronies of the regime. Secondly, the government should recover nonrenewable natural resources that are being mindlessly exploited by foreign multinationals with little spillover effect in the domestic economy. The export sector should be reorganized so that the direct producers—farm workers, miners, lumberjacks, and fishermen—can influence and benefit from production, rather than being, in most cases, the most exploited and disorganized sectors of the labor force. The earnings from the export sector should be returned, to finance the expansion and deepening of the domestic market for the many, as well as to increase the industrial diversification of the domestic economy.

In the countryside, co-ops, processing plants, and sideline industries should manage the agroindustrial complexes, providing full-time employment and extending social services (day-care, health, housing, and education) currently at abysmally low levels. New class and gender representatives—particularly in farm labor, co-ops, and neighborhoods—should manage macroeconomic policy, imposing discipline on capital to invest, increasing taxes on profits, interests, and rents while financing social services in health, education, recreation, and ecological recovery. Workers' control over the nearly US$15 billion in social security and pension funds currently being managed by the Administradoras de Fondos de Pensiones (AFPs), dominated by Chilean and transnational finance capital, would inject significant resources into the economy for activities oriented toward the satisfaction of human needs.

A new consensus of social pacts among self-managed, co-operative, and private enterprises based on meeting decent living standards of working people should form the basis for governability. Economic strategy should shift from the current export policy, based on cheap temporary labor working in raw materials, to increased public and private investment in research and development, linked to a more diverse, technologically advanced industrial and commercial economy.

In effect, the social pyramid should be reversed in order to free the political sphere from the narrow elite constraints that exclude the majority from the benefits of export production. Production linked to social participation and material rewards can replace financially and ecologically high cost incentives currently bestowed by the state on the private investors to motivate investment.

Export strategies linked to welfare and popular participation; economic diversity linked to the liberation of civil society from neocorporatist constraints; linkages between rural employment and the expansion of backward and forward linkages to primary product exploitation—these and related changes are based on transformation of the institutional parameters of Chilean society. As long as Chile's investor elites, linked to the international circuits and the existing state, are in power, no major enduring structural change is possible—incrementalism is the only choice.

The alternative self-managed social economy is not organized through a state-centralized detailed plan. Rather, the public sector coordinates with the decentralized co-operative and with self-managed and private enterprises; resources and financing coordinate around strategic goals; then, each sector and region autonomously pursues its implementation. Given Chile's skilled and productive labor force, the quality and competence of its professionals, and the deep commitment to democratic social values, there are prospects for successfully pursuing a democratic alternative to the current technocratic neoliberal model.

Conclusion

Though aware of the existence of these four problem areas, Aylwin's economic team has chosen to address these choke points by relying on the same old neoliberal medicine: greater opening to international capital flows, expansion of guarantees to foreign and local private capital, privatization, and subordination of popular demands to the profitability of private capital. Though such policies might prove effective for symptomatic treatment of short-term macroeconomic problems, they will inevitably intensify the deeply rooted conflicts inherent in the Chilean economic model. Short-term economic success and maintenance of the open economy development strategy are being achieved at the cost of structural imbalances and an increasing subsumption of the social demands of workers and of the impoverished to the large conglomerates that control the economy.

From a broader perspective, each of the four limitations of the growth with equity development strategy briefly delineated above condenses the persistent contradictions of the export-led model. On the one hand, these contradictions embody the chronic antagonism between the continuity of neoliberal policies and the real democratization of Chilean society; on the other hand, they spur the search for alternative modes of organizing Chilean social life and the economy.

Notes

1. See *La Nación*, November 19, 1991.

2. Oscar Landeretche, a member of Aylwin's economic team, made such a statement in a presentation to the Second Annual Conference of the Sociedad Chilena de Economía Política, January 11, 1992, Santiago, Chile.

3. For critical perspectives on Chile's export-oriented economic model see, among others, Fernando Ignacio Leiva, "La Crisis de América Latina y el Caribe en el Contexto del Nuevo Orden Mundial," *Materiales para la Discusión* no. 18 (Santiago: Taller PIRET, 1991); Alvaro Díaz, *El Capitalismo Chileno en los 90: Crecimiento Económico y Desigualdad Social* (Santiago: Ediciones PAS, 1991); and Gustavo Marín, "Chile Hacia el Siglo XXI: Crisis del Capitalismo y Recomposición de las Clases Sociales," *Documentos de Trabajo* no. 43 (October) (Santiago: PRIES-CONO SUR, 1991). For a critical look at other Latin American export-oriented models of capital accumulation, see James M. Cypher, "The Debt Crisis as 'Opportunity': Strategies to Revive U.S. Hegemony," *Latin American Perspectives* 16, 1 (1989), pp. 52–78.

4. Patricio Meller, "Revisión del Proceso de Ajuste Chileno de la Década del 80," *Colección Estudios CIEPLAN* no. 30 (Santiago: CIEPLAN, 1990), p. 24.

5. Ibid., pp. 31–32.

6. Gustavo Marín, op. cit., p. 25.

7. See *Indicadores Económico-Sociales* no. 96 (November) (Santiago: PET, 1991).

8. *El Mercurio*, November 16, 1991.

9. In January 1992, the Central Bank was forced to revalue the peso at 5 percent. For an explanation of this measure, see the interview with the vice-president of the Banco Central, Juan Eduardo Herrera, in *Página Abierta*, February 3–16, 1992. Among other measures considered was giving permission to the AFPs to invest up to 10 percent of their holdings in international markets within a decade.

10. *Indicadores Económico-Sociales*, op. cit., p. 2.

11. The US$4.5 billion was bought by expanding the internal debt through the sale of Central Bank promissory notes. However, the interest paid on those notes by the Central Bank was more than the amount obtained by depositing the purchased dollars in foreign accounts. This difference cost the Central Bank approximately US$100 million.

12. The gap between the rhetoric and the reality of the state's role in the neoliberal strategy was pointed out by Diaz-Alejandro. See his essay, "Some Unintended Consequences of Laissez-Faire," in *Development, Democracy and the Art of Trespassing: Essays in Honor of Albert O. Hirschman*, eds. Alejandro Foxley, Michael S. McPherson, and Guillermo O'Donnell (South Bend: University of Notre Dame Press, 1989). This idea was later expanded and reformulated by Diaz 1991, op. cit.

13. It is called subordinated debt (*la deuda subordinada*) because the law stipulates that the Central Bank shall be paid only after the salvaged banks have paid their debts to all other institutions (i.e., the private transnational banks).

14. Presentation by Marcel Claude, adviser to Carlos Ominami, at a seminar organized by SOCHEP, June 12, 1991. For a detailed and eye-opening analysis of the scope and implications of the subordinate liability see Fernando Carré, Felipe

Peralta, and Patricio Rozas, "El Problema de la Obligación Subordinada de la Banca Comercial: Diagnóstico y Propuestas Alternativas," in *Documentos de Trabajo* no. 42 (Santiago: Programa Regional de Investigaciones Económicas y Sociales del Cono Sur [PRIES-CONO SUR], 1991).

15. Dilmus James and James L. Dietz, "Latin American Lessons from the Far East: Substance or Illusion" (paper presented at the Sixteenth Congress of the Latin American Studies Association, April 4–6, 1991, Washington, D.C., p. 3).

16. See Banco Central, *Boletin Mensual* no. 767 (January 1992).

17. A stimulating comparative study of the Latin American and Southeast Asian experience in export-growth models is presented by James and Dietz, op. cit., and in Rhys Jenkins, "The Political Economy of Industrialization: A Comparison of Latin American and East Asian Newly Industrializing Countries," *Development and Change* 22 (April 1991), pp. 197–231.

18. Rhys Jenkins, op. cit., p. 200.

19. Interview with Alejandro Foxley, *Newsweek*, March 26, 1990, p. 56.

20. On the topics of "flexibilizing" and informalization, see the following illuminating articles: Guy Standing, "Global Feminization through Flexible Labor," *World Development* 17, 7 (1989), pp. 1077–1095; Juan Carlos Fortuna and Suzana Prates, "Informal Sector Versus Informalized Labor Relations in Uruguay," *The Informal Economy: Studies in Advanced and Less Developed Countries*, eds., Alejandro Portes, Manuel Castells, and Lauren A. Benton (Baltimore and London: Johns Hopkins University Press, 1989).

21. Increasing manufactured exports is no replacement for economic development and social justice. Textile, clothing, and leather exports reached US$31.9 million in 1991. To export that amount, Chile had to import US$8 million in denim and US$15.2 million in raw cotton (See Banco Central, *Boletin Mensual* no. 767 [January 1992], p. 16). In other words, there is no guarantee that the increase of *maquiladora* production, given its character, will have significant backward linkages with local production.

9

Conclusion

The critical edge of most assessments of the Aylwin regime has been severely dulled by a widespread misconception: The continuity of neoliberal policies in post-Pinochet Chile is merely a "tactical maneuver" in the face of insurmountable political constraints erected by the exiting Pinochet dictatorship. Though soothingly seductive, this conception is seriously flawed. It completely ignores some of the major developments that, unfolding under the Pinochet dictatorship, determine the nature of the Aylwin regime and shape the current context for democratic struggles in Chile. A comprehensive understanding of the last two decades of Chilean history needs to acknowledge, not ignore, the defining characteristics of that history.

1. The violent process of capitalist restructuring and the dramatic change in the correlation of forces between capital and labor through state terror under Pinochet defines the social, political, and economic foundations of the elected Aylwin regime.
2. The intellectual conversion of opposition economists and intellectuals from critics of the model before 1981 to active crusaders in the defense of export-oriented accumulation, after recanting and reshaping their conceptual matrix, has created new constraints on the prospects for change.
3. The nature of the Chilean transition can best be understood by clarifying the difference between state and regime: In Chile juridical-institutional changes (change in regime) were grafted upon socioeconomic, class, and state continuities, a fact that engenders multiple contradictions and reveals the limited democratic character of such a process.
4. The existence of an electoral regime should not be carelessly equated with democracy: In Chile electoral politics has served as a mechanism for social ascension of the political class and for the control of popular demands through clientelistic and electoral means.

If each of these elements is not duly examined, it is impossible to obtain significant insight into the complex relationship between poverty and democracy—two powerful and recurrent themes—in the practice of Chile's social movements, as well as in that of both elite and popular political forces.

Our review of the Aylwin administration's economic policies during these first two years reveals that its purported aim of humanizing Pinochet's "savage capitalism" has been consistently subordinated to the overriding goals of safeguarding investor confidence and deepening the internationalization of the Chilean economy along the lines dictated by global capital. In the process, the much-propagandized concern for redistribution in Aylwin's economic strategy has given way to a reissue of neoliberal trickle-down and growth-oriented developmental discourse.

Whereas the current expansive phase of the Chilean economy and the elected character of the political regime allow leeway for marginal improvements in social conditions, the parameters of political space continue to be defined by the requirements of the conglomerates that dominate the economy. Hence, the main obstacles to the full establishment of popular sovereignty and popular citizenship today in Chile are not the "authoritarian enclaves" left by Pinochet. Rather, a more comprehensive and incisive analysis of recent political and economic transformations would argue that full democratization of Chilean society is blocked by the enthusiastic Christian Democratic-Socialist support for the neoliberal economic model and the open economy development strategy originally implanted under the military regime.

The Limits to Elite Democracy

The emerging model of Chilean society thus combines neoliberalism with neocorporatism: the deregulation of the economy and state regulation of civil society. The regime privatizes public enterprises, enlarges the opportunities for overseas investors to control national resources, and at the same time imposes controls over wages, union organization, and strikes. Neocorporatism harnessed to neoliberalism has led to the one-sided outcomes of the "social pacts" (concertación) agreed to by capital, labor, and the state. Asymmetrical concessions and benefits—wage increases that barely keep up with the cost of living—accompany profit margins that exceed productivity gains. Given the inequality of the bargaining agents, particularly with the regime's strong investor orientation, the notion that social pacts could ensure stability and equity have proven false.

Notions such as social pacts and "political consensus," framed in the context of consolidating the vast inequalities of power and wealth, tend to freeze relations and to block change. The politics of "consensus," as it has been practiced in Chilean politics, is based in the first instance on the pre-mise of securing the cooperation of the investor classes, of guaranteeing the existing balances in external accounts and the domestic budget. Hence, to begin with, labor concedes 90 percent of what there is to bargain over: the existing unjust parameters of social income, land tenure, prop-erty ownership, profit margins, and so on define the basis of any possible agreement. Consensual politics in this environment is the politics of the status quo. The regime's rejection of the positive role of conflictual politics and its active role in intervening in conflicts against striking workers re-veal the conservative nature of consensual politics. In Chile, consensual politics reached its high point in the first year of the Aylwin regime and subsequently began to gradually deteriorate because of regime-employer opposition to wageworker demands. The breakdown of consensual poli-tics is inevitable, given the broader policy framework in which it operates.

Along with "social pacts" and "consensus," the next-favorite term used by regime ideologues to define the goals of the Aylwin government is "governability." Essentially, this notion emphasizes the state's capacity to control and channel citizen activity through routinized political chan-nels. In practice, "governability" has been translated into a policy of inte-grating and linking local grass-roots organizations to the state. In effect, governability has become a formula for societal immobility and the bu-reaucratization of civil society.

Neocorporatism, insofar as it broadens the state's role over civil society and neoliberalism, and insofar as it extends the investor elites' reach within the economy, reflects the authoritarian-pluralist configuration of post-Pinochet Chile. Surrounding the pockets of political freedom are hi-erarchical economic and state institutions retaining all the authority and influence of the pre-electoral era.

The great accomplishment of the Pinochet Right was to convert the op-position to the notion that socioeconomic conformity and individual mo-bility was the basis for political realism. From that it was a short step to the Aylwin regime's embrace of supply-side economics, an open door policy for foreign investment, and the trickle-down theory of social ameliora-tion. What was defined as macropolicy largely involved managing aggre-gate investment and consumption within existing institutional bound-aries. Incomes, budgets, and living conditions of the poor were arbitrarily relegated to the level of micropolicies—to receive residual consideration after major allocations were made to the investor class. Macropolicy, as it is defined in Chile, not only subordinates working-class interests to inves-tor incentives but subjects Chile's natural resources to unprecedented pil-lage: timber, maritime, mining, and rivers have all been subject to unregu-lated exploitation by overseas capital as a means of establishing favorable macroeconomic results.

Demystifying the notion of "macroeconomic variables" revolves around identifying the principal class actors subsumed under the categories of "investment," "consumption," "savings," and so forth. The concentration of capital leaves little doubt whose "interests" are being "managed" when the finance minister speaks of managing macroeconomic variables.

The economic growth in Chile is based on an unstable and unequal expansion of primary commodities and on the influx of foreign capital in speculative, nonrenewable, resource-rich regions. Chile's aggregate expansion in the late 1980s and early 1990s has been built on the exclusion and low pay of its labor force, not on entrepreneurial investment in innovative technologies. The concentrated wealth in Chile is based on the dispossession of a significant number of former small producers and on their subordination to the productive-distributive networks of hub firms through subcontracting. The large influxes of capital are increasingly matched by growing outflows; Chile's open economy and overdependence on primary goods exports is susceptible to downturns in the world economy. The scarcity of quality high tech manufactured products in its export mix suggests that the modernization accompanying Chile's export expansion is narrowly specialized.

The societal configuration in Chile reproduces the divisions in the workplace: a super rich elite at the top; a substantial minority of upwardly mobile professionals tied to the private sector and aspiring to link up with those at the top; an impoverished, relatively downwardly mobile public sector of employees (teachers, public health employees, and so on); an alienated, underpaid, and insecure industrial working class; and a mass of highly exploited seasonal farm, timber, and packing house workers.

The class structure reveals a pattern that is segmenting the middle class into public and private; that is fusing the ruling class, bringing together traditional wealth, the nouveau riche Pinochet cronies, and the new upwardly bound "high tech" entrepreneurs associated with the current government. The path to ruling class power follows a dual course: the first begins with inherited wealth and is expanded through political office, ending in large-scale enterprise; the second begins with political outsiders, converts political influence into economic opportunities (via privatization, among other instrumentalities), and leads to directorship of major enterprises. The relative economic openness of the ruling class to individual mobility is matched by its collective obduracy about labor.

The class struggle in Chile continues to be waged, mostly from the top down. The electoral political formulas that emphasize conciliation with the military, consensus, and social pacts have temporarily obscured the deep class divisions that define the two worlds of contemporary Chile: the world of private schools, country clubs, summer homes, private clinics, overseas vacations, and maids and servants for the affluent upper and middle classes; and the shantytown poverty, dusty streets, and the crowded, understaffed, and underfunded clinics and schools of Chile's working classes.

Any statement of "success" in Chile has to be put in context. The economic and military elite in Chile "succeeded" in negotiating a political transition in which privileges, property, and profits were guaranteed and legitimated. The political right "succeeded" in dividing the opposition and securing the cooperation of influential leaders to pursue free market economics, while isolating antisystemic forces. The center-left "succeeded" in securing the return of electoral politics and access to public office, as well as securing their acceptance by domestic and overseas economic elites. Washington "succeeded" in brokering a transition that retained political support for its regional strategy of a free trade zone and an exemplary propaganda model for arguing the virtues of free market economics.

For most Chileans in the formal and informal economy, in the factories, urban slums, fields, and canneries, the electoral transition has not produced the substantial changes in working or living conditions that they expected. Trade union rights are still highly restricted; promises of income and welfare programs have been largely forgotten. Patronage politics has replaced programmatic changes as the principal vehicle for securing lower-class voter allegiances. The basic question facing any analyst evaluating the Chilean experience is the ancient issue: Success for whom? The continuities in the state and society speak to the perpetuation of the vast inequality in wealth, power, and prestige concentrated in the new and old conglomerates. The political and legal changes in parliament, the electoral system, and party competition have been grafted onto the underlying structures of socioeconomic power and the institutions of the state. In government, the civilian politicians imitate the economic behavior of their predecessors, vying to outdo them in offering incentives to foreign investors, boasting of their bonds and close ties to private investors, publicizing their success in managing the macroeconomic accounts by holding down wages and salaries of impoverished workers. Chile is passing through a period of political conformism: Innovative and transformative styles are dubbed "utopian" or "anachronistic." The conformist political style engages the upwardly mobile former reformers and former radicals because it opens new "social spaces" for political and economic deal making. Christian Democratic party leaders have frequently become partners and directors of lucrative business enterprises. "Renovated" Socialists compete for bureaucratic posts, basking in the sympathetic coverage of the conservative media. Communists and former MIR revolutionaries who have discovered the virtue of "realism" are invited to sip pisco sours in the suburban country clubs. The stability of the Chilean transition is linked to the co-optation of the former Left to supporting neoliberalism and the exclusion of the major exploited classes from effective influence over the allocation of state resources. The flexibility of the Chilean elite in providing social opportunities and political space for the upwardly mobile professionals of the center-left is complemented by elite intransigence in resisting the emergence of broad-based social movements with substantive redistributive programs.

The conformist political style characteristic of contemporary Chilean political culture has deeply influenced, and has been influenced in turn, by the middle class. During the 1960s and early 1970s significant segments of the middle class felt the need to balance commitments to social equality with personal aspirations to achieve moderately affluent private lives.

In the 1990s, under the influence of the neoliberal ethos, many middle-class professionals have resolved such public-private contradictions by channeling most of their energies toward professional success and private gain. Ostentatious consumerism and individual enrichment is flaunted in a fashion unimaginable earlier. The drive for personal success has largely overcome previous guilt feelings about affluence in the midst of mass poverty. As part of the professional middle class, Chile's intellectuals have not been immune to the same *arribista* (social-climbing) pursuits. Ensconced in externally funded institutes, those with the right political connections to the parties have moved into the government bureaucracy or serve as paid consultants. From their new positions of influence, the intellectuals-turned-functionaries provide the ideological rationale for government policy. At the highest levels, the former reformist intellectuals have become the macroeconomic managers for the investor elites. At the middle levels they write the speeches and programs for the congressional and party leader. At the bottom, they conduct surveys and manage poverty organization in the popular neighborhoods to preempt popular discontent. Today in Chile, the critical intellectuals are a minority—dissent from the neoliberal course frequently means marginalization or even expulsion from the government parties, exclusion from research funding, and even termination of state-related employment.

The civilian regime's quest for "reconciliation" with the military and secret police figures responsible for mass killings stands out as an example of what can best be described as the highest immorality. The Aylwin regime's investigation of massive human rights violations by the Pinochet regime took the form of the Rettig Commission, which collected information on several thousand homicides but was prohibited from even naming the perpetrators. Subsequently, the issue of human rights crimes was laid to rest: The report was referred to the Pinochet-controlled judicial system, which predictably took no action. The Aylwin regime proffered symbolic and inconsequential gestures to the victims and their families and offered substantive positions and promotions to the military victimizers. This peculiar blend of hypocritical moralism and self-righteous realism captures the immorality of the conformist middle class in and out of government. At a practical level, the notion that democracy is consolidated by absolving its enemies is an invitation for future military coups.

The Challenge Confronting the Chilean Left

The Left has not recovered from the political defeat of 1986. On the contrary, the triumph of the electoral coalition has deepened the crisis in the Left: Fragmentation, external paralysis, and internal divisions continue to plague the Communist party, MIR, the Christian Left, as well as the many independent Socialist nuclei. The crisis in Eastern Europe and the USSR has further disoriented those sectors of the Left influenced by statist versions of socialism. Four issues divide and fragment the Left to one degree or another: (1) strategy and tactics in the context of the electoral-civilian regime, (2) internal organizational principles under the new conditions, (3) responses to the changes at the global political level, and (4) alternatives to the neoliberal policies—new conceptions of socialism.

In the immediate post-Pinochet period both MIR and the Communist party were divided between those who wanted to continue armed struggle and those who argued for a shift toward "mass mobilization." Whereas this division persisted up until 1990, the new debate revolves around those who are oriented toward supporting the regime coalition (albeit "critically") and those who are in favor of outright opposition. Within the Communist party and MIR, sectors of the "political" (as opposed to the guerrilla) sector have positioned themselves to enter the Socialist party.[1] In an extreme case, sectors of MIR (political) have even offered to reveal names, activities, and dates of past guerrilla activity in order to gain acceptability by the ruling parties.[2] In the Communist party, a significant sector, led by Luis Guastavino, has already prepared the groundwork for reentry into the parliamentary universe through a full-scale attack on the "electoral abstentionism" of the party.

No less important, the Communist party is riven by dissension on the right to dissent within the party: The issue of internal party democracy or the lack of it is an issue that unites socially disparate groups, who share little in common otherwise. The party leadership's attempt to restore bureaucratic centralist practices in the present national and international context is an act of self-destruction—and is alienating many militant young Communists, as well as the dissident Social Democrats.[3] Absorbed by the internal struggles and divisions (the three MIRs are, in turn, internally divided), the Left has been unable to intervene in the neighborhood struggles or to provide a coherent critique of the current regime and conjuncture.

The growing discontent of the pobladores with the social insufficiencies of the electoral regime and with the increase in trade union organization is occurring independently of the leftist parties and their leadership. The Left has yet to devise a strategy that moves from local community struggles through a set of transitional demands toward the long-term goal of a socialist transformation. The external crisis of Stalinism and statist socialism has disoriented the leftist intelligentsia, which has failed to examine the micromodels of socialism in its own country and history: There are successful examples of popular power exercised in the neighborhoods, factories, and co-operatives between 1965 and 1973.[4] The Left has not yet confronted the need for a transition program based on developing an alternative state budget based on popular needs, or an alternative investment and industrial development program that is under democratic control and that subordinates the export market to deepening the domestic market. Instead, there is empirical criticism of particular regime policies or continual complaining about the "need for an alternative model."

The Left, in the new context, has the difficult course of steering between two dangerous reefs—between continuation of a self-defeating armed struggle at a time of ebbing popular support and absorption by the electoral machines of the state parties. The fundamental challenge for the Left is to decide how to reinsert itself into the social movements, how to manage the loyal reconstruction of those movements (not merely to enter and cannibalize members), and how to elaborate a realistic transitional program that links local demands to the reallocation of state resources and the expansion of sociopolitical terrain for struggle (the right to strike at harvest time, a new labor code, and so on).

The Search for Democracy

At the center of this reconstructed Left is the question of democracy. A full-scale critique of the current regime's flawed self-definition of democracy is fundamental. Procedural changes in an authoritarian state framework do not define a democratic political system. The Left could draw on its collective historical memory in defining a new agenda and in criticizing the renovated Socialists' embrace of neoliberal democracy.

In the 1940s and 1950s sectors of the Socialist party claimed to have "renovated" their ideas by joining center-right coalitions. Socialists, led by Bernardo Ibañez, supported President González Videla, and Clodomiro Almeyda later joined Ibañez's cabinet. Both experiences ended badly.[5] Without power, prestige, or popular support, Socialist support withered. In the early 1930s and in the 1960s and 1970s an alternative Socialist tradition emerged that combined electoral politics with independent class organization. A vibrant Socialist movement grew and gained mass support, but was defeated by military force, not by its own political compromises.

The crucial issue, of course, concerning any substantial and enduring social democracy in Chile revolves around democratizing the permanent institutions of the state: No serious democratization of the economic system can take place under the elite-controlled, authoritarian military, judicial, and civil bureaucracies. Unless the Left can begin to build on the emerging conflicts between movements and regime, the Right, firmly entrenched in the affluent sectors, as well as in the sectors of the very poor, will capitalize on the discontent and on the regime crisis, and it will return to power, possibly even through electoral processes with the help of military pressure.

But prior to and accompanying any critique of the flawed nature of "existing democracy" in Chile today, the Left, and particularly the Communist party, must subject its own past and present political organizational practices to a thorough critical examination. Unless the leftist parties open up democratic debate inside and deepen their downward ties with the popular movement, there is little hope that they can reconstitute themselves as a hegemonic force among the popular classes. Democracy within the Left is an essential ingredient in developing a credible critique of the absence of democracy in the larger society.

Over the past two decades, Chile has experienced two political transitions—one in which the military transferred office to the civilians and another in which the new electoral political class transferred its allegiances from the populace to the neoliberal economic elite. The result is the emergence of a growing gap between the political class, which banters and bargains over the scope and depth of private gains in the corridors and tearooms of Congress, and civil society, where the populace, marginalized from power, struggles to organize political alternatives. In the short term, the political elites will continue in power: bargaining, dividing, and coalescing. In the middle run, the inequalities, cleavages, and exclusion that divides civil society from the political class could become the basis for the return of class-based politics. The collective memories of the past—of participatory democracy and social ownership—are still present in the minds of the Chilean poor.

Notes

1. Interviews with leaders of MIR (political wing) and dissident Communists, July 1990.

2. Patricio Rivas and José Miguel Moya, spokespersons of MIR, made this offer on June 23, 1990, at a press conference.

3. On August 6, 1990, 40 percent of the Central Committee of the Young Communists resigned. Three days later, the Central Committee expelled two other dissidents, and a week later, 488 militants, led by former Central Committee member Fanny Pollarolo, publicly rejected the "repressive attitude" of the Political Commission in confronting the crisis.

4. Very little commentary about these experiences was made in my discussions with Communist and Socialist dissidents. On the 1970s experience, see Andrew Zimbalist and Juan Guillermo Espinosa, *Economic Democracy in Chile* (New York: Academic Press, 1978).

5. See James Petras, *Politics and Social Forces in Chile* (Berkeley: University of California Press, 1965).

Epilogue

More than a year has passed since we completed the last chapter of this book. Yet events during 1992 and 1993—the second half of the Aylwin government's tenure—have been rich in elements that serve to deepen and validate our study of the Chilean transition.

An Elitist Electoral Regime

A major theme explored in the preceding chapters has been to examine how the reconstituted political class made agreements with, and concessions to, the military before 1989, which severely undermined the newly elected regime's democratizing potential. As we approach the final months of the Aylwin government's four-year term in office, many Aylwin supporters have been forced to accept the fact that the post-Pinochet electoral regime has not necessarily led to a profound democratization of Chilean society. A recent document of the Socialist Party's Women's Department reflects this bitter discovery, lamenting:

> Ensuring stability of the transition has been given priority over promoting citizen participation in the decision-making process over crucial social and political matters. The outcome after three and a half years of this practice has been the increasing oligarchic-type control exercised over key social sites of power. In fact, the results have been the growing distancing of the government from the people, the ebb and disarticulation of social movements, as well as the increasing elitization of politics.[1]

Rising discontent with the elitist "style of politics" of Concertación—which we have argued is a consequence of the nature of the transition and of commitments made by the renovated Christian Democratic and Socialist leadership—led to the first desertions from the government coalition. During 1993, two small parties, first the Alianza Humanista-Verde and then MAPU, decided to abandon Concertación to join the emerging leftist opposition to the Christian Democratic-Socialist alliance and its policies.

After almost four years of government by an elected regime, there is a growing feeling that Concertación's campaign promise La Alegría Ya Viene still remains to be fulfilled for Chile's 4 million poor, for teachers and health workers, for miners and small agricultural producers, and for the majority of workers, human rights activists, and victims of human rights violations under Pinochet. The campaign pledges to reform the 1980 constitution in order to democratize the binomial electoral system and the designated Senate, to ensure a civilian majority over the Pinochet-nominated National Security Council, and to bring the military under effective civilian control remained untouched. Minor changes in Pinochet's labor law have neither significantly improved workers' rights nor provided adequate protection from ongoing arbitrary firings and workplace repression.

Continued Military Tutelage

The limits of the electoral regime, as well as the pusillanimity of the Aylwin coalition, have also become apparent as Pinochet has sought to consolidate and increase the army's tutelage over the political system. Faced with imminent legal proceedings against military officers accused of human rights violations, Pinochet and the army decided to flex some military muscle: On May 28, 1993, heavily armed troops and tanks were deployed around the army's Chief of Staff Headquarters only a few blocks away from La Moneda, the presidential palace. Through this display of military force, later dubbed as *el boinazo* in reference to the berets worn by army commandos, Pinochet and the army sent a forceful political signal to the government and to the Chilean people: The military would resist any attempt by the civil society or the government to prosecute the military officers responsible for past crimes. The boinazo and the servile political response on the part of the Aylwin administration illustrate that three and one-half years into the transition, Pinochet and the army will not give up their autonomy. After a series of meetings between Pinochet and President Aylwin, in August the government decided to send a law proposal to Congress for its urgent approval—a proposal that, fashioned in close consultation with the army, would establish Special Courts to accelerate pending human rights cases. These Special Courts would guarantee the absolute secrecy of their proceedings and the anonymity of those testifying; only under these conditions would the military recognize the location of the remains of the hundreds of disappeared political prisoners in exchange for immediate application of Pinochet's 1978 amnesty for human rights violators. Human rights lawyers immediately denounced the "Ley Aylwin" (Aylwin's law), as the president's proposal came to be known, as a quick route to impunity. Human rights lawyers explained to Socialist members of Congress the many loopholes built into the law—the most salient of these being the possibility for the Special Courts to exclusively seat military judges on the bench. After learning of this possibility, Socialist Deputy Camilo Escalona is reported to have said, "If that happens, and we approve it, they will hang us from the lampposts."[2] Pressured by mass protests and hunger strikes against impunity, the Socialist party withdrew its support for passage of the law at the last minute, choosing to face being accused of having betrayed President Aylwin by Christian-Democratic allies rather than suffering the electoral consequences of betraying the rank and file.

In the wake of the *boinazo,* ensuring impunity for over sixty officers in active duty facing pending trials in civilian courts was only one of Pinochet's concerns. During the commemoration of his twentieth anniversary as commander in chief of the army, Pinochet outlined a plan for the armed forces' continued political role in coming decades. In his August 20, 1993, speech, Pinochet complained that the army had not been able to deploy all of its abilities in meeting its constitutional mandate, "probably because the tendency persists to reduce the army's contribution exclusively to the defense of national sovereignty and territorial integrity, which significantly undercuts its action, advice and cooperation in other key areas of national life."[3] Pinochet offered the army's cooperation to the government and Congress in defining the goals and priorities of Chile's defense, foreign relations, and environmental protection policies, as well as in the nation's long-term development strategy. Concertación leaders were quick to celebrate Pinochet's speech and manifest their willingness to implement his proposals.

The success of Pinochet's latest politico-military operation, begun with the boinazo, can be gauged by the pro-army and pro-Pinochet discourse suddenly discovered by Concertación policymakers. Socialist leader Ricardo Lagos, who gained notoriety by wagging his finger at Pinochet during a 1988 television interview and asking for his immediate resignation, in a September 1993 interview praised the veteran general's role: "I believe that Pinochet has been a barrier of contention against those officers who wanted to seek more autonomous solutions within the military."[4]

It is not a farfetched scenario to imagine that the March 1994 ceremony, in which a new civilian president is sworn in as Aylwin officially finishes his mandate, will transpire under the gaze of Pinochet, dressed in full regalia as commander in chief of the army, as key power broker and guardian of a "democratic" Chile.

Economic Performance

During the second half of the Aylwin administration, the Chilean economy entered into its ninth year of expansion: GDP grew at a rate of 10.4 percent in 1992 and a 5 to 6 percent growth rate is expected by year's end, 1993. Although high growth and investment rates attest to succulent profits to be reaped by private capital in the aftermath of the politico-economic transformation of Chilean capitalism, the first recognizable signs that such a pattern of accumulation are not sustainable over time have begun to appear.

In 1993, Chile's fresh-fruit export boom received its first knockout punch at the hands of declining world prices and increasing protectionism by the European Economic Community. For the second consecutive year, fresh fruit exports declined from US$992 million in 1991 and US$982 million in 1992 to an estimated US$860 million in 1993.[5] Apple exports will plummet from US$249 million in 1992 to US$102 million in 1993.[6] A 38 percent decline in the exchange rate from 1987 to 1993 has forced many producers of apple and kiwi, once touted to be the crop of Chile's future, to leave their fruit to rot unpicked in order to cut their losses. Other key exports also confront a lower demand and declining prices. Copper, fishmeal, and cellulose prices are at a three-year low, and in terms of dollar value, total Chilean exports are expected to decline by 6 percent in 1993, signaling that the decade-long cycle of growth based on primary exports is losing momentum.

The decline in the level of poverty—measured in terms of income—has been celebrated as a major success of the Aylwin government's macroeconomic management and social policy. Whereas 44.6 percent of the population was under the poverty line in 1987, this proportion had declined to 40.1 percent in 1990 and to 32.7 percent as of November 1992, according to the August 1993 CASEN report.[7]

These positive results need to be critically examined from four different angles to place them in proper perspective.

First, the proportion of Chileans living in poverty in 1992 remains higher than in 1968, when the figure was 28.5 percent of the population. At the end of 1992, when Chile's average annual per capita income stood at US$3,300, there still were 4.37 million Chileans receiving annual per capita incomes below US$820, the amount that the government has defined as the poverty line.[8] Of these, 1.2 million were indigent poor, that is, they had incomes of less than US$410, the amount required to acquire foodstuffs providing the minimum internationally established standards of caloric and protein intake to adequately sustain human life. Poverty and misery, which in the late 1960s fueled massive social and political mobilizations, still remains a central trait of Chilean society.

Second, the mechanisms which over the past five years were used to augment income—increased employment and social spending—face significant structural limitations in the future. The unemployment rate, for example, stood in June 1993 at 3.9 percent of the labor force, a level considered by many analysts to be full employment. The decisive role increased social spending plays in reducing poverty (and the limits of trickle-down economics) is illustrated by the following comparison: During the 1987–1990 period, GDP grew at an accumulated rate of 20.6 percent, whereas poverty declined only 5.5 percent; for the 1991–1992 period, when social spending was increased, accumulated GDP grew at a rate of 17 percent, and poverty decreased at a rate of 16 percent.[9] On the basis of this experience, any consistent effort to combat poverty should strive to increase social spending, especially when the resources for such an increase are readily available. Recall that at the beginning of 1993 Chile enjoyed a fiscal surplus of 2.5 percent of GDP (or US$700 million) and possessed international reserves topping US$10 billion.

There are two powerful reasons, however, to suggest that in coming years significant resources to combat poverty will not be forthcoming. First of all, Foxley has openly admitted that "we have the money and we are not going to spend it"[10] to give the population "a long term-pedagogical exercise."[11] Behind Foxley's political decision is the Aylwin government's intent to discipline workers and the poor, breaking their expectations for rapid improvement in their living standards, quashing any attempts at escalating popular demands from the state. On the other hand, there are structural constraints imposed by Chile's open economy development strategy on the options for macroeconomic management. Such limitations (analyzed in Chapter 8) have been recently acknowledged by Juan Villarzú, economic adviser to Eduardo Frei, Jr., and Foxley's likely successor. Addressing a breakfast meeting of Chilean–U.S. Chamber of Commerce representatives, Villarzú recognized, "The only instrument that we can manage internally with some flexibility is our fiscal policy. Monetary policy ... is determined in practice by fluctuations in interest rates abroad. ... The exchange rate is another variable that local action cannot control."[12] Hence, a stable fiscal policy is considered the key to sustaining growth, i.e., profits. Not mentioned by Villarzú, however, was the fact that governmental control over fiscal spending was further constrained by the constitutional obligation to turn over 10 percent of gross copper sales to the military and by the lingering financial costs of the 1985 salvaging of the private banks. Consequently, of all the components of fiscal spending, expenditures on social services remain the only variable fully under governmental control. As external shocks increasingly require that the economy adjust its level of expenditure, it seems safe to conclude that social spending will not grow at the same rate as the past three years. "Trickle-down" economics will once again be the major poverty alleviation mechanism.

Persistent and growing distributional inequality constitutes a third reason to critically assess the Concertación poverty-fighting scorecard. As we have indicated in previous chapters (see Table 8.2, for example), the participation of wages in GDP decreased at a yearly average of 0.3 percent during the 1987–1992 period and at an average of 0.2 percent during the 1990–1992 period.[13] From 1987 to 1992 real wages did rise, but these increases have been below the rise in average productivity. Thus, if other factors are taken into account, such as the functional distribution of income or access and quality of services like education and health, then the accomplishments of the Aylwin government fall dramatically short of original promises.

But above all, the central reason for criticizing Concertación's performance vis-à-vis poverty is that the pattern of accumulation that it has endorsed is itself at the root of poverty-creating processes. Nowhere is this more starkly clear than when the social effects of the development of capitalism in the countryside are examined. The recently concluded 1992 Sixth Agricultural Census allows comparison with the previous census carried out in 1976. The picture that emerges of the 1976–1992 period is one in which rapid capitalist expansion in agriculture resulted in widespread impoverishment; expulsion of rural population from the land; concentration of landownership; loss of productive potential; environmental degradation; and a growing threat to 250,000 small peasant-producers. In terms of land use, for example, the area of land destined for traditional crops declined by 280,000 hectares, whereas the use of land for pine plantations expanded by 348,000 hectares.[14] The rapid expansion of forestry and lumber exports has become a veritable "satanic mill" that has ground peasant producers into masses of dispossessed. According to Guillermo Díaz, president of a small producers' organization, the Asociación Gremial Agro del Valle, in Chile's Sixth Region: "There is great pressure by the transnationals to buy the land from those of us that remain between the pine plantations, and the temptation to sell is great because they offer good money."[15] But he adds that many producers resist selling because they know that "in the best of all possible cases, the money will last them two or three years, and then they become either an emigrant to the city or a rural squatter who works wherever they invite him."[16]

This profound reconversion of the agricultural sector is celebrated as a sign of increasing productive efficiency by Ivan Nazif, Socialist head of the government's Bureau of Agricultural Policy and Analysis (ODEPA). His response to the plight of the 250,000 traditional peasant producers is that they must either lower unitary costs according to the competitive requirements dictated by the world market, or they will have to disappear. Repeating the approach of the Chicago Boys in their most dogmatic period, Nazif clarifies that if this tendency of agricultural reconversion "makes us face deficits in certain areas, we will import those foodstuffs, since we will found our policy less and less on the concept of food security."[17]

The Reemergence of the Left

During 1992 and 1993, the mobilization of teachers, health workers, copper miners, Mapuche Indians, ecological groups, workers, and students continued without a significant breakthrough in the social and political coordination of these movements. Leftist parties and movements reorganized, egged on more by the upcoming December presidential and congressional elections than by profound self-criticism and reestablishment of links with social sectors. As a result of this top-down operation, three different presidential candidates emerged: Reverend Eugenio Pizarro, candidate of the Communist party and MIDA; Cristián Reitze, supported by the Nueva Izquierda (composed of former Communist party and MIR leaders) and the Alianza Humanista-Verde; and economist Manfred Max-Neff, representing a loose coalition of ecological, cultural, trade union, Mapuche, and other urban social movements. The profound self-criticism and reassessment of the past, which we deemed necessary for a new relationship between leftist parties and social movements, has been preempted by electoral urgency. The fact that in spite of all the obstacles (each candidate had to present 50,000 signatures) the Left was able to field three candidates, striving to represent different constituencies, is a significant development. However, the challenges of building and rebuilding strong social movements that, articulated by a common political project, are able to democratize Chilean society will not be addressed by the electoral campaign; but this prefigures a rich discussion after the electoral contest has passed.

Pinochet's binomial political system guarantees that the next president of Chile will be either Concertación's Eduardo Frei, Jr., or Arturo Alessandri, who represents a rightist coalition made up of Renovación Nacional, UDI, and the Union de Centro Centro. Frei and Alessandri openly recognize that, in terms of economic policy, there are no significant differences between their campaign programs. Yet, the fact that Chileans will once again be forced to choose between a Frei or an Alessandri as their next president is a vivid metaphor of the conservative character of the electoral regime and speaks of the rigidity of the political system.

Blood on the Alamedas

September 1993 has marked the twentieth anniversary of the military coup. While in the rich neighborhoods, the wealthy celebrated their "liberation from communism" and toasted Pinochet in a swank gala dinner at Santiago's plushest hotel, in the dusty streets of popular neighborhoods, workers and the poor remembered Allende and the fallen with candle-lit vigils, barricades, and protests. On September 11, 1993, several thousand young people (many of whom had not been born when the coup took place) marched onto Santiago's main avenue, the Alameda, and attempted to reach the presidential palace to pay their respects where Salvador Allende and the defenders of La Moneda had fallen. The police, under the direction of Aylwin's minister of the interior, brutally repressed the marchers. Two people were killed—one shot in the chest, another crushed by a police armored vehicle. The outcome was over ten people wounded by police bullets and 200 arrested, in what has been recognized as the Aylwin government's first act of repression. The ensuing condemnation-defense of the brutal police action revealed that twenty years after the coup, Chilean society remains bitterly divided. The wounds opened on September 11, 1973, have not been healed by almost four years of the electoral regime. Healing those wounds requires much more than the rhetoric of reconciliation proffered by Chile's political class; healing those twenty-year-old wounds requires a new, more vigorous relationship between democracy and poverty—one that both materially and symbolically, both politically and economically opens up the "grandes alamedas" to the new generation of Chileans.

Notes

1. Vice-Presidencia de Asuntos de la Mujer, Partido Socialista de Chile, *Programa Socialista de la Mujer: Participación y Protagonismo para los Cambios (Borrador de Discusión)* (Santiago: Partido Socialista, 1993), p. 4.

2. *El Mercurio*, August 22, 1993, p. D–14.

3. "Ejército Quiere Asesorar a Poderes del Estado: Proposición Fue Hecha Ayer por el General Pinochet durante una Charla," *La Epoca*, August 20, 1993, p. 17.

4. *El Mercurio*, September 5, 1993, p. D–20. Twenty years earlier, another Socialist leader, Salvador Allende, had reached the same erroneous conclusion and named Pinochet commander in chief of the army, with the tragic consequences we all know about.

5. *El Mercurio*, July 11, 1993, p. D–15.

6. Ibid.

7. Ministerio de Planificación y Cooperación, "Evolución de los Ingresos de los Hogares y de la Pobreza Regional: 1987–1992." Press release, August 25, 1993.

8. See Jaime Ruiz-Tagle, "La Pobreza: Tareas Pendientes," *La Nación*, August 7, 1993, p. 39.

9. *El Diario*, July 28, 1993, p. 32.

10. *La Epoca*, July 21, 1993, p. 20.

11. Ibid.

12. U.S.–Chilean Chamber of Commerce, *The Journal*, August 1993, p. 12.

13. Rafael Agacino, "El Modelo No Garantiza la Equidad," *Los Tiempos*, May 9, 1993, p. 26.

14. Teresa Espinoza, "El Profundo Proceso de Cambio Productivo del Sector Agrícola," *La Epoca*, July 30, 1993, p. 2–B.

15. Aldo Anfossi, "Los Parias de la Modernidad Agrícola Agonizan en Lolol," *La Epoca*, August 19, 1993, p. 2–B.

16. Ibid.

17. Teresa Espinoza, op. cit., p. 2–B.

About the Book and Authors

The critical issues concerning the development of a substantial and enduring democracy in Chile are those of strengthening civil society, democratizing the permanent institutions of the state, and building an economy geared to effectively satisfy human needs. In this book, the authors offer a critique of the Chilean transition and of the Aylwin electoral regime, analyzing the linkage between political compromises made prior to the civilians' assumption of power and the choice of socioeconomic policy in the post-electoral period. They argue that the decisive factor underlying the Chilean transition is the contrast between the legal-political changes and socioeconomic and institutional continuities, a contrast that perpetuates the vast inequalities of wealth and power generated under Pinochet's sixteen-year-old military dictatorship. They also challenge the myth of the "Chilean miracle"—the purported success of neoliberal policies in promoting sustained growth and social justice—and therefore in laying the basis for long-term social harmony and enduring political stability.

James Petras is professor of sociology at the State University of New York–Binghamton and author of numerous books on Latin America. **Fernando Ignacio Leiva** is the founder of Promoción e Intercambio de Recursos Educacionales y Tecnológicos (PIRET) in Santiago, Chile, and a doctoral candidate in economics at the University of Massachusetts–Amherst. **Henry Veltmeyer** is professor of sociology and coordinator of International Development Studies at St. Mary's University in Halifax, Nova Scotia.

Series in Political Economy
and Economic Development in Latin America

Series Editor

Andrew Zimbalist

Smith College

Through country case studies and regional analyses this series will contribute to a deeper understanding of development issues in Latin America. Shifting political environments, increasing economic interdependence, and the difficulties with regard to debt, foreign investment, and trade policy demand novel conceptualizations of development strategies and potentials for the region. Individual volumes in this series will explore the deficiencies in conventional formulations of the Latin American development experience by examining new evidence and material. Topics will include, among others, women and development in Latin America; the impact of IMF interventions; the effects of redemocratization on development; Cubanology and Cuban political economy; Nicaraguan political economy; and individual case studies on development and debt policy in various countries in the region.

Index

ACI. *See* Agencia de Cooperación Internacional
Acuerdo Marco Tripartito, 120–121, 122
Acuerdo Nacional, 78(n38)
Administradoras de Fondos de Pensiones (AFP), 179
AFP. *See* Administradoras de Fondos de Pensiones
Agencia de Cooperación Internacional (ACI), 119
Agrarian reform, 10, 24, 41(n6), 88, 154–155
Agricultural Census (1992), 198
Agriculture, 3, 32, 152–157, 159, 166(n41), 198–199
Ahumada, Juan, 155, 165(n36)
Alessandri, Arturo, 199
Alianza Democratica, 99(n2)
Alianza Humanista-Verde, 193, 199
Allamand, Andrés, 46
Allende, Salvador, 9, 41(n10), 59, 200, 200(n4)
  regime of, 9, 18–20, 23, 27
Almeyda, Clodomiro, 190
Annual National Assembly of Private Enterprise (ENADE), 57
Arellano, Juan Pablo, 47
Argentina, 19, 21, 27, 39, 41(n5), 97
ASEXMA. *See* Association of Exporters of Manufactures
Association of Exporters of Manufactures (ASEXMA), 172
Aylwin, Patricio, 2, 4–5, 101(n30), 104, 106. *See also* Aylwin government
Aylwin government, 2, 4–5, 8–9, 139(n53), 144–145, 147–148

debt under, 11, 174, 181(n13)
and democratization, 133, 135, 183–184, 187–188, 190–194, 200
demonstrations against, 90, 105, 145, 159–162
economic development strategy of, 106–108, 110, 112–117, 132–135, 136(n8), 169–171, 173, 178–180, 184, 185, 197
economy under, 109–112, 136(n15), 167, 168(table 8.1), 169–174, 196
export policy of, 169, 171, 175–180, 182(n21)
and human rights abuse prosecution, 10–11, 94, 96–98, 100(n14), 102(n49), 103(n53), 188–189, 194–195
labor reform under, 57–58, 90, 119–122, 152–153, 155–156, 158, 166(n38)
military in, 194–195, 200
and neoliberalism, 46–49, 53–54, 61–64, 66, 73–75, 87, 88, 91–94, 98, 105, 122, 133, 144, 161, 183–184, 188
neostructuralism in, 66, 73
political class creation in, 121, 143–144, 162–163
political parties under, 88, 91, 118, 121–122, 144
politics under, 140, 141, 150–152, 162–163, 184–185
social inequalities under, 93–94, 108, 112
social programs of, 108, 117–119, 122–128, 132, 133, 167, 173–175, 197–198
state role in, 118–119, 123